The Cubs Quotient

How the Chicago Cubs Changed the World

Scott Rowan

D1417266

sherpa

MULTIMEDIA, INC.

This book is available in quantity at special discounts for groups and organizations. For more information please contact:

Sherpa Multimedia
(773) 977-8570
info@sherpamultimedia.com
www.sherpamultimedia.com

Printed in United States of America

First American Paperback Edition

Edited by Blythe Hurley
Designed by Patricia Frey

ISBN: 978-0-9895003-0-2

LCCN: 2013910134

To Drew,
Thank you for your support.
I love you more than pizza.

— S.R.

Contents

Section III: Race

Section IV: Vice

Section V: Innovation

Section VI: Entertainment

Foreword

Question everything. Assume nothing.

Those were the two directives that eventually guided me through the research of this book. But that was far from my initial goal, which was to write the ultimate braggart's resource for Chicago Cubs fans. I grew up working in bars, restaurants and pubs during high school, college and in the years after I graduated from Virginia Tech. I've had every job, from busboy to general manager of a sports pub in Colorado.

The bar banter was always a blast even if the actual work was often not. From Fairbanks to Maui's Hana Highway, Key West to Lake Titicaca, I learned that bar stories are one thing everyone has in common. You may not be able to speak the language, but when you've found a good bar you always feel at home. I've shared tall tales in many languages and learned that everyone always wants to one-up a good story.

So this book began as a series of baseball stories for bar fans. (Or was it bar stories for baseball fans? I was never quite sure.) But early in the process I found that the most interesting stories were actually serious ones, not merely barroom tales. Through my research on the Chicago Cubs, I found myself learning more about White House scandals that involved former Cubs executives. Psychology, architecture, medicine, mental epidemics and even voodoo became more intriguing than hitting totals or pitching feats. What started as a book of great bar stories morphed into an examination of American and global history as seen through the prism of the Chicago Cubs. While other teams may be able to brag about owning more World Series championships than the Cubs, I discovered that no other sports team has altered global history to the degree the Cubs have.

I have lived a couple of blocks from Wrigley Field for a decade; I am a Cubs fan. But I was also a journalist for six years so I made sure to take as unbiased a stance as possible. I simply reveal the facts, connect the dots and, as often as possible, allow the comments of established historians to fill in the details. Not every story is one that Cubs fans will be proud to learn. Some will change the thoughts you held for years and may force you to question many things. The good guys aren't always good, the bad guys aren't always bad and many so-called facts taught in schools are more myth than truth.

Billion-dollar fields such as marketing, broadcasting, fast food, medical science and religious evangelism evolved they way they did due to The Friendly Confines.

Al Capone would have improved baseball if he had not been sent to prison.

Jackie Robinson was *not* the first African American major-league player.

And it was all because of the Chicago Cubs.

Question everything. Assume nothing. Enjoy.

—The author

Introduction

What is GeoVerse™? How can I live a book?

GeoVerse™ is the latest evolution in book publishing that helps readers take the reading experience to places it has never been by guiding them to locations in the real world. Each book powered by GeoVerse™ contains sections that allow readers to learn more about a specific topic through either online video and/or audio or, by using a GPS-enabled device (Global Positioning System), they can be guided to a location in the real world that corresponds to the section.

Created in conjunction with teachers seeking to make learning more enjoyable and publishers seeking to enhance the book-reading experience, GeoVerse™ works with traditional printed books as well as ebooks.

Scattered throughout each GeoVerse™-powered book are coded entries set apart from the text by parentheses that begin with the name GeoVerse™ and are followed by a number — for example, (GeoVerse™286). In the ebook version of a GeoVerse™ book, the reader merely needs to click the hyperlinked entry. The hyperlink will open up the GeoVerse™ page at SherpaMultimedia.com that corresponds to that coded entry. On that Web page the reader will find a hint about what the entry is or where it is located and either a video to watch, audio to hear or a pair of GPS-friendly files that can be used with any smartphone or GPS device to guide the reader to the location in the real world. The pair of GPS files each contain the same information but allow the reader the choice of how he or she wishes to experience the location in real life: either via a Google Map that offers instant directions on any GPS-enabled handheld (smartphone, iPad, etc. Note: not all Kindles are loaded with GPS software) or a GPX-coded file that can be downloaded and synced to any traditional GPS device (Garmin, Magellan, etc.) for later use.

For a traditionally printed book, the reader merely needs to go to the GeoVerse™ page at SherpaMultimedia.com (SherpaMultimedia.com/GeoVerse) and scroll down to find the code for the entry in question.

GeoVerse™ is a complementary and enjoyable way to extend your learning experience beyond the printed page. You decide how much you want to participate, or even at all. You can easily skip right over the GeoVerse™ entries and continue reading if you have no interest in viewing any online videos, listening to any online audio or being guided to locations in the real world. Or you can experience GeoVerse™ after you've finished reading the book. Or you can enjoy each GeoVerse™ entry as you come across them in the book. It's your choice.

—The Publisher, Sherpa Multimedia

Section I

Politics

Chapter 1

Cubs Spring Training Led to End of Communism

How Cubs Spring Training on Catalina Island
Changed the Course of History

Before the Chicago Cubs settled on the more geographically friendly city of Mesa, Arizona, for their spring training location beginning in 1952, the team called Catalina Island home during that season. Located approximately 22 miles off the coast of Los Angeles, California, Catalina Island may look familiar to movie fans, as more than 200 films have been shot there over the past century, including *Pearl Harbor* (2001), *The Hunt for Red October* (1990) and *Jaws* (1974). But Catalina Island was not always so welcoming to film studios and tourists. Before movies took over the island, the Cubs were the most famous temporary residents there.

In 1919, Cubs owner William Wrigley spent $16 million to buy and renovate the tropical island to create his version of a baseball haven, though it was far from that in the minds of the players and coaches. Beautiful for vacations, Catalina Island was remote and rugged, hardly the place to play baseball. It was a great place to climb mountains. But run on level baseball fields? Not really. Players hiked mountains for conditioning, something they were neither accustomed to nor needed in their line of work. Gabby Hartnett once tried to joke his way out of mountain hikes by asking the coaching staff if the National League base paths were inclined.

Wrigley eventually built the baseball home of which he had dreamed on Catalina Island; however, the remote location would prove to be too difficult for the team to manage. Lack of competition within driving distance, the cost of travel, and unpredictable weather made scheduling a nightmare for the organization and their opponents. In 1952, the team moved spring training to

3

the mainland. Today little remains of the Cubs' former presence on Catalina Island, now a playground for the wealthy and film companies. In 1975, William Wrigley's son, Philip, donated 88 percent of the island to the Catalina Island Conservatory, a nonprofit organization whose goal is to ensure that the island is preserved for posterity.

What few people are aware of is that this tiny island—and, more specifically, the difficulty of accessing it—changed the course of history.

Ronald Reagan, the 40th president of the United States, was not just one of the most popular U.S. presidents ever, but also helped end the Cold War with the Soviet Union. He negotiated an historic reduction in nuclear weapons, and his famous 1987 "tear down this wall" speech helped lead to the eventual dismantling of the Berlin Wall. What many people don't know about him is that his career began in part because of remote Catalina Island.

An avid sports fan, Reagan was born in the small town of Tampico, Illinois, in the western part of the state. After graduating from college, he managed to get a job with WHO radio out of Davenport, Iowa, as its sports director. Eager to make his way to the West Coast to get a shot at Hollywood fame and fortune, Reagan negotiated a deal with the station to let him cover the Cubs for ten days during spring training.

A violent storm was blasting Southern California upon Reagan's arrival at Los Angeles in 1937. Safety concerns prompted local authorities to forbid boats and planes from attempting to reach the island, where mudslides had cut off the Cubs' hotel from town.

The future president made an executive decision and decided to stay at the Biltmore Hotel, the Cubs' hotel on the mainland. While staying there, he called on a former WHO coworker, Joy Hodges, who was breaking into the movie business. Over dinner, Hodges promised to get Reagan a screen test while he was in California if he was serious about starting a career in show business. The next day, Reagan met with agent Bill Meiklejohn, who was instantly impressed. Meiklejohn got Reagan a meeting with Max Arnow, casting director for Warner Brothers. Arnow was equally impressed and asked Reagan to stay in town for a few more days. Nervously and politely, Reagan explained that he could not do so. While he desperately wanted to work for Warner Brothers, his obligations to the Cubs required him to get to Catalina Island and then back to Iowa. He gave Arnow his contact information and hoped for the best.

"At the end of the day, when I finally arrived on Catalina, Cubs manager Charlie Grimm chewed me out for being absent without leave," Reagan later wrote in his autobiography, *An American Life.* "I couldn't bring myself to tell him that my mind was somewhere else; it was exploding with visions of a future of which he wouldn't be a part."[1]

Reagan's future was anything but assured. After all, countless young acting hopefuls flocked to California, dreaming of the chance from which he had just walked away. He had just told one of the most powerful men in Hollywood that he would not stay the night in Los Angeles to wait for an answer. This was someone who was not accustomed to being told *no.* Reagan admitted in his autobiography that on the train ride home to Iowa, he called himself "a damn fool" for leaving.

Two days later, a telegram arrived from Hollywood with an acting contract for seven years at $200 per week. Reagan was eventually featured in more than 70 Hollywood films, and later used his acting experiencing to become one of the most popular politicians of the twentieth century. Dubbed "The Great Communicator" due to his oratory skills, which he had honed during his time broadcasting Cubs games on the radio and his acting days in Hollywood, Reagan became a household name around the world.

By working together to negotiate, sign, and enact the 1987 Intermediate-Range Nuclear Forces Treaty (which limited the production of nuclear weapons by the world's two greatest powers at the time), Soviet Union leader Mikhail Gorbachev and Reagan changed the world more than any leaders had since World War II. In 1989, the Berlin Wall did finally come down. In 1990, Gorbachev became the first elected president of the Soviet Union, which collapsed a year later, allowing open markets to flow into the former Soviet countries, freeing millions of people from communist regimes.

The world will forever remember the dismantling of the Soviet Union as one of the most important political events of the twentieth century. Gorbachev achieved the political influence to realize such a dramatic change through years of negotiations to end the Cold War with the United States—led at the time by Ronald Reagan, a former Cubs broadcaster whose own career was launched by foul weather off Catalina Island during spring training in 1937.

Chapter 2

The Teapot Dome Scandal

One of the Worst Political Scandals in American History Revealed Deep Corruption that Led All the Way to the Oval Office—And Right in the Middle of It All Was a Former Cubs Owner

The connection between the Chicago Cubs and the White House wasn't always as rosy as the relationship that former president Ronald Reagan enjoyed with the team. In fact, the connection between the Cubs and the Oval Office includes one of the biggest scandals in the nation's history, an event that changed the way our government is run thanks to new laws and regulations that seek to ensure such illegal activities cannot happen again.

The Teapot Dome Scandal of the 1920s revealed the truth behind the long-suspected practice of big business "buying" politicians through campaign financing and bribes. Given the atmosphere of corruption that permeated American business at the turn of the twentieth century, some people may not blame former Cubs co-owner and oil tycoon Harry Sinclair for his desire to use his vast fortune and connections to become the richest man in the nation.

Sinclair had made it clear that he was out to amass a fortune larger than that of the man he saw as his competitor, John D. Rockefeller—the founder of Standard Oil, one of the richest men in history, and a pioneer in the practice of big business buying the White House. According to Rockefeller biographer Ron Chernow (author of *Titan: The Life of John D. Rockefeller, Sr.*), Rockefeller contributed more than $250,000 to Republican presidential candidate William McKinley, governor of Ohio, in 1896. This single contribution was greater than half of what opposing candidate William Jennings Bryan, a Democrat, was able to earn. Bryan sought to curb the monopolies that Rockefeller and other tycoons such as Andrew Carnegie and J.P. Morgan maintained. McKinley won the election, ensuring congress never passed legislation preventing expansion of big business monopolies, and Bryan's fight for the average person became a footnote in history.

That dusty past was merely a prelude to the nefarious business tactics Harry Sinclair would eventually attempt.

The year 1905 saw big changes all over the world. An unknown scientist named Albert Einstein published papers revealing his famous equation, $E = MC^2$, which would alter science forever. Russia's Bloody Sunday slaughter hinted at the Bolshevik Revolution soon to come, which would alter the world's political landscape. The Cubs, too, were undergoing a major change in leadership.

Due to failing health, Cubs owner Jim Hart sold the Cubs to former Cincinnati sports reporter C. Webb "Charlie" Murphy and his financial backer, Charles P. Taft, in 1905. Taft was the brother of William Howard Taft, 27th president of the United States, who took office four years after the Murphy-Taft duo bought the Cubs. Charles Taft's relationship to the Cubs, along with the political guidance he gave his brother's presidential campaign, would eventually lead to a national conflict that has lasted more than a century and counting—but that is the topic of our next chapter.

The Cubs experienced some of their best (and worst) days during the Murphy-Taft ownership, winning the 1907 and 1908 World Series thanks to eventual Hall of Famers Mordecai "Three-Finger" Brown, Frank Chance, Johnny Evers, and Joe Tinker. By 1912, however, the team was on the decline, and Chance had taken over as manager. Worse yet, rival baseball leagues threatened to steal the limelight from the Cubs, including the Federal League, which had placed a team in Chicago. By 1914, the Federal League, formerly a minor league, had added enough teams to call itself a major league.

Meanwhile, Murphy, who handled the business of the Cubs (Taft preferred to remain in the shadows in his office in Cincinnati), was unloading the Cubs' best players in an attempt to stay financially solvent. Murphy either released or traded Tinker, Brown, and Ed Reulbach; each of them signed eventually with Federal League teams, simultaneously improving the new league's player pool and weakening the talent base of the established National League. Enraged at Murphy's actions, the other NL owners were eager to find new custodians for the Cubs and end the Murphy-Taft reign.

Making things even worse for the Cubs was the fact that a new, beautiful ballpark debuted in Chicago in 1914: fan-friendly Weeghman Park, which would eventually be renamed Wrigley Field. An immediate hit with baseball fans, Weeghman Park was home to the Federal League's Chicago Whales, a team that had not only some of the best talent in baseball, but an ideal stadium in which to play.

If the Cubs were allowed to continue in their skinflint ways, the entire National League was at risk of falling victim to the expanding Federal League. Something had to be done, and quickly.

Lawsuits between the Federal League and Organized Baseball (a consortium of the National League, the American League, and their affiliated minor league teams) were filed throughout 1914 and 1915, with both sides losing money in the process. On December 22, 1915, all the fighting ended with a $600,000 buyout of the Federal League by Organized Baseball and the agreement that two Federal League owners would be allowed to buy existing major league franchises and merge their baseball interests. Pursuant to this agreement, St. Louis Terriers owner Philip Ball bought the American League's St. Louis Browns (which became the Baltimore Orioles in 1953) and Chicago Whales owner Charles Weeghman, along with partner Harry Sinclair, bought the National League's Cubs. They moved the team into their beautiful new ballpark in January 1916.

The total cost to major league owners to destroy the Federal League reached approximately $5 million. That may sound expensive, but it was worth it in order to finally begin to organize the largest professional baseball leagues—the NL and the AL—into one coherent management structure overseen as two equal halves of Major League Baseball.

However, while the major league owners didn't realize it at the time, they had just let the wolf into the chicken coop. As innovators in their respective industries—Weeghman in fast food and Sinclair in oil—both of the new owners of the Cubs had large personal fortunes. They also brought a great deal of dirty laundry to the league—secrets that would eventually lead to incredible scandals in both baseball and politics.

Weeghman was friends with a number of powerful Chicago gamblers, particularly Mont Tennes, a known colleague of underworld boss Arnold Rothstein. Weeks before the 1919 World Series, Tennes told Weeghman that Rothstein and his cronies had fixed the upcoming World Series between the Chicago White Sox and the Cincinnati Reds. Weeghman revealed that he had known about the fix before the Series during his grand jury testimony in the wake of the infamous "Black Sox Scandal." Yet investigators failed to follow up on Weeghman's clear connections with organized crime. Those connections will be the subject of future chapters, but suffice it to say, by his own admission, Weeghman had high friends in low places. What's more, Sinclair, his business partner, would prove to be one of the most infamous criminals in American political history.

And there was yet another problem with Weeghman's purchase of the Cubs: he couldn't afford it. Weeghman was a showman who enjoyed portraying himself as a mover and a shaker in industry—an innovator and a marketer rather than a financial manager. Indeed, the restaurateur turned baseball owner changed the future of both fast food and baseball with his ideas (which will be explored further in later chapters). He was also a smart marketer, which allowed him to develop his greatest strength: the ability to raise capital. After experiencing success with his Weeghman lunch counters, the young businessman sought to expand his financial empire, investing in movies and poolrooms, among other exploits. Unfortunately for him, these investments never proved financially successful. Before he died, Weeghman boasted that he had a net worth of $8 million—but the claim was never substantiated.

While Weeghman recognized the opportunity to buy the Cubs for $500,000 in early 1916 as a worthwhile investment, he did not have the cash on hand to pull off the deal by himself. Undaunted, Weeghman approached some of the most wealthy men in Chicago—including J. Ogden Armour (a meatpacking tycoon), William Walker (a wealthy fish monger who later became Cubs president), Julius Rosenwald (a partner in Sears and Roebuck and founder of Chicago's Museum of Science and Industry), Albert Lasker (an advertising pioneer), William Wrigley (a chewing gum magnate), and Harry Sinclair (an oil baron and former owner of the Federal League's Newark franchise who netted $100,000 from the negotiated demise of the Federal League)—and convinced them to become investors in his ballclub.

Despite these high-powered associates, World War I changed everything for Weeghman and Sinclair. Government rationing of food caused reductions in supplies, and fewer men working in Chicago's downtown "Loop" area needed quick lunches because the army had drafted them into the war effort—both of which took a toll on Weeghman's lunch counter earnings. His restaurants began closing and his ability to finance the Cubs eroded.

For Sinclair, however, the war was a boon, increasing the consumption of oil and gas beyond anything he could have hoped for earlier. Sinclair founded the Sinclair Oil & Refining Corporation in 1916, eventually becoming the leader of a billion-dollar company and propelling himself toward the highest echelons of the wealthy elite.

Weeghman began selling off shares of his stake in the Cubs to Wrigley, who was known for maintaining his fortune by shunning investments in other companies and instead keeping his money in large cash reserves. Sinclair, intent on becoming wealthier than Rockefeller, allowed his investments in the Cubs to diminish along with Weeghman's. Many baseball historians contend that Sinclair's only interest in baseball was monetary—that he never had a love of the game—unlike Wrigley, who was a true fan of the sport. Whether Sinclair had a passion for baseball or not, his investment in the Cubs as a partial owner was over by 1921, when Wrigley took complete control of the organization, forcing Albert Lasker, the last partner from Weeghman's takeover of the club in 1916, to sell his portion of the team.

Parting ways with Sinclair proved to be fortuitous for Weeghman, Wrigley, and the rest of the investors when it was revealed that Sinclair had bribed a member of President Warren Harding's cabinet to gain oil rights in the largest American land lease scandal of the twentieth century.

By the fall of 1923, details emerged that Sinclair had paid Alfred Fall, Harding's secretary of the interior, $100,000 in bribe money to secure the rights to drill for oil on portions of land in Wyoming (the Teapot Dome oil field) and California (Elk Hills and Buena Vista oil fields) that were owned by the government. Fall resigned his cabinet position in January 1923, but not before giving Sinclair a five-year contract to buy the oil rights in the Teapot Dome reserves, amounting to roughly two million barrels of oil a year. Worse yet, the contract was renewable. Sinclair's bribes were successful at first, but not for long.

On August 2, 1923, President Harding died from a stroke. Biographers and researchers have differed for decades about whether or not the former president was aware of Sinclair's bribes and the illegal acquisition of the Teapot Dome oil rights. But, as Laton McCartney explained in his book *The Teapot Dome Scandal*, the fact that Harding's widow, Florence, immediately returned to the White House after the president's funeral to burn any papers that might besmirch her dead husband's legacy does not shed a positive light on Harding's possible role in the scandal.

Vice President Calvin Coolidge assumed the office of president after Harding's death, knowing that the Teapot Dome scandal was a mess that would likely doom his political career. Unsure of how to handle the situation so as to minimize its impact on both his career and the Republican party, Coolidge turned to another politician (and Cubs fan), former president William Howard Taft—whose brother, Charles, had sold the team to the Weeghman-Sinclair ownership group seven years earlier. According to McCartney, Taft's reply was simple: "Do nothing."[2]

Was Taft urging Coolidge to go easy on Sinclair because of the baseball connection the men shared? It's doubtful. After all, Taft is the only U.S. president to also serve as Chief Justice of the United States. Upholding the law was Taft's mission in life. However, it is both odd and noteworthy that Taft's advice to Coolidge would benefit the oilman who also owned the baseball team that Taft's family had been involved with for nearly two decades.

An official government investigation into the Teapot Dome scandal began in October 1923; it would take six years for the U.S. government to finally deliver justice. In 1930, Alfred Fall became the first-ever member of the cabinet to be sent to prison for his actions in office, eventually serving nine months in a New Mexico jail. He was also fined $100,000, the amount of Sinclair's bribe. But the former cabinet member may have gotten off easy, considering Sinclair eventually paid Fall as much as $269,000, according to McCartney.[3]

But the heart of the scandal was Sinclair, who refused to cooperate with authorities and investigators. He and his lawyers did everything possible to draw out the investigation. In the end, he was found guilty of contempt of the U.S. Senate and contempt of court. In May 1929, Sinclair went from being known as one of the richest men in the nation to being known as inmate No. 10520 in the District of Columbia Jail & Asylum. Sinclair served seven months in prison, where, according to McCartney, he wore silk pajamas to bed at night.

Despite his jail sentence, Sinclair seems to have had the last laugh. After departing prison in November 1929, he went on to expand his fortune several times over. In fact, at the time of his death in 1956, his net worth was estimated at more than $400 million.

What the Watergate Scandal was to American politics in the second half of the twentieth century—a revelation of deep-seated corruption at the highest levels of government, possibly even including the president of the United States himself—the Teapot Dome Scandal was to the first half of the century. In fact, in some ways, Teapot Dome was worse than Watergate. The Watergate scandal proved that politicians would stoop to spying on and stealing from their own citizens to preserve their power. But Teapot Dome revealed that elected officials and the power they carried was literally for sale to the highest bidder, making the rich even richer while denying average Americans access to and profits from valuable public lands. At the center of this dark period in U.S. history stood a former Cubs owner, Sinclair, who proved he would use any and all means at his disposal to secure what was best for his own interests. Too bad for Cubs fans that his main focus was oil fields and his fortune instead of baseball and championships.

Chapter 3

Rift Between Republicans and Democrats

American Politics Is Now a Bipartisan, Contentious Battle with Both Sides Unwilling To Work with the Other. It Did Not Used To Be that Way, and the Start of the Current State of Affairs Was Largely Due to the Chicago Cubs.

American politics in the twenty-first century is a combative spectacle with both sides waging verbal battles and refusing to cooperate. But it wasn't always like that—until the Chicago Cubs entered the story, at least.

Of course, politics has always involved heated competitions between two or more parties fighting to win people over. When careers and reputations are at stake, powerful men often stoop to petty tactics. For example, during the 1800 presidential campaign, Thomas Jefferson's supporters accused then-president John Adams of being a hermaphrodite. Adams' son, John Quincy Adams (the first son of a president to become president himself), continued the tradition of verbal sniping by calling opponent Andrew Jackson a murderer, his mother a prostitute, and his wife a mistress during the 1828 presidential campaign.

Passionate politicians have always been at odds with each other, but many historians regard the 1912 presidential campaign as the start of a rift in the political fabric of the United States. Neil Steinberg of the *Chicago Sun-Times* explained it succinctly:

> Before 1912, presidential elections were low-key affairs, with candidates rarely campaigning in person, and never attacking each other directly. Then former president Teddy Roosevelt leapt into the race between President William Howard Taft and Woodrow Wilson, calling Taft a "fathead" with the "brains of a guinea pig." Taft returned fire, calling Roosevelt supporters "neurotics." [Taft] became the first sitting president to actively campaign for re-election, determined, he said, "to keep a madman [Roosevelt] out of the White House."[4]

15

Why the acrimony? Teddy Roosevelt, the 26th president of the United States, felt he had been betrayed by his handpicked successor, William Howard Taft— who also did more than any other president to popularize the game of baseball. And why wouldn't he? After all, his brother was part owner of the Chicago Cubs. Charles Taft, the younger half-brother of the president, also founded the *Cincinnati Post*, the cornerstone of a media empire. In 1905, Charles Taft loaned $125,000 to Charles Murphy to buy the Chicago Cubs, making the newspaper publisher a key yet behind-the-scenes part of team management from his home in Cincinnati. Murphy repaid the loan without incident, but nine years later, Charles Taft decided he wanted to go from financier to outright owner, buying the Cubs from Murphy in 1914.

Charles Taft was a shrewd businessman and political adviser, abilities that benefited his older brother but also led directly to an eventual rift between two of the times most important political leaders. The assassination of President William McKinley in 1901 vaulted the 43-year-old Roosevelt into the Oval Office, where he remained until 1909. William Howard Taft was one of Roosevelt's trusted colleagues, and the man whom Roosevelt hoped would succeed him in the White House. Publicly backed by Roosevelt and with his brother helping to direct his campaign, William Howard Taft easily won the 1908 presidential election against Democrat William Jennings Bryan.

The first letter William Howard Taft wrote after winning the election was to Roosevelt. According to biographer Herbert S. Duffy's book, *William Howard Taft*, the letter said in part:

> The first letter I wish to write is to you, because you have always been the chief agent in working out the present state of affairs and my selection and election are chiefly your work. You and my brother Charley made that possible which in all probability would not have occurred otherwise.[5]

Little did President Taft know that this simple letter of thanks would forever alter the course of American politics.

It is a little known fact that Teddy Roosevelt hated baseball and anyone or anything associated with it, calling the sport mollycoddle (by which he meant that the game was not manly). Even worse, Roosevelt had a huge ego and never forgot a slight, whether real or imagined. Roosevelt deeply resented Charles Taft's involvement in his brother's campaign. What's more, being mentioned in the same sentence with a baseball man was an insult Roosevelt would not forget. "[Roosevelt] hated baseball, a game much too slow for his impetuous nature," wrote Richard D. White Jr. in his book *Roosevelt the Reformer.*[6] Baseball was not the only rift between these two presidents. But the lines in the sand were drawn that fateful day when Taft dared to put a baseball person on the same plain as the former president.

Roosevelt's cronies and companions quickly exacerbated the conflict; they too harbored resentments, as they had expected Taft to toe the line created by his predecessor, particularly when it came to preserving the national parks that Roosevelt had established and rehiring Roosevelt's advisers. Wrote Duffy:

> Almost immediately after the election, Taft began the trying task of organizing the Cabinet. [Taft] wanted around him men with whom he could work to the best advantage, in his own way. To find them was not easy, for he was hampered by the exaggerated expectations of subordinates in the Republican ranks, who, believing [Taft] to be a sort of "crown prince," thought that he should carry on not only the policies but also the appointees of his predecessor [Roosevelt].[7]

Besieged by Roosevelt appointees seeking to keep their jobs and maintain the status quo, President Taft set up a remote office in Augusta, Georgia, to put some distance between himself and his Republican subordinates. Taft insisted on running his presidency in his own way with his own selected cabinet members. Roosevelt's former cabinet members went to the previous president several times in the hopes that he would help stave off their replacement. Roosevelt, however, did not intervene until Taft replaced Secretary of the Interior James Rudolph Garfield with Richard Ballinger.

Convinced that Roosevelt had overstepped his authority in turning millions of acres of privately owned land into national reserves, Taft and Ballinger controversially reversed those decisions, opening up large tracts of land for private and commercial use. Gifford Pinochet, a close friend of Roosevelt whom the president had appointed to oversee the U.S. Forest Service, was vehemently opposed to Ballinger's actions and openly questioned whether the Taft administration was for sale to the highest bidder when it came to real estate.

While no evidence was uncovered proving Pinochet's accusations, they do underscore the ominous advice ("do nothing") that Taft later gave President Coolidge during the Teapot Dome scandal later in 1923. While it may be mere coincidence, it is highly suspect that the same accusations—selling public land for private oil development—were made against both Taft (whose brother owned the Cubs) and Harry Sinclair (who, along with Charles Weeghman, bought the Cubs from the Taft family). It would appear that baseball connections helped to create skeletons in Taft's political closet.

Taft fired Pinochet for his insolence and open accusations of the White House, an act that only created more rancor between Roosevelt and his successor. Wrote Duffy, "Taft had long possessed misgivings as to Roosevelt's sincerity and . . . wondered if Roosevelt were not dissembling, and in truth seeking for an excuse, or a number of excuses, for an open break with the President."[8]

When Taft asked personal friends who knew both men what the root of the growing rift between them was, the answer shocked him. Archibald Butt, who had the rare distinction of being an aide and adviser to both Roosevelt and Taft, told Taft that Roosevelt deeply resented the letter that gave credit for his election to both Roosevelt *and* Taft's brother, a man who worked in the ignoble and "mollycoddle" sport of baseball. Wrote Duffy:

> That Roosevelt should regard this letter as an occasion for feeling bitter toward Taft, because he had dared to include his brother in the same class with Roosevelt, surprised [President Taft]. It seemed petty that a letter written in the fullness of gratitude, as this letter was, should hurt his vanity because Taft had included his own brother as entitled to gratitude. Taft could hardly believe that a man of Roosevelt's capacities would stoop to such a trifling excuse for breaking with him.[9]

Trifling or not, the rift between the two was real and would only get worse. By the time the 1912 election came around, Roosevelt had reversed his previous assertions that he would never again run for president. When the Republicans nominated Taft for a second term, Roosevelt started the Progressive Party, nicknamed the Bull Moose Party in reference to Roosevelt, and in so doing split the Republican party in two and practically handed Democratic nominee Woodrow Wilson the presidency.

Calling the sitting president a "fathead" and "puzzle-wit" during his 1912 election campaign, Roosevelt set the derisive tone that political campaigns have had ever since. Taft retaliated by calling Roosevelt unethical and unprofessional. It was a new low for some of the most important men in the world, and the tone of political discourse has not changed much in more than a century.

Relax on the Titanic

President William Howard Taft was actually not in attendance for one of the baseball firsts with which he is credited—which was why it was a first. Confused? We'll explain.

Taft was the first president to throw out the first pitch for a baseball game, doing so at the Washington Senators' home opener in 1910 and again in 1911. But as mentioned previously, he was not on hand in 1912 to throw out the first pitch. Taft was attending the funeral for personal friend and former aide Archibald Butt, whose death was so dramatic that it reads like fiction—though it is all true.

After a career as a journalist and army major, Butt became an aide to President Teddy Roosevelt, accompanying the president everywhere and becoming a trusted friend. When Taft assumed the duties of president, he kept Butt on as an adviser and they became close friends as well. When Taft and Roosevelt became bitter rivals, Butt found himself torn between two men whom he deeply respected and considered friends.

Never married, Butt wrote letters nearly every day to his sister, Clara, about his life in the White House. His letters are an historic glimpse into the inner workings of the Oval Office at the turn of the century and, perhaps more importantly, the conflict between Roosevelt and Taft.

Butt was so close to both men that the simmering feud between the two actually caused their mutual friend health issues; in fact, Butt was on the verge of a nervous breakdown. Like a child caught between divorced parents, Butt was constantly asked by Roosevelt what Taft was saying and doing, and Taft did the same about Roosevelt. The stress took such a toll on the loyal aide that doctors urged him to take an extended vacation in Europe to relax his nerves. Eager to help his friend, Taft arranged a six-week trip to Europe for Butt, including a visit to the Vatican to hand deliver a note of thanks to Pope Pius X for three new cardinal appointees in the United States.

Before sailing for Europe, Butt sent a note to Clara jokingly reminding her of the location of the library of letters he had sent her in case his ship sank. Unfortunately for Butt, his reminder soon became no joke. Being a close friend of the White House meant Butt received first-class treatment, included during his trip home from Europe, which was booked on the most exclusive transportation in the world at that time: the H.M.S. *Titanic*.

Butt died in the icy waters of the wreck. Numerous accounts say that the former army officer helped several women and children into the lifeboats, his only request being that the survivors remember him to his family. Butt's trip abroad permanently relieved him of all his White House–related stress and made him a part of history, but it just goes to show that having friends in high places doesn't always work out for the best.

While Roosevelt may have his likeness carved into Mount Rushmore, as the president who started more baseball traditions than any other, Taft's legacy is arguably more ingrained in American society. In fact, Taft's connections with baseball were so numerous that when baseball officials determined in 1920 that they needed to hire a commissioner to oversee the game, they offered the position to the former president. (When he declined, they turned to their second choice, Judge Kenesaw Mountain Landis, who accepted the job.)

Of course, there have always been connections between our national pastime and our leaders. George Washington played a game called "rounders" at Valley Forge that fans today would recognize as an early form of the game. John Adams, Andrew Johnson, and Abraham Lincoln all either played or watched baseball. According to the White House's official website, in 1892 Benjamin Harrison became the first sitting president to attend a game (rather than Taft, as many reports have claimed). However, it was Taft who did the most to create acceptance among the American public for the simple act of attending a baseball game.

Prior to Taft, presidents were concerned that being seen sitting still for several hours would be bad for public relations or that the taint of widespread gambling within the game would tarnish their reputation if they were to attend a contest. Taft, who pitched at Yale University and loved baseball (although his passion for golf was even stronger), refused to subscribe to such concerns. He attended three games in 1909, six in 1910, and fourteen in total during his presidency—each of those numbers becoming firsts for a president.[10]

On May 29, 1909, Taft became the first president to watch a game in a city other than Washington, D.C., attending a Pittsburgh Pirates game. Instead of meeting with local business leaders as planned, Taft attended the Pirates game in an effort to portray himself as an average fan like his constituents—making him the first president to use baseball as a form of propaganda. Taft's aide, Butt, rearranged the president's schedule and secured seats in the grandstands to create an image of Taft as a man of the people. Officials with the Pirates and the visiting club reworked the game's schedule to accommodate the president. It wasn't hard to do, since the opponent that day was the Chicago Cubs. (The Cubs won 8–3 in 11 innings.)

On September 16, 1909, Taft became the first sitting president to attend a baseball game at Wrigley Field, watching the New York Giants' Christy Mathewson outduel the Cubs' Mordecai "Three-Finger" Brown in a 2–1 Giants victory. Brown and Mathewson, the two best pitchers in the NL at that time, had one of the most storied baseball rivalries of the twentieth century. The two Hall of Fame hurlers played each other 24 times overall, with Brown winning 13 of their meetings, including 9 in a row between 1905 and 1908. Like Presidents Taft and Roosevelt, Brown and Mathewson were destined to have their careers revolve around each other, squaring off in what proved to be the final major league game for both on September 4, 1916. Brown, whose hand was mangled on his family's farm in Nyseville, Indiana, was one of the best pitchers of all time despite having no index finger above the knuckle and being unable to control his pinky. His baseball accomplishments, achieved despite this handicap, earned him a monument in his honor in southern Indiana. (GeoVerse™022)

Taft's two most enduring contributions to the game began on the same day: April 14, 1910, Opening Day, when he threw out the first pitch of the season to future Hall of Famer Walter Johnson. Since then, it has been a tradition for the president to throw out the first pitch of the Major League Baseball season. The second tradition credited to Taft that day may be more myth than fact, as evidence about the occurrence is anecdotal. Legend has it that during the game, Taft, who at more than 300 pounds was the heaviest president in history, couldn't stay seated any longer and needed to stand up and stretch his legs, doing so during the seventh inning. Seeing the president stand, fans also stood and stretched. Thus allegedly began the tradition of the seventh-inning stretch.

Taft threw out the first pitch once more on Opening Day in 1911, but the *Titanic* disaster in 1912 forced him to miss that year's first game, giving Vice President James S. Sherman the opportunity to become the first man in that office to throw out the first pitch. (See sidebar, "Relax on the Titanic.") Other presidential baseball firsts for Taft included being the first to attend two games in one day (in St. Louis on May 4, 1910) and the first to see a game in his hometown (May 7, 1912, in Cincinnati).[11]

Much like his presidency, however, Taft's baseball legacy included questionable and suspicious decisions.

Taft was the only president to also serve on the Supreme Court, where he held the office of chief justice from 1921 to 1930. It was during his tenure in that role that the Supreme Court handed down its most important and controversial ruling ever regarding professional baseball: the ruling that defined Major League Baseball as a sport, rather than a business. This ruling is still widely questioned by legal experts. Opponents to the ruling point to the Taft family's ownership of the Chicago Cubs as a conflict of interest that might have swayed the decision. As author Eldon L. Ham wrote in his book *Broadcasting Baseball:*

> Taft was chief justice when [Oliver Wendell] Holmes wrote the "baseball is not a business in interstate commerce" opinion in the landmark *Federal Base Ball* ruling of 1922, effectively exempting major league baseball from the U.S. antitrust laws. This was an especially ironic if not suspicious ruling since the Taft presidency was known for its aggressive trust-busting practices with the filing of no fewer than 67 antitrust actions. Interestingly, Taft himself had been offered the job of the first commissioner of major league baseball, but turned it down to stay on the Court, at which point the owners turned to Chicago federal judge Kenesaw Mountain Landis.[12]

Despite all that Taft did to advance baseball, historians remember him more for the falling out with Roosevelt, which split the Republican Party and gave birth to the current antagonistic atmosphere in American politics. According to BaseballAlmanac.com, the difference between Roosevelt and Taft is clear when you consider Roosevelt's only first in baseball history: on May 6, 1907, then-President Roosevelt was issued the first presidential lifetime pass, allowing him entrance to any game for free. The pass was never used.

Chapter 4

The President and the Birth of Fantasy Baseball

Ever Hear of the First Baseman Who Went on To Become, Among Other Things, The U.S. Ambassador to the United Nations, U.S. Envoy to China, Director of the Central Intelligence Agency, Vice President of the United States, and President of the United States? Yet the Quiet Coach of that Same Yale Baseball Team Changed the World as Well.

Some sports fans may recall Ethan Allen as a former outfielder for the Chicago Cubs. A few more knowledgeable fans will remember him in his role as a Yale baseball coach for 23 years, where he led the Bulldogs to the 1947 and 1948 National Collegiate Athletic Association finals (the first two NCAA championship series in history)—and coached future president George H. W. Bush in his turn at first base to boot.

Considering that Allen only played one of his thirteen seasons in Chicago, you can forgive fans for forgetting his stay in the Windy City. And since the most notable player to take the field for him at Yale didn't go on to play in the major leagues—instead earning the slightly less prestigious honor of becoming the president of the United States—his Yale career is an esoteric memory to most. But you would be hard pressed to find anyone in the civilized world who has not heard about the industry he pioneered: fantasy sports. In fact, the genesis of the idea for all such gaming took place within the "Friendly Confines" of Wrigley Field just prior to World War II.

While patrolling the outfield at Wrigley during his playing days, Allen envisioned a game in which a player's statistics could be used in a competition between two people who would pretend to be a general manager or team owner, "drafting" players for their teams. This was during the 1930s, before computers, so Allen's vision was for a board game. Each player would have a circular cardboard disk that would fit around a spinning arrow. The "owner" of each team would spin this pinwheel, and the location where the arrow stopped would determine the action in the game.

"While I was with the Cubs in 1936, I went to various manufacturers with the hope of selling the idea to them as a game," Allen recalled in a 1983 interview with *The Sporting News'* Bill Madden, "only to have most of them practically kick me out of their offices."[13] Undaunted, Allen continued to pursue his dream as if it were a long fly ball. In 1940, Allen reached an agreement with game manufacturer Cadaco-Ellis to manufacture a board game based on his idea; in 1941, the world's first fantasy sport game, called simply All-Star Baseball, hit the marketplace.

An instant success, All-Star Baseball remained in production until 2004. The company printed new cards for all Major League players each year; since each disk was the same size, gamers could pit players from different eras against each other.

Success always spawns competition and rivals. In 1951, a similar gamed called American Professional Baseball Association appeared, and in 1961, the Strat-O-Matic game debuted. Rotisserie baseball was created during the 1980s. But before all of those games, there was Allen's All-Star Baseball. "While other similar games, such as Strat-O-Matic and APBA, have had more staying power with the public, All-Star Baseball predates them as a realistic, stat-based facsimile of actual baseball," *Wall Street Journal* writer Mike Sielski explained in 2011.[14]

Board game expert Erik Arneson called All-Star Baseball "one of the most historically and culturally significant games published since 1800."[15] Why? Because it was the first of what would become one of the world's most famous pastimes: fantasy sports.

In 2011, the Fantasy Sports Trade Association estimated that 32 million people play fantasy sports in North America. The following year, MSN.com reported that 2 million new members join the ranks of those playing fantasy sports in North America each year, meaning that the total should reach approximately 40 million by 2015—more than the number of people who voted for the 1992 reelection of George H. W. Bush, the former Yale captain whom Allen called "a one-handed artist at first base."[16] In 1992, Bush lost his re-election bid, garnering just 39 million votes to Bill Clinton's 44 million.

Allen died in 1993 at the age of 89. But thanks to his creativity while manning the outfield at the Friendly Confines, millions of fantasy sports players around the world have experienced the thrill of "owning" their own baseball team for the small cost of buying a game.

Chapter 5

The First Flyover in Aviation History

When the Chicago Cubs Met the Boston Red Sox for the 1918 World Series, a New Tradition Was Born that Has Lasted Until This Day. This Spectacle Is Still a Jaw-Dropping Experience for Young Fans and Military Enthusiasts Alike.

What began on the sandy beaches of Kitty Hawk, North Carolina, in 1903 continues on to this day, with the only difference being that Orville and Wilbur Wright's first plane—little more than a glider with a small, home-built engine—has morphed into F-15 Eagles and other fighter jets screaming across the sky. Either way, the result is the same: man-powered flight and the awe it inspires in witnesses on the ground.

Game 1 of the 1918 World Series between the Chicago Cubs and the Boston Red Sox featured the very first military flyover in world history. On September 5, 1918, 60 army biplanes flew over Chicago's Comiskey Park as a demonstration of patriotic pride, urging support for U.S. soldiers and sailors serving in World War I. Today, the military flyovers that fans everywhere enjoy are often the highlight of the game. F/A-18A fighter jets, C-17 cargo jets, F-117 stealth fighters, B-2 stealth bombers, UH-60 Black Hawk helicopters, and even historic prop planes frequently grace professional sporting events and major entertainment gatherings across the country. All of that pageantry began back in 1918 with the Cubs and the Red Sox.

Let's get the most obvious question out of the way first for Cubs fans: Why was the game played at Comiskey Park rather than the Cubs' home field, Weeghman Park (later renamed Wrigley Field)? As usual, the answer is money. Comiskey Park was larger and could therefore hold more spectators. Charles Weeghman, whose restaurants were losing money at the time because of food rationing and depletion of the homeland work force, needed the extra income. So he bargained with White Sox owner Charles Comiskey to use their larger ballpark to allow increased ticket sales.

With that out of the way, the next question is: Why have a flyover at all? The answer was the same in 1918 as it is today: moral support for our military and an attempt to increase recruitment. Military leaders recognized the potential that sporting events present: a captured audience that can be influenced to act after being inspired by a demonstration of military might. Wendy Varhegyi, a member of the air force's public affairs department, explained the "why" behind flyovers to the *Orlando Sentinel* in 2008:

> We look at these events as a way to get our message out to a more diverse audience than traditional routes. We look at sporting events as a way to reach a unique audience that is typically of recruiting-age interest.[17]

In other words, the military hopes that the awe-inspiring moment of seeing some of the most sophisticated aircraft in the world will make many in the audience want to enlist.

Such sentiment would have been overwhelmingly true in 1918, when the sight of 60 planes ready for war was a true show of force by the United States government. After all, the flying machine had only been invented 15 years earlier. The government created the U.S. Air Force in 1907 and gave it the overview of "military ballooning, air machines, and all kindred subjects." In 1912, the air force had only nine planes in its fleet (they had built eleven, but the first was given to the Smithsonian Institute and the second was destroyed in a crash). By 1915, the number of planes had risen to 23.

Sadly, there is now a chance that this grand tradition may come to an end. One of the first acts undertaken as part of the 2013 government sequestration budget cuts was to halt any participation in flyovers or air shows by the air force's Thunderbirds, the navy's Blue Angels, the army's Golden Knights, and any other similar groups. Proponents of flyovers and air shows argue that they are the only chance civilians have to see many of our military assets in action, hopefully inspiring some young people to join the cause. Opponents say that these shows are extravagantly expensive and accomplish little more than turning gasoline into noise. Either way, 1918 saw the first jingoistic show of force in the form of a flyover in both global aviation and baseball history.

Chapter 6

A Supreme Court Justice Proven Wrong

A Headhunter, a Baby, and a Supreme Court Justice Went to a Baseball Game Where History Was Made. It Sounds Like the Set Up to a Joke, but One of the Most Influential Judges in American History Confirmed this Famous Moment in Sports History as Fact. The Only Problem Is, the Judge Was Wrong. And Cubs Fans Couldn't Be Happier.

Lifelong Cubs fan and former Supreme Court Justice John Paul Stevens swore it happened. History can't have a better witness than a judge, especially since he saw it in person. Stevens wanted to close the book on Babe Ruth's famous "Called Shot" home run.

"Justice John Paul Stevens has shaped more American history than any Supreme Court justice alive," said CBS reporter Scott Pelley in a November 2010 episode of *60 Minutes*. "It was Stevens who forced a showdown with President [George W.] Bush over the prisoners at Guantanamo Bay, and Stevens who tried to stop the court from deciding the presidential election of 2000."

After discussing terrorist case rulings, the legality of corporations contributing to political campaigns, Guantanamo Bay, and the 2000 election controversy, Pelley and Stevens finally turned to a topic closer to Stevens' heart: the Chicago Cubs. A 12-year-old at the time, Stevens was in the grandstands for Game 3 of the 1932 World Series when New York Yankee slugger Babe Ruth appeared to point to center field during the fifth inning before belting a towering shot into the Wrigley Field bleachers, giving New York a 7–5 win en route to winning the Series. Ruth's "Called Shot" is one of the most famous plays in baseball history, as well as a source of endless debate.

Did he really call his shot to center field? Is it a myth? Was it retaliation for the nasty treatment the Cubs players gave their Yankee counterparts during that Series? A grainy video unearthed during the 1990s did nothing to settle the matter.

27

(GeoVerse™011) But Justice Stevens never needed to see a video or even hear what anyone else thought. And since there is no higher law in the nation than the Supreme Court, if Justice Stevens says it happened, it must be true. Right?

"He took the bat in his right hand and pointed it right at the center-field stands and then, of course, the next pitch he hit a home run in center field," Stevens told Pelley. "There's no doubt about the fact that he did point before he hit the ball."

"So the 'Called Shot' actually happened?" Pelley asked.

"Oh, there's no doubt about it," Stevens confirmed. "That's my ruling."

"Case closed?" Pelley double-checked.

"That's the one ruling I will not be reversed on!" Stevens insisted.

Home plate umpire Roy Van Graflan agreed with Stevens. "Let him put this one over and I'll knock it over the wall out there," Van Graflan quoted Ruth as saying, according to the book *Cubs Journal* by John Snyder.[18] The only problem was, Van Graflan was the only witness who heard that.

Pat Pieper, the former Cubs public address announcer and another witness, emphatically agreed that Ruth did call his shot. Years later, several Yankees agreed. So did several newspapers reporters, though only the ones from outside of Chicago.

Former Scripps-Howard reporter Joe Williams wrote, "With the Cubs riding him unmercifully from the bench, Ruth pointed to center and punched a screaming liner to a spot where no ball had ever been hit before." *New York Times* writer John Drebinger wrote a similar account.[19]

Justice Stevens may have been one of the most pivotal American figures of the twentieth century. His rulings set precedent and are part of law school lessons. Yet he was wrong about Ruth's home run.

Who said so? Ruth himself.

The story really starts with the man on the mound for the Cubs that day, Charlie Root, who earned the nickname "Chinski" because he was always ready to fight on the field and never hesitated to brush back a hitter. According to his fellow players, he was a nice guy off the field, but Root was a headhunter when crossed. His willingness to go after batters was so well chronicled that he created a myth of his own that rivaled the "Called Shot."

In Peter Golenbock's book *Wrigleyville,* former Cubs trainer Ed Froelich shared the story of a game years earlier in which Root showed his famous temper. Angry at being hit by opposing pitcher Adolpho Luque, Root took first base and told New York Giants first baseman George Kelly: "George, when you get back in the dugout, you tell your guys to be plenty loose up there because I'm going right down the batting order, twice, each man." Root was true to his word, knocking each player down twice. After he had knocked the ninth man down for the final time, umpire Cy Rigler called time, walked out to Root, and said, "Charlie, you said you were going to knock nine guys down, and that's the ninth guy. No more." Root consented and resumed pitching as normal.[20]

No box score exists to support this anecdote, but there is one from the second game of a doubleheader against the Brooklyn Robins at Ebbetts Field on July 16, 1930, in which Root hit five batters, including Luque, the winning pitcher in that 5–3 Cubs loss. Even if Froelich exaggerated his story from five hit batters to nine, and remembered it happening against a different New York team, it only underscores how richly Root deserved his "Chinski" nickname.

When a headhunter is on the mound, no hitter wants to antagonize him. Not even Ruth, who finally revealed the truth about his "Called Shot" to Froelich years after the event in question. In 1938, Froelich was the trainer for the Brooklyn Dodgers, who made their facilities available to Ruth after he retired to help him with his aches and pains. One day, Froelich asked Ruth about the "Called Shot"; he recalled Ruth's answer in *Wrigleyville*:

> [Ruth] said, "You tell those people for Baby"—he always called himself Baby— "that Baby says they're full of crap right up to their eyeballs. I may be dumb, but I'm not that dumb. I'm going to point to the center-field bleachers with a barracuda like Root out there? On the next pitch, they'd be picking it out of my ear with a pair of tweezers."
>
> He said one final word, "No."[21]

According to Froelich, the source of the "Called Shot" myth was Grantland Rice, the famous sportswriter and journalist who reveled in creating sports legends such as his famous "Four Horsemen of the Apocalypse" column in 1924 that likened Notre Dame's quartet of backfield teammates to the unstoppable four Horsemen from the Bible's Book of Revelation. Froelich said that after Game 3, Rice and the journalists from New York went straight to Ruth's locker, trying to bait him into claiming he had called his home run. Ruth wouldn't bite.

Froelich recounted that Rice said to Ruth, "Babe, damn if it didn't look like you pointed when you hit the ball."

Ruth said, "The hell I did."

Said Froelich, "That's all he said. And the newspapermen created a legend from that."[22]

None of the Chicago newspapers reported anything resembling a "Called Shot." None of the Cubs players confirmed it either, especially Root, who insisted so emphatically that it didn't happen that he refused to play himself in a scene in the 1948 movie *The Babe Ruth Story*.

Over the years, the myth of that home run grew with every telling; Ruth, realizing the story wasn't going away, embraced the revision of history that became one more part of his legend.

But what really happened that day?

Tempers were very high between the two teams even before the start of the Series. Former Yankee shortstop Mark Koenig, who played on New York's championship teams in 1926, 1927, and 1928, joined the Cubs late in the 1932 season, sparking the team to the World Series. Since Koenig was with the team for only 33 regular-season games, the Cubs didn't vote him a full World Series share. The rest of the story is best told by the Cubs players who were there that day (as quoted in *Wrigleyville*).

Cubs second baseman Billy Herman: "We were a young team and a fresh team. We had some guys on the bench that got on Ruth as soon as the Series started. And I mean they were rough. Once all that yelling starts back and forth, it's hard to stop it, and of course the longer it goes, the nastier it gets. What were jokes in the first game became personal insults by the third game. By the middle of the third game, things were really hot."

Cubs third baseman Woody English: "We were surprised when [the Yankees] came out in the paper the day before and called us the 'cheap' Chicago Cubs, 'penny-pinching' Cubs, and that's why we got on them from our dugout so badly. So we were retaliating from what they had said in the papers. When Ruth came up there, we really got on him, boy. [Commissioner] Judge Landis was really upset by the profanity around the Cubs dugout."

Cubs manager Charlie Grimm: "One of the nicknames [Ruth] didn't like was 'Big Monkey.'"

Ruth belted a first-inning home run followed by a third-inning homer by Lou Gehrig in the third, tying the game 4–4. When the Yankees came up in the top of the fifth, Root hurled two strikes past Ruth, and then the myth began.

English: "[Ruth]'s got two strikes on him. The guys are yelling at him from our dugout. He's looking right in our dugout, and he holds up two fingers. He said, 'That's only two strikes.' But the press box was way back on top of Wrigley Field, and to the people in the press, it looked like he pointed to center field. But he was looking right into our dugout holding two fingers up. That *is* the true story."

Herman: "What Ruth did was hold up his hand, telling them that was only two strikes, that he still had another one coming, and that he wasn't out yet."

Cubs pitcher Charlie Root: "Sure, Babe gestured to me. We had been riding him, calling him 'Grandpop' and kidding him about not getting to be manager of the Yankees. We wanted to get him mad, and he was when he came to bat. . . . Babe pointed at me and yelled, 'That's only one strike.' Maybe I had a smug grin on my face after he took the second strike. Babe stepped out of the box again, pointed his finger in my direction, and yelled, 'You still need one more, kid.'"

English: "Ruth hit the heck out of the ball."

Herman: "But [Ruth] didn't point. Don't kid yourself. I can tell you just what would have happened if Ruth had tried that—he would never have got a pitch to hit. Root would have had him with his feet up in the air. I told you, Charlie Root was a mean man out on the mound."

Cubs infielder Dick Bartell (who played for Chicago in 1939 and was friends with Root): "For years, nothing made Root madder than hearing about how Ruth called his shot. But he just had to live with it."

Froelich: "As a rule, Ruth didn't hit the ball into center field. Almost never. Would he be pointing to a spot where he almost never hit the ball? It doesn't make sense. But see, it's a legend. People like to believe in fantasy, even newspaper reporters."[23]

Which brings us to one of the best resources in baseball, former *Chicago Tribune* Cubs beat writer and Major League Baseball historian Jerome Holtzman. Holtzman researched the "Called Shot" and gave his verdict in a column on November 1, 1987:

Babe Ruth's called-shot home run is a myth, a fairy tale conjured from the imaginative spirit of sportswriters who, of necessity, possess a flair for the romantic and dramatic. If it never happened, why then has this fiction taken root? Because people gild lilies and sometimes remember seeing things they didn't see.[24]

It just goes to show, if the story is good enough, apparently even a Supreme Court Justice will buy a fantasy.

Chapter 7

D-Day and the Cubs

*Only One Former MLB Player Helped Defeat the
Nazis on D-Day—And He Was a Cub.*

It only seems appropriate that a baseball player named Larry French should be remembered and honored for his service in France.

D-Day, the largest amphibious assault in military history, occurred on June 6, 1944. An eye-popping panorama of 5,000 boats and 13,000 airplanes carrying 160,000 soldiers landed on the beaches of Normandy, France, to give the Allies a foothold against German forces. The cost of victory was very high: 9,000 Allied soldiers died in just a few hours.

"After fighting the Nazis, facing Major League hitters didn't seem so tough," said future Hall of Fame pitcher Warren Spahn, who was one of 500 major leaguers who served their country during World War II (although he was not part of the D-Day assault). Most baseball fans are aware that several future Hall of Famers—including Ted Williams, Bob Feller, and Spahn—had their playing careers interrupted while they served in the military. However, Cubs fans can be proud of the fact that only one former major leaguer was part of the 160,000-person force that stormed the beaches of Normandy—and he was a Cubs pitcher.

According to historian Gary Bedingfield's site BaseballInWartime.com, at least 24 Chicago Cubs served in the military during World War II. But French was the only one to take part in the greatest show of military force in recorded history. French, who served in the navy, was also the only player in history—not just the only Cub, but the only known baseball player at all—to end his playing career when he joined the military. Realizing his playing days were done, French stayed in the navy for 27 years (22 in active duty) before retiring in 1969 as a captain.

Leaving baseball was not an easy decision for French. He had 197 career wins (and 171 losses) over 14 seasons with the Pittsburgh Pirates, the Brooklyn

Dodgers, and the Cubs, and he desperately wanted to reach the benchmark milestone of 200 wins. He asked the navy to let him return to professional baseball long enough to get three more victories. He even offered to donate his military salary ($8,000) if he could just get the time to earn those three more wins. The military gave most former baseball players stateside assignments, with very few seeing action. But not wanting to set a precedent for future situations, the navy denied French's request.

French started Game 6 of the 1935 World Series, which the Cubs lost in the ninth inning, giving the Detroit Tigers the championship. He also pitched in relief in the 1938 World Series. French went 17–10 for the Cubs in 1935 and followed that with an 18–9 mark in 1936, his two best seasons for Chicago. His lone record-setting achievement was an ignoble one, his 10–19 performance for the 1938 Cubs. It was the most losses ever for a starting pitcher for a pennant-winning team, accounting for nearly a third of the Cubs' losses that season, which they finished with an 89–63 record.

French was a jovial guy who loved playing practical jokes on unsuspecting teammates and anyone unfortunate enough to be staying in the same hotel when the Cubs were on the road. Fans may remember that he actually bought a bear cub as a pet and kept him in his Chicago apartment. The idea was as horrible as it sounds: the young bear ripped his home apart. French unloaded the cub on teammate Ripper Collins; the bear quickly destroyed his home as well. Thankfully, Collins had the good sense to give the bear to a conservation organization.

Despite antics such as launching water balloons at unsuspecting fellow hotel guests from the rooftop, ignominious accomplishments like losing 19 games in a season, and laughable blunders like buying a bear cub, French goes down in history as the most patriotic Chicago Cubs player ever for serving in both the European and Pacific theatres during WWII. Next Memorial Day, Cubs fans would do well to raise a glass to the only baseball player to give up his playing days for military service; French lived to tell the story for the next four decades until his death in 1987.

According to Bedingfield, the other 23 former Cubs who served in World War II were: Dale Alderson, Hi Bithorn, Cy Block, Dom Dallessandro, Pete Elko, Marv Felderman, Bill Fleming, Charlie Gilbert, Paul Gillespie, Al Glossop, Emil Kush, Mickey Livingston, Peanuts Lowrey, Clyde McCullough, Russ Meers,

Vern Olsen, Whitey Platt, Marv Rickert, Bob Scheffing, Johnny Schmitz, Lou Stringer, Bobby Sturgeon, and Eddie Waitkus.

There was also a future major leaguer among the 160,000 soldiers on the beach that bloody day at Normandy: a diminutive 18-year-old known as Larry to his fellow navy sailors. He tried to convince his comrades that he was a minor league player back in Virginia, but none of the sailors believed this short guy—with even shorter legs. After the war, the 5'7" Larry Berra went on to have a Hall of Fame baseball career, starting as a catcher for the New York Yankees, where he became known as Yogi Berra.

While Berra's baseball career started after WWII, French's ended because of it, making him the only former baseball player at Normandy. Leon Day, a Negro League player who was elected to the Hall of Fame, served as a member of the army amphibious assault team that provided support for the D-Day attack; however, Day's unit didn't arrive until six days after D-Day on June 12, 1944.

Chapter 8

Named After and Portrayed by a President

Only One Baseball Player Was Named After a President and Portrayed by Another in a Movie—And He Was a Former Cubbie, of Course.

One of the best pitchers in history was also one of its most notorious despite having served his country in World War I. Grover Cleveland Alexander was named for U.S. President Grover Cleveland, the 22nd and 24th president of the United States (the only president to be reelected after leaving office). In 1952, two years after Alexander's death, Ronald Reagan, the 40th president of the United States, starred in a biopic about the right-handed hurler called *The Winning Team*.

Reagan appeared in 77 films during his career, but the list of those he was most proud of was quite short. *The Winning Team* was one he showed to guests at the White House on several occasions. In his 1990 autobiography *An American Life*, Reagan said he was "especially proud of" *Kings Row*; *Knute Rockne, All American*; *The Voice of the Turtle*; *John Loves Mary*; and *The Hasty Heart*.

A lifelong Cubs fan, Reagan referred to *The Winning Team* often over the years. He never forgot some of his lines from the film. When talking about his deep love for his wife, Nancy, Reagan wrote: "I can sum up our marriage in a line I spoke when I played the great pitcher Grover Cleveland Alexander, a line spoken by him in life to his wife, Aimee: 'God must think a lot of me to have given me you.'"[25]

Why did Reagan have such affection for "Alex," as he was given to call Alexander? Perhaps it was because Alexander was a damaged and pained person who overcame amazing obstacles to become in 1938 the first Cub ever inducted into the Hall of Fame.

Alexander's drinking problem was legendary, but often forgiven. Because he was the best pitcher in the game, his fellow players chose to overlook the fact the he often showed up for games extremely hungover or still drunk from the previous night. Fans forgave him because he was a war hero who played just three games—including starting for the Cubs on Opening Day in 1918—before shipping off to France to serve during World War I.

Drafted into the war, Alexander worked on the frontlines in the artillery as a sergeant and was gassed by the enemy. When he returned home after the war, Alexander was deaf in one ear, suffered from epileptic fits and posttraumatic stress, and became a chain-smoker and an alcoholic. Yet despite these flaws, almost everyone loved the guy—well, anyone who didn't have to work with him too much, that is.

Much like young players at the turn of the twenty-first century, Alexander wore his baseball cap to the side and made sure to get it one size too small so that he would stand out. He was also completely disdainful of authority figures, blatantly ignoring his coaches and manager and even smoking in the clubhouse. He was known to stash bottles of gin anywhere he could.

Through all of that, the pitcher earned the nickname Alex the Great because of his performance on the mound. Any athlete who has suffered a strained ligament can appreciate Alexander's toughness. During the early 1900s, the pitcher reportedly had a torn ligament "snapped back into place" by a "specialist." Even that injury couldn't derail a career that spanned 20 years and 373 victories (No. 1 all-time in the NL, and tied for No. 3 all-time overall with Christy Mathewson) and included three 30-win seasons. Despite his drinking, smoking, and mental and physical problems, Alexander was a guy's guy who didn't make a fuss about anyone else and definitely didn't want anyone making a fuss about him.

Alexander's personal routine before games was a perfect example of his old-school baseball mentality. "The most vivid memory I have of Grover Alexander is of him sitting in front of his locker watching the clock and waiting for exactly 20 minutes before game time," said Ed Froelich, former Cubs clubhouse boy, in the book *Wrigleyville*:

> Alex didn't believe in going to the trainer's room, and he would take a bottle of Sloan's liniment out of his locker and start pouring it onto his right shoulder and his pitching arm. He'd work and work and work until he had just the right degree of warmth, and then he'd go in and wash his hands and return to the stool in front of his locker. Then the other part of the ritual began.
>
> He'd light a Camel cigarette and sit there and smoke it, and that would consume about five minutes, and now it would be 10 minutes to three, and he'd

put on his undershirt, his uniform shirt, pick up his cap and his glove and he'd start out for the field to warm up. He'd have less than 10 minutes to get warm, and then he'd begin.[26]

An introvert who didn't socialize with his teammates or do much talking, Alexander eventually drank himself out of baseball. By the age of 42, he was broke. The moneyless pitcher was forced to work for Hubert's Flea Circus in New York's Times Square, recounting his baseball exploits to rowdy crowds. He died penniless at age 63 in his home state of Nebraska.

In *Wrigleyville*, Froelich recalled a conversation with former Cubs manager Joe McCarthy during which he asked the skipper how good Alex the Great could have been had he not been such a hard drinker. "'Who knows? Maybe he might not have been so good,' McCarthy said. 'Maybe that was one of the things that helped make him as good as he was.' He added, 'In the final analysis, how much better could he have been?'"[27]

Chapter 9

The Most Powerful Secret Society in Sports

Secret Societies Have Existed for Centuries, but There Is Only One in History that Boasts the Most Powerful Membership in the United States—And It Exists Solely Because of the Chicago Cubs.

Skull & Bones. The Bilderberg Group. The Freemasons. The Illuminati. The Knights Templar. Thanks to books, movies, and television shows, millions of ordinary people around the world know about these secret societies, whose rich, powerful members supposedly shape the world we inhabit. But there is one more secretive group that Chicago Cubs fans should care about more than any other: the Emil Verban Memorial Society.

Founded in 1975 by lobbyist David Ladd as a way to get a foot in the door with powerful Washington, D.C., politicians, the Emil Verban Memorial Society began with the sole interest of gathering high-ranking individuals in political circles to talk about and celebrate the Chicago Cubs and their players. How high-ranking? The membership of roughly 700 individuals has included former President Ronald Reagan, former Vice President Dick Cheney, former First Lady and Secretary of State Hillary Clinton, former Secretary of Defense Donald Rumsfeld, Supreme Court Justice Antonin Scalia, Senator John McCain, Senator Dick Durbin, and, to the surprise of vocal Chicago White Sox fans, President Barack Obama.

Almost everyone in the Emil Verban Memorial Society is connected to politics in some fashion, either as a politician, a lobbyist, a lawyer, a reporter, or some other kind of Beltway insider. There are some members outside of politics, but even they are heavy hitters in their own right, including actors Gary Sinise and Joe Mantegna and journalists Bryant Gumbel and George Will.

Other members have less illustrious claims to fame, including current and former federal inmates Nos. 25338-016, 16627-424, and 40892-424 (otherwise known as former Governor George Ryan, former U.S. Representative Dan Rostenkowski, and former Governor Rob Blagojevich, respectively). Despite their guilty convictions, only Blagojevich was "respectfully dumped from the club by a phantom committee," Ladd told *Wall Street Journal* reporter Ben Austen. The reason for his ejection was stupidity: "There's a difference between regular, normal Illinois graft and being an idiot," Ladd added.[28] Ladd's "phantom committee" comment was a light-hearted reference to the fact that he himself serves as the entire "committee"—Ladd is the club's only official, acting as founder, historian, and secretary, and writing more than 250 newsletters over the years to keep his 700 members connected.

Belting just one home run in his 2,911 at-bats over a seven-year playing career, Ladd selected Verban as the perfect example of Midwestern perseverance amid mediocrity. Ladd added the "Memorial" part because he wasn't sure if Verban was alive or not at the time (he was), and he thought it made the club name sound better. Before he died in 1989, Verban became aware of the club and was not happy, fearing the organization was mocking him rather than honoring him. Verban changed his mind about the club after Ladd invited the former Cubs second baseman to a luncheon during which he was ushered to the White House to meet Reagan, then in office as president.

Created to share a common affection for the Cubs, the Emil Verban Memorial Society has only a few rules: a current member must nominate new members; nominees must live in the Washington, D.C., area (a rule that has been relaxed over the years); members must be Cubs fans; and they must have a sense of humor.

The last requirement is one that both Ladd and Obama have had to learn personally. Beginning as early as 2000, Ladd tried to end the Emil Verban Memorial Society several times, only to have his members respond in an uproar, asking that the cabal of Cubs fans continue into the twenty-first century. Despite retiring from his lobbying efforts, Ladd consented to continue the society.

"The nice part of the club is that we don't do anything," Ladd, told the *Chicago Tribune*'s Shannon McMahon. "We meet every two years. That's it, and that's the nice part—no dues, no committees, no obligations."

Holding luncheons every two years made the events popular with members, who turn out by the hundreds to meet the former Cubs player or two on hand to meet members, talk about the team, and autograph baseballs. Yes, even though its members include some of the most powerful people in the world, the Emil Verban Memorial Society allows them to act like children again, meeting their baseball heroes, swapping stories, and getting autographs. Hilary Clinton even invited the society to the White House, where they surprised President Bill Clinton in the Oval Office.

Surprises from the Emil Verban Memorial Society have continued until very recently, with Obama becoming a member despite his open affection for the Chicago White Sox. When an unnamed member of the society nominated Obama for inclusion, Ladd decided to let the White Sox fan into the group without going on record as to which member was responsible for his nomination.

"I know it will be hard for him to accept this accolade," Durbin told *The Wall Street Journal*. "It's like telling him he was elected to the board of directors of the Republican National Committee." After learning of his inclusion in the society, Obama had staff members contact Ladd to find out how he could be removed. Ladd's answer to the White House was simple: "He can't."[29]

The organization presents two tongue-in-cheek awards at the society's luncheons: the Ernie Banks Positivism Award (recipients include Harry Caray, Joe Garagiola, Reagan, and Hillary Clinton, among others) and the Brock-for-Broglio Award, given for the most egregious display of bad judgment. Winners of the latter award have included former president George W. Bush (for his decision while with the Texas Rangers to trade away Sammy Sosa) and former Cubs general manager Larry Himes (for not re-signing five-time Cy Young Award winner Greg Maddux, allowing the greatest pitcher of his generation to flee Chicago for Atlanta). While the society's luncheons are biennial, periodic newsletters and some good-natured jokes—such as the one played on Obama—are the hallmarks of the group.

There have also been serious moments that benefited Cubs fans around the Beltway, even if they didn't know it. Having that much political sway gathered in one organization has its benefits—a fact that every Cubs fan in the Mid-Atlantic area had reason to be thankful for during the 1980s, according to *The Wall Street Journal*. At that time, the cable provider in Washington, D.C., that carried WGN-TV—the only source for televised Cubs games in those days—decided to drop WGN from its lineup. Refusing to lose their beloved Cubs games, several

Verban Society members intervened, making phone calls and setting up private meetings with company executives. Not surprisingly, the company restored WGN and Cubs fans, both in elected office and in the civilian population, did not miss any games.[30]

Chapter 10

Betrayed by Their Own Fans

One of the Most Powerful Men in the World—and a Lifelong Cubs Fan—Threw Out the First Pitch of the Cubs' 2004 Season Opener. But Instead of Wearing a Cubs Jacket, He Wore the Colors of the Cincinnati Reds.

While the Chicago Cubs opened the 2004 season on the road in Cincinnati, they seemed to have one small edge to boost their confidence that day: one of the world's most powerful men, who also happened to be an avowed Cubs fan, was on hand to throw out the first pitch. However, to the disbelief and consternation of Cubs fans everywhere, this "fan" went to the pitcher's mound wearing Cincinnati's colors. Vice President Dick Cheney proved that, for himself at least, politics is sometimes more important than personal preference. In a move apparently intended to appease future voters in Ohio, Cheney—a founding member of the Emil Verban Memorial Society who has been a Cubs fan since seeing his first game in 1958 as a teenager—chose a Reds jacket instead of a Chicago one.

Kerry Wood and his teammates shrugged off the slight and won the season opener, 1–0. But Cheney's actions came as a shock to anyone who knew of his love for the Cubbies. After all, as Cheney explained in his autobiography *In My Time,* his love for the team had begun way back during the summer between his junior and senior years at Natrona County High School in Wyoming, when he was selected for a special five-week program at Northwestern University for advanced students. Cheney, who was born in Lincoln, Nebraska, and moved to Wyoming with his family when he was young, was eager to see the world beyond his hometown of Casper. He jumped at the chance to visit Illinois, boarding a Union Pacific train in Rawlins that took him to Chicago. That summer, Cheney went to his first Cubs game, where the sights, sounds, and smells of the Friendly

Confines hooked the future politician. In fact, his love for the Cubs was so well-known to Washington insiders that when lobbyist David Ladd began the Emil Verban Memorial Society, he invited Cheney to become one of the founding members. Cheney was member number four of the secret group that would eventually boast more than 700 members.

While Cheney may be best known to the world as a hawkish Republican with an impressive career that included serving as vice president (twice), congressman, chairman of the Republican National Convention, secretary of defense, and CEO of Halliburton, he is also one of the most power-wielding Cubs fans in the world. Still, political historians may not blame Cheney for wearing the Reds' colors on Opening Day in 2004, considering that Cheney and Bush were re-elected that year for a second term while the Cubs lost seven of their final nine games to miss the playoffs.

Chapter 11

Only Player Traded for a Vote

A Future Hall of Fame Pitcher with One of the Most Unusual Careers in Baseball History Was Also Part of the Only Trade in Baseball History in Which No Player, Product, or Payment Exchanged Hands—The Only Trade in Baseball History that Was About Office Politics.

Baseball history is littered with strange trades that have left fans scratching their heads, but in every single case, there was some sort of compensation bartered between the two teams. A November 2008 issue of the magazine *Mental Floss* hilariously chronicled many of the sport's weirdest trades, including the infamous swap of Hall of Famer slugger Dave Winfield when Minnesota traded him to Cleveland for a player to be named later in 1994. Since a player strike ended the season early, Winfield never actually played for the Indians and the other player to be traded was never named. Club officials from both teams settled the matter with a nice dinner, for which the Cleveland organization foot the bill.

John Odom was traded for ten baseball bats in 2008 when a Canadian minor league team realized the pitcher had a felony on his record (aggravated assault in 1999) that prevented him from entering Canada. Eager to get something for the player, the team traded him to the Laredo, Texas, Broncos for ten maple bats (worth roughly $700). Opposing fans besieged him with taunts and the theme from "Batman" was played over the PA system at rival stadiums when he took the field. Odom left the team within three weeks. Sadly, within six months, he was dead of an overdose of heroin, methamphetamine, benzylpiperazine (a stimulant), and alcohol, according to NBCSports.com.

In 1998, Ken Krahenbuhl was traded by the Pacific Suns to the Greensville Bluemen for a player, cash, and ten pounds of catfish. In 1931, Johnny Jones was traded by the Chattanooga Lookouts to the Charlotte Hornets (of the Piedmont League, not the NBA) for a 25-pound turkey that was served to the local media.

At the end of the meal, Chattanooga owner Joe Engel declared that Charlotte had got the better end of the bargain, since the turkey was too dry for his taste.

Even in these weird—and, in Odom's case, sad—stories at least something changed hands. But in the strangest trade in baseball history, future Hall of Fame pitcher Grover Cleveland Alexander was traded for a vote and an endorsement. Alexander, one of the most extraordinary characters ever to play baseball (much less reach the Hall of Fame), was known for many things: alcoholism so severe that the Cubs were used to sending him home instead of playing him because he often showed up still drunk from the night before; smoking like a chimney minutes before taking the field; open disdain for all authority figures; his service during World War I; epilepsy; and one of the strongest arms of all time. His 373 wins are unlikely to ever be topped by a Cubs pitcher. His 90 lifetime shutouts are second only to Walter Johnson's 110. He averaged more than 19 wins per season for 19 years despite pitching in hitter-friendly parks such as Wrigley Field and Philadelphia's Baker Bowl, where the right-field fence was only 290 feet away.

Alexander, known to friends as "Dode" or "Pete" (and then "Old Pete" in his later years), was also country strong. He grew up in Elba, Nebraska, where he taught himself to pitch by throwing rocks at chickens to catch the family's dinner. (To be fair to the birds, he let the chickens get a head start.) As a teenager, he earned $5 per game pitching local teams to victory in popular hometown contests.

Despite his father's urging, Alexander refused to become a lawyer like his namesake, former President Grover Cleveland. He instead signed to play for the Galesburg Boosters of the Illinois-Missouri League. He was having a good rookie season, throwing six shutouts and amassing a 15–6 record, before his career took an unfortunate turn on July 28, 1910. Galesburg was playing their rivals, the Pekin Celestials. Alexander belted a single in the eighth inning. The next batter dribbled an infield hit; in the process of trying to turn the double play, the Pekin shortstop hit Alexander between the eyes with the ball, knocking him unconscious. He awoke in the hospital with double vision and migraines. Many baseball historians believe this incident was what led to his eventual fits of epilepsy (which is discussed in more detail later in the book).

"I was unconscious for 36 hours," Alexander said later. "When I revived, I saw everything in double. If you had put out your hand to shake with me, I would have seen two hands. I didn't see how I was going to pitch to two hitters at the same time when there was only one at the plate."[31]

Alexander's double vision ended his tenure in Galesburg, and the team sold his rights to the Indianapolis Indians of the American Association. It was obvious that something was wrong with Alexander when he reported in Indianapolis. An eye specialist determined that the blow to his head had damaged two optic nerves but that with sufficient rest, he should recover. After two months of recuperation, Alexander tested his pitching, taking the mound for a local team three times and winning all three games. With his vision clear, Alexander was ready to play. He then reported to Indianapolis for the 1910 season—only to learn that Indians manager Charlie Carr had other plans for him.

In addition to managing the local baseball team, Carr was also the owner of a local manufacturing company that made baseball equipment. Eager to get his baseball declared the official ball of as many minor leagues as possible, Carr offered Syracuse Stars manager Ed Ashenback his pitcher, Alexander, in exchange for the Stars' endorsement and Ashenback's vote to approve Carr's product as the official ball of the New York State League.

Both parties got what they wanted. Carr got the vote his company needed and Syracuse got a star pitcher without giving up any players, cash, catfish, equipment, or dinner. Alexander went 29–11 for the Stars with a 1.85 ERA during what would be his only season in Syracuse. The Philadelphia Phillies then drafted him based on his impressive season with the Stars and were rewarded for their efforts. Alexander's 1911 rookie season was arguably the strongest major league pitching debut of the twentieth century: he went 28–13 with 31 complete games, seven shutouts, and a third-place finish for the NL MVP.

Chapter 12

World War II Led to Cubs' First Night Game

Contrary to Popular Belief, the First Night Games at Wrigley Field Were Not Played in 1988. They in Fact Happened Decades Earlier, and Were the Direct Result of World War II.

Cubs fans proudly recite the historic date of the supposed first nighttime game at Wrigley Field. The date, 8/8/88, is easy to remember. Countless baseball writers and fans around the world have continued the story, saying the Cubs played their first game under artificial lighting at Wrigley Field on August 8, 1988. The Cubs asked 91-year-old fan Harry Grossman to throw the switch, powering on the lights for what even the Cubs own website calls "the first home night game in team history."

It's a nice story—except for the fact that it isn't true.

As fans will recall, that game on August 8, 1988, against the Philadelphia Phillies was halted in the fourth inning due to rain. After a two-hour and ten-minute rain delay, home plate umpire Eric Gregg called the game. Baseball rules stipulate that for a game to be official, it must at least reach the fifth inning. Since the 8/8/88 game was suspended in the fourth inning, the Cubs' 6–4 win against the New York Mets the following night was actually the first official game played at Wrigley Field under the lights.

That, *too*, would be a nice story—except for the fact that it isn't true, either.

Long before the Internet and computers were invented, before every player in the Cubs organization (and most coaches) were even born, and even before the Nazis were defeated in World War II, Wrigley Field had night games. In fact, the first two night games in Wrigley Field history were actually played during one week in 1943.

On June 25, 1943, the Chicago Cubs played their first night game at Wrigley Field. Game time was 6:00 p.m. because the nation was at war and President

Franklin D. Roosevelt had urged baseball teams to start games as late as possible so that factory workers manufacturing war supplies would be able to enjoy the American Pastime at the end of their shifts. The Cubs obliged, and picked that date to play the organization's first "twilight" game, as it was called then—today we would simply call it a night game. Management picked that date to take advantage of the summer solstice, the day of the year with the most sunlight. Hi Bithorn threw a two-hitter that night, leading the Cubs to a 6–0 win against the St. Louis Cardinals; all accounts are that the 6,620 fans in attendance were able to see the action just fine during the two-hour 17-minute game, which lasted until nearly 8:30 p.m.

A week after Bithorn's two-hitter, on July 1, 1943, temporary artificial lights were erected for the first nighttime game under lights at Wrigley Field, allowing an estimated 7,000 fans to watch the All-American Girls Professional Baseball League's All-Star game. The league was the brainchild of Cubs owner Philip Wrigley.

Not only was the first baseball game under lights in the Friendly Confines played by women instead of men, but the attendance figures were higher than regular-season Cubs games that same week, according to documents at the Chicago Baseball Museum.[32] There was good reason for this, as more than 500 major league players had been drafted or enlisted into the war effort, watering down the talent base for major league games. The women who played in the AAGPBL took their game as seriously, taking it as a point of pride to prove that they were not a joke. Immortalized in director Penny Marshall's 1992 movie *A League of Their Own,* the AAGPBL was created by Wrigley, who announced the league's formation on February 20, 1943. Wrigley was motivated by private worries that the war effort, which forced several minor league teams to disband for lack of players and fans, would turn ballparks like Wrigley into white elephants in their hometowns.

A financial heavy-hitter in his own right, Wrigley was joined by financiers and other baseball men who shared his concerns, including Brooklyn Dodgers president and general manager Branch Rickey, who served on the league's board of directors. The AAGPBL was set up as a nonprofit organization and had four teams in 1943, the league's first season: the Kenosha, Wisconsin, Comets; the Racine, Wisconsin, Belles; the Rockford, Illinois, Peaches; and the South Bend, Indiana, Blue Sox.

That the government allowed the AAGPBL to play a night game during wartime was shocking and evidence of the conflicted interests that a nation must juggle while at war. The government had ordered power brownouts for large portions of the country's coastal areas and around the Great Lakes in order to conserve resources, as well as to disguise all manufacturing efforts just in case any spies were lurking about. But the government also knew that its work force needed entertainment to maintain both morale and production quotas.

The idea of holding a nighttime All-Star Game at Wrigley Field appeared to appease the government's concerns. As former AAGPBL player Dottie Hunter recalled in Sue Macy's book *A Whole New Ballgame*, the temporary lights were not very bright and not much good for lighting a baseball field. Apparently, playing under temporary lights in 1943 wasn't much different from a brownout—but at least in provided entertainment for the public.

It would take another 45 years for the Cubs to erect permanent lights, making them the last nonexpansion organization to do so. Why did it take so long? Because Philip Wrigley was as much an American patriot as he was a businessman—which is the subject of our next chapter.

Chapter 13

Cubs' Patriotism Cost Them Championship Manager

The Cubs' Lack of Lights Was Initially an Act of Patriotism of Which Fans Can Be Proud; However, that Act Became a Self-Destructive One that Led to a Rival's World Series Title.

The installation of lights at Wrigley Field would have happened in 1942 instead of 1988 had it not been for the bombing of Pearl Harbor. Cubs owner Phillip Wrigley had already bought the lighting equipment, and the installation was scheduled to begin on December 8, 1941. But when the Japanese bombed Pearl Harbor on December 7, 1941, Wrigley instead unflinchingly donated the 165 tons of steel, 35,000 feet of copper wire, and other pieces of equipment to the government for use in the war effort. "We felt that this material could be more useful in lighting flying fields, munitions plants, or other war defense plants under construction," Wrigley explained.[33]

Wrigley was not a fan of nighttime baseball, so his donation, as patriotic as it may have been, was a way for him to keep day baseball *and* help his country. Even if the lights had been installed, his intention was to start more "twilight" games at 6:00 p.m., with the lights helping in the fading dusk. Disgusted by the "freight yard" appearance lights gave stadiums, Wrigley openly preferred the simplicity of day games.

Lights were nearly installed during the 1937–38 renovation of the stadium, according to team historian John Snyder, but with some caveats: Wrigley wanted to hide the lights. Two ideas were proposed but never put into action: camouflaging the lights as trees, which was deemed too impractical, and using hydraulics to raise and lower the lights as needed, which proved too costly. So the idea of lighting Wrigley Field was shelved, while the team's crosstown rivals, the Chicago White Sox, installed lights in Comiskey Park in 1939.[34]

Fearing that baseball might need to shut down for the remainder of the war, commissioner Judge Kenesaw Mountain Landis wrote to President Franklin D. Roosevelt asking the commander in chief what to do so that baseball would not hurt the war effort. A baseball fan since his youth, Roosevelt replied with his famous "Green Light" letter on January 15, 1942, urging that baseball continue:

> There will be fewer people unemployed and everybody will work longer hours and harder than ever before. And that means that they ought to have a chance for recreation and for taking their minds off their work even more than before. Baseball provides a recreation that does not last over two hours or two hours and a half, and which can be got for very little cost. And, incidentally, I hope that night games can be extended because it gives an opportunity to the day shift to see a game occasionally.[35]

Responding accordingly, Landis announced that the league would allow teams to expand nighttime games from seven games to fourteen per season starting in 1942.

With no way of satisfying the government's desire for evening baseball games, Wrigley and the Cubs set aside their pride and attempted to negotiate a lease allowing them to use the White Sox's Comiskey Park. It was embarrassing, but when the president of the United States said he liked the idea of evening games, even the Cubs realized they needed to try everything—no matter how distasteful the idea of playing "home" games at Comiskey would feel. "It would be a considerable blow to our pride to play elsewhere than in our own park," said Cubs general manager Jim Gallagher, "but we feel that under the circumstance, this would be the only sane and logical thing to do."[36]

Talks reached an impasse, however, when Landis ruled that 14 nighttime games *per stadium* was the limit, regardless of what teams were playing. Since every "home" game for the Cubs was one less home game for the White Sox, the South Siders politely told the Cubs to go back to their unlit stadium.

Wrigley tried one more time to install lights, this time in 1944. But by then, the war was at its zenith and permission to buy the supplies required the approval of the War Production Board's recreation section, headed by George W. McMurphey—who denied Wrigley's request after careful consideration, writing:

> The release of materials alone was not the deciding factor. While materials may be available, this office also took into consideration that construction could not

be completed before August, which would leave only 21 weekday dates available to the Cubs in their home park. Under such circumstances, the expenditure of material and labor does not seem justified for so few night games.[37]

McMurphey invited the Cubs to petition his office again in 1945, but by then the war had ended, and the organization no longer needed permission to buy supplies. What's more, by that time, Wrigley had had enough. He hadn't really wanted lights in the first place, yet had tried several times to have them installed; now that he was free to do so, he refused.

By 1948, the Cubs were the only team in the league playing home baseball games exclusively during the day. In 1962, other NL owners implored Wrigley to install lights, noting that the Cubs' home attendance was dead-last in the league (609,802), while the top eight teams in the league—many in much smaller markets such as Minneapolis, Pittsburgh, and Detroit—had more than one million in attendance. By even more direct comparison, the White Sox, located less than ten miles to the south in the same city, were seventh in attendance, yet had nearly twice the Cubs' attendance, at 1,131,562. Wrigley still refused, citing the Cubs' 16 consecutive seasons with a final record of .500 or less. "We don't need lights in Wrigley Field; we need a contender," Wrigley infamously quipped.

Wrigley also used the ballpark's neighborhood as an excuse, combined with some good old-fashioned wrong thinking: "Number one, I don't think they're necessary. If you'll check the figures, I think you'll see that lights are just a novelty shot in the arm. If you have a winning team, I think you'll draw as many people in the long run without lights. Number two, we're in a residential neighborhood."[38] Wrigley would continue to use the neighborhood as his biggest excuse for not installing permanent lights for years, despite the fact that he leased out use of Wrigley Field for numerous events that made use of temporary lights.

In 1966, a 27-year-old lawyer named William Shlensky—who had held two shares of Cubs stock since he was 14—filed a lawsuit against Wrigley seeking to force the owner to install lights. The court noted that while it might not agree with Wrigley's decision, it would not overturn it. Wrigley Field remained unlit. Wrigley died in 1977 having never installed permanent lighting at Wrigley Field.

The Cubs were sold to the Tribune Company in 1981, prompting the lighting debate to flare up once again. In 1982, Cubs general manager Dallas Green hinted that the Cubs might leave Wrigley Field if lights were not installed. That sparked years of political strife between the neighborhood, the team, and politicians that went as far as Governor James Thompson—who was intent on preventing nighttime baseball at Wrigley—signing new noise pollution regulations.

The debate raged for years until November 1987, when Mayor Harold Washington made public his support of limited night games at Wrigley Field. On February 25, 1988, the Chicago city council voted 29–19 to allow night games at Wrigley, but limited them to 18 per season. In 2003, the number of night games allowed was increased to 30. In 2013, the total was increased to 40, with a possibility for more to be added, along with a giant electronic screen, more advertising signage, and additional parking.

It took decades of legal battles for the Cubs to finally achieve what they wanted, and it may have cost them postseason success along the way. At the very least, the lack of lights surely cost the organization the chance to hire a manager who led a rival, instead of the Cubs, to the World Series. Whitey Herzog, who led the Cardinals to the 1982 World Series championship and three National League pennants, in addition to guiding the Kansas City Royals to three straight division titles, was the top choice for the Cubs open manager role for the 1980 season.

Cubs general manager Bob Kennedy had narrowed his search to Herzog and Sparky Anderson, both of whom passed on the chance to join the North Siders. When *Chicago Tribune* reporter Bob Verdi interviewed Herzog years later to find out why he rejected the Cubs, his answer was simple: Wrigley Field's lack of lights:

> I love Bob Kennedy, and I thought a lot of Mr. Wrigley, too, but there's no way I could have handled Chicago. Chicago wasn't for me, and I knew it. And I don't mean the fans or the city or the ballpark. None of that. All that's terrific. It's those 81 day games. I'd have wasted away. I wouldn't have lasted.
>
> You know me, I like to wake up early in the morning here in St. Louis, fish or play golf. Mostly fish. Then I go home for a nap, have something to eat and head for the ballpark. At night after the game, I go home, then get up and do the same thing all over again. Now, could you have imagined me in Chicago?
>
> I'd wake up, go to Wrigley Field, manage, then what do I do at 4 o'clock when it's over? I ain't gonna drive home and fight that traffic, so I'd have gone across the street to the saloon to have a few. Then I'd drive home about 7 and have a few more, and lie down on the couch in the soup and wake up in the morning. Same

thing all over again. See what I mean? Fishing ain't the greatest exercise in the world, but that Cub thing, that would have driven me to drink.[39]

Countless baseball players and managers echoed Herzog's complaints about daytime games at Wrigley Field over the decades. In fact, during spring training before the 2012 season, Cubs president Theo Epstein told the *Chicago Tribune's* Paul Sullivan that day games meant players had time to carouse at night, "and that [he's] sure it's been an impediment to the Cubs in winning."[40]

Daytime games were a Wrigley Field tradition. But so, too, is more than a century of failing to attain a World Series victory. Can it be a coincidence that only one organization in the league has such a depressing history despite the abundant sunshine at games?

Section II

Society

Chapter 14

Public Enemy (and Cubs Fan) No. 1

America's First Celebrity Criminal, an Aspiring Shortstop,
Became the Focus of the Kind of International Attention
That Even Players Rarely Receive. But This Cubs Fan
Proved to Know More About Safes than Saves.

Scotland Yard hunted him, worried he was within their jurisdiction.

German newspapers used him as an example of why a country with low morals such as the United States should have no place in European politics.

J. Edgar Hoover made him the Federal Bureau of Investigations' public enemy No. 1.

Little did authorities around the world know that all they had to do to catch John Dillinger back in 1934 was spend the day at Wrigley Field.

One of the most fervent Cubs fans of the twentieth century was also one of the most notorious bank robbers of all time. Dillinger used the north side of Chicago as his playground, using more than 50 locations as hideouts there while getting away with the most audacious string of bank robberies in the country's history to that point.

Why the north side of Chicago?

Simple: that's where the Cubs play baseball.

Dillinger was such an ardent Cubs fan that even though Chicago's newspapers were printing headlines about his gang's exploits, he still chose to relax by watching the Cubs take the field rather than laying low, as caution would have dictated.

On the run from the law and convinced he would soon be a resident of Mexico (after pulling off one final big heist that never came together), Dillinger decided to make his home in and around Wrigley Field, using nearby apartments as his home base while he and his gang robbed banks in the Midwest. Baseball, bank robbing, and the back roads of Indiana and Illinois were what Dillinger knew best.

Growing up in Mooresville, Indiana, Dillinger became bored with country life in his hometown and used baseball to pass the time. Shy and withdrawn as a young child, Dillinger eventually found that he was a good athlete, playing second base before becoming Mooresville's starting pitcher. Barely into his teens, Dillinger fell in love with two things that never left him: baseball and the nightlife.

Dillinger's mother died when he was only three years old, leaving him to grow up with his father in a cold, lonely house. In baseball, he found for the first time in his life that he was good at something at which people would help him excel. Unfortunately, being the team's star player soon led the young man to stay out later and later at night, learning to enjoy postgame parties with young women and wild times.

By age 21, Dillinger was married, but not ready to give up baseball. He and his wife, Beryl, were living with her parents in Martinsville, Indiana, while the future outlaw played shortstop for the Martinsville baseball team. Baseball and crime meshed in Dillinger's world: he committed his first robbery with one of the league's umpires, Ed Singleton. They were quickly caught. Within days, Dillinger pled guilty and was sentenced to 10 to 20 years in the Pendleton Reformatory.

During the next eight years, Dillinger did his best to become both an ideal inmate and a top-shelf baseball player. At that time, it was customary for prisons to have organized baseball teams that played other prisons or local semipro teams. By 1929, Dillinger had become such a good shortstop that Indiana Governor Harry Leslie, who was on hand to watch Dillinger play on the day of his parole hearing, told an *Indianapolis News* reporter, "That kid [Dillinger] ought to be playing Major League Baseball."[1]

Despite this praise, Leslie was not impressed enough to grant Dillinger parole. But the governor did acquiesce to an unusual request by Dillinger: to be transferred to Michigan City State Prison so he could "go up there and play baseball. They have a real good team."[2]

Still thinking that Dillinger could be a professional baseball player after his incarceration ended, Leslie relented to the unexpected request. "It might be a good profession for him later," Leslie said.[3]

The governor's transfer approval did aide Dillinger's future profession—but as a bank robber, not a base stealer. At Michigan City State Prison, Dillinger befriended two of the first members of his eventual bank robbing gang, Harry Pierpont and Homer Van Meter.

Dillinger's passion for baseball never flagged. In addition to playing on the prison team, he "followed the Chicago Cubs with avidity, and conducted a baseball pool in the penitentiary," historian G. Russell Girardin revealed in his book *Dillinger: The Untold Story.*[4]

After his parole in 1933, Dillinger immediately began robbing banks, the first one coming less than three weeks after his release. Over the next 13 months, Dillinger and his gang robbed more than 12 banks, killed ten men (including one sheriff), wounded seven more (including two guards), raided two police arsenals, and had multiple shootouts with police. Dillinger was named public enemy No. 1—but he still made sure to attend as many Cubs games as he could.

During the 1933 and 1934 seasons, "Dillinger attended ball games at the Cubs' park on three or four occasions,"[5] according to Girardin, including all or part of the Cubs homestand against the Phillies on July 22–23, 1933.[6] As the 1934 season commenced, Dillinger seemed to have become fearless about appearing in public. On June 8, 1934—the same day a headline reading "DILLINGER GANG GUNMAN SLAIN BY IOWA POLICE" appeared in the *Chicago Daily Tribune*—Dillinger decided to take in a Cubs game (a 4–3 loss to the Cincinnati Reds) to relax. Never mind that gang member Tommy Carroll had been shot dead in Waterloo, Iowa. Never mind that the Cubs lost. Dillinger felt rejuvenated by seeing his first game of the 1934 season, and tried to convince his gang members to go with him to another Cubs game. But none of them dared act as brazenly as he did.[7]

On June 26, 1934, Dillinger's name again appeared in the *Chicago Daily Tribune* under a headline reading "DILLINGER, FLOYD RAID ON OZARKS TIP IS FRUITLESS." The notion of police officers chasing false leads must have put Dillinger in a good mood that day, because he decided to go to the Friendly Confines for another day game, disregarding the $10,000 bounty on his head. The fugitive joined 17,000 other Cubs fans who saw Kiki Cuyler homer to help Chicago beat the Brooklyn Dodgers 5–2. It was the last Cubs game that Dillinger, who was killed less than a month later, is known to have attended. It also proved to be his most dangerous public appearance, considering that one Cubs fan, Robert Volk, recognized Dillinger and considered alerting his friend, a Lake County deputy sheriff sitting in another section of the stands. Volk was convinced by a friend with whom he was attending the game to ignore Dillinger and not raise an alert for fear of the criminal's reprisal. Dillinger left after the seventh-inning stretch and avoided any conflict.[8]

Dillinger celebrated his 31st birthday with his new girlfriend, Polly Hamilton, while his beloved Cubbies were in the midst of a season-high seven-game winning streak. But the good times were about to run out for this notorious criminal.

Hamilton's close "friend," Ana Cumpanas—aka Anna Sage or the Lady in Red—was the manager of a brothel. She later claimed she had recognized Dillinger despite the plastic surgery he had undergone. But in reality she was part of an elaborate set up to finally bring Dillinger to justice. She was by his side when he was killed less than a month later outside the Biograph Theater blocks from Wrigley Field on July 22, 1934. It was a sad day for Cubs fans everywhere: Chicago lost to Philadelphia 6–5 in 12 innings.

Chapter 15

The Woman in Orange

The Most Infamous Femme Fatale in American History Was a Byproduct of the Chicago Cubs and Nightlife Culture.

"The Lady in Red" has long been a significant patch in the quilt of American morality, a story repeated for generations that titillates as much as it teaches. Along the way, the phrase became a part of everyday conversation, entertainment, and pop-culture history. Details about the most infamous FBI informant of all time seemed to matter little to most people, who instead simply remember that a notorious woman helped plot the downfall of America's first celebrity bank robber. What has been lost in the decades since the fateful night of Dillinger's shooting was that Anna Sage, "the Lady in Red," owed her notoriety in no small way to the popularity of the Chicago Cubs and the nightlife that the team helped spawn—the cornerstones of her infamous occupation on Chicago's north side.

While Dillinger became America's first celebrity criminal, Sage became the nation's first femme fatale. In fact, millions know and use the phrase "the Lady in Red" without being aware of the term's origin. The prostitute turned madam turned snitch was a key part of the plan to capture (and kill) Dillinger. She avoided arrest for years thanks to the protection of her boyfriend, corrupt East Chicago police officer Martin Zarkovich. The tale of Dillinger, Sage, and Zarkovich only underscores the fact that Wrigley Field has been at the center of the entertainment universe for more than a century. Both Dillinger and Sage (born in Romania as Ana Cumpanas) were in the Cubs' neighborhood for the same reasons: nightlife and female companionship. For Dillinger, the women were a pleasant distraction; for Sage, they were a source of income.

By July 4, 1934, Dillinger was hiding from the law and in need of a place where he could recover from his recent facial plastic surgery. Considering that his girlfriend, Evelyn "Billie" Frechette, was serving a two-year jail sentence, he wouldn't have minded having some female companionship as well. Dillinger trusted his crooked lawyer, Louis Piquett, with the arrangements. Piquett turned to Zarkovich, who had a quick answer: his girlfriend, Sage, would be glad to help. An experienced madam who ran prostitution rings in Indiana and Illinois, Sage was accustomed to unsavory situations and questionable people. After more than a half dozen arrests in Indiana for prostitution, she had relocated her business to Chicago. However, her problems had now escalated beyond the state police. Her multiple arrests had led immigration officials to begin deportation proceedings against her. She hoped that helping the authorities capture Dillinger would persuade them to let her stay in the country. In retrospect, trusting a crooked lawyer, a corrupt cop, and a prostitute/madam who was in trouble with the law was perhaps not the brightest plan on Dillinger's part. But then again, that is part of both the mystique and the lesson of the story behind "the Lady in Red": trusting the wrong people can get you killed. Dillinger didn't have a problem trusting Piquett and Zarkovich. That was no surprise, as the duo had helped Dillinger before.

Despite swearing to uphold the law, Zarkovich had never met a vice he didn't like. He had met Sage at her place of business, the Kostur Hotel in northwest Indiana. Dubbed the "Bucket of Blood" by local authorities due to the amount of violence that took place there, the Kostur Hotel was frequented often by Zarkovich, who took a liking to Sage. Zarkovich and Sage were perfect for each other: she ran multiple houses of prostitution, and his badge protected him even though he was nothing more than a criminal himself. Dillinger biographer Girardin described Zarkovich as "a hoodlum in police officer's clothing,"[9] in part because of his involvement in shakedowns of bootleggers. In 1930, Zarkovich had been one of more than two dozen East Chicago police officers and public officials—including the chief of police and the mayor—investigated for charging local bar owners and bootleggers with specific prices for protection.

Legend has it that Dillinger escaped from the Crown Point County Jail on March 3, 1934, using a fake wooden gun. However, historians now believe that Dillinger actually used a real gun smuggled into the jail. Piquett has been widely suspected of being the mastermind behind that plot, while Zarkovich may have been the one to actually sneak the gun into the jail. Whether Zarkovich was part of Dillinger's escape or not is uncertain, but there is no debate about Zarkovich's crooked background past and future.

As Sage faced deportation, Zarkovich successfully intervened on her behalf with the Crown Point prosecutor's office, buying his girlfriend some time. But the U.S. Department of Immigration was going to be more difficult. Zarkovich's influence with corrupt officials could help in local matters, but had no sway with the federal government. By the summer of 1933, immigration had issued a warrant for Sage's deportation to Romania.

To put distance between herself and northwest Indiana, Sage moved her base of operations to Chicago's north side, near Wrigley Field, to take advantage of the nightlife in the area. Despite being wanted by the government, Sage returned to doing what she did best: running a prostitution ring. She maintained multiple addresses on Chicago's North Side, including 3504 Sheffield Avenue (just two blocks from Wrigley Field) and 3436 N. Lincoln Ave. (four blocks from Wrigley Field).[10] The addresses were in the neighborhood, including two alleged brothels, where her relocated prostitutes from the Kostur Hotel found no shortage of clients.

One of the women who made the move from the "Bucket of Blood" to Wrigleyville was Polly Hamilton, who worked as a waitress by day at the S & S Cafe eight blocks from Wrigley Field. It was at that cafe that Hamilton claimed to have met Dillinger, who was using the alias "Jimmy Lawrence" and telling people he was a clerk at the Chicago Board of Trade. Or at least that was the story Hamilton told authorities. But many historians claim that Dillinger and Hamilton's meeting was actually arranged by Sage.

With Frechette in jail until 1936, Dillinger was eager for female company while recovering from his plastic surgery. He took Hamilton to Cubs games during the day and out on the town at night. The couple went to north side watering holes such as the French Casino and Chez Paree, where Dillinger often danced but refused to have more than one drink. Wanting to stay mentally alert in case the situation ever called for quick action, Dillinger often made orange juice his drink of choice.

Hamilton enjoyed her time with Dillinger so much that she started to call him her boyfriend. It's doubtful that Dillinger felt the same way about her. Frechette was still his first choice, despite her absence. Hamilton was little more than a pleasant distraction—or, more likely, a frequent "business associate," given the nature of Sage's occupational background.

Dillinger and Hamilton lived with Sage and her son, Steve, in the third-floor apartment at 2420 N. Halsted Street. (GeoVerse™030) When it became clear that her deportation problems were not going away, Sage approached authorities claiming that she knew where public enemy No. 1 was hiding. She also claimed that she had recognized Dillinger despite his recent plastic surgery. Portraying herself as merely an observant citizen, Sage did not reveal that she knew Dillinger's whereabouts because he was living with her. Nor did she reveal that her boyfriend, an associate of Dillinger and Piquett, had facilitated the arrangement. Sage and Zarkovich had been biding their time, waiting for the right moment to use their secret as a bargaining chip with authorities.

Dillinger was apparently unaware of the conspiracy building against him. Despite a $25,000 reward for his capture, he and Hamilton appeared to continue to enjoy their time together on the town. Hamilton later claimed that she had been ignorant of Sage's plans, which seems unlikely given her sordid background and the fact that she too lived in Sage's apartment. Yet Hamilton's motives for associating with Dillinger are unclear. Was she a young woman in love? A prostitute paid for her time? Or a pawn forced by Sage and Zarkovich to distract and entertain the notorious Dillinger? Whatever Hamilton might have stood to gain, it was nothing compared to the benefits that Zarkovich and Sage would reap if Dillinger was arrested or (especially in Zarkovich's case) killed. "Both [Zarkovich and Sage] stood to benefit substantially from selling [Dillinger] out," Girardin explained in *Dillinger: The Untold Story*. "The federal government was preparing to deport Anna for her activities in the realm of vice. The state of Indiana was investigating corruption in East Chicago and was casting menacing looks in the direction of Sergeant Zarkovich and others."[11]

Whether he knew it or not, the net was closing in around Dillinger. If he did know, he didn't let on to anyone around him. In between Cubs games and trips to the popular Riverview Amusement Park, where he showed a particular skill at shooting-range games, Dillinger enjoyed home-cooked meals of chicken and biscuits, steaks, and ice cream prepared by Hamilton and Sage. He also acquired a love of the movies, and often took Hamilton, Sage, and her son to movie theaters at night to escape the summer heat. What Dillinger didn't know was that while he was treating his supposed friends to Cubs games, movies, and nights out on the town, his hostess was meeting with the FBI, planning to turn him in.

Among the other details that Sage managed to keep from the authorities was a small but important detail that she and Hamilton could not have helped but notice. Wrote Girardin:

John Dillinger always carried thousands of dollars about his person and in a leather billfold in his left hip pocket. This was his "get" money, in case he was spotted and had to take flight. Anna Sage must have known of this money during the weeks he lived in her house, for he was constantly redistributing it in the pockets of his coats and trousers.[12]

This would be yet another secret that Sage and Zarkovich would share.

Sage agreed with FBI officials to wear her favorite orange skirt the next time Dillinger treated her and Hamilton to a night at the movies to make the group recognizable to the waiting authorities. On July 22, 1934, Dillinger offered to take Sage and Hamilton to see *Manhattan Melodrama* at the Biograph Theater. Sage wore her orange skirt, and in so doing set in motion the death of one of the most well-known criminals in history.

At the end of the movie, Dillinger walked out of the theatre with Hamilton and Sage. Seeing her, the authorities knew they were within moments of capturing the most wanted criminal in America. Accounts vary as to whether or not they even called out Dillinger's name, much less tried to arrest him, before gunning him down on the street in an explosion of bullets.

Zarkovich was the first officer to reach Dillinger's slumped body in the alley beside the Biograph. (GeoVerse™041). Corrupt to the core, Zarkovich he rifled through Dillinger's pockets, looking for the money he knew was hidden on his body. It will never be known how much money Zarkovich stole from Dillinger's limp body; some accounts say $3,000 while other historians claim even more. What was not in doubt was that "Zarkovich searched [Dillinger] and took some money from his pockets."[13] When the authorities turned over Dillinger's body to his family days later, they claimed that public enemy No. 1 had only $7.71 on his person at the time of his death. Zarkovich had gotten away with yet another theft.

During the chaos of the shooting, Hamilton and Sage were able to escape into the crowd that gathered to witness the death of America's first celebrity bank robber. Attesting to the level of fame that Dillinger had achieved, witnesses actually dipped pieces of clothing and paper into the pool of his blood to collect a morbid souvenir of his death.

Hamilton later claimed she retreated to the S & S Cafe after the shooting. By contrast, the methodical Sage knew what to do first: she grabbed the cache of weapons that she had been hiding for Dillinger and dumped them in Diversey Harbor. The illegal arsenal included a Thompson submachine gun, a .45-caliber automatic, a colt super .38 automatic with the serial numbers sanded off, five clips of ammo, one loaded machine gun drum, 75 rounds of .45 automatic shells, and a bulletproof vest.[14] While the authorities would later discover that the two keys in Dillinger's pockets opened the doors to Sage's apartment, they would find no evidence of any firearms there.

The FBI acknowledged that Sage had helped apprehend Dillinger, and awarded her $5,000 of the reward (while Zarkovich and East Chicago Police Captain Timothy O'Neill received $2,500 each). But they did not choose to intervene whatsoever in her deportation process. In 1936, the government sent her back to Romania. Kissing his lover and accomplice one last time at the train station—smoking a cigarette in his full-length camel hair coat, fedora, and leather gloves—Zarkovich looked more like a gangster than a police officer. One can only wonder if he had purchased his outfit with the money he stole from Dillinger after helping to gun down his former accomplice. In the aftermath of the shooting, Zarkovich was promoted to detective.

Sage never offered any words of regret for turning Dillinger in, but she was concerned about one fact that reporters consistently got wrong. The skirt she wore that night was orange, *not* red. It may seem odd that she would be so adamant about such a minor detail, but history has proven her fears correct: journalists latched onto the idea of "the Lady in Red," turning her story into a moralistic tale of avarice, greed, and sex. While Dillinger became a Robin Hood–esque hero to the public, Zarkovich was promoted, and the federal agents involved were celebrated, Sage was struck with the unsavory role of the untrustworthy friend. Banished to Romania, she was never able to defend her actions or point out that she had been only one part of a team of conspirators. Wrote Elliott J. Gorn in his book *Dillinger's Wild Ride:*

> Even more than the unmanly feds, it was Anna Sage who bore the stigma of betrayer. The red dress was the outward sign of a fallen woman, one who took money for love, sold out for cold cash the man who trusted her. There is a powerful misogyny here, a fear that women might abandon their true roles as nurturers. Again, implicit is the notion that greed eroded all other values, and the city, with its riches and blandishments, was the breeding ground of avarice.[15]

Perhaps Dillinger was destined to die in gunfire. But the city of his demise was determined by his love of the Cubs and his desire to live as close to the Friendly Confines as possible.

Chapter 16

The Underground Railroad and the Cubs

Trying to Evade the Authorities Isn't Always a Bad Thing.
Only One Player in MLB History Is Known to Have
Family Members Who Used the Underground Railroad to
Escape Slavery—And He Is Not African American.

On July 21, 1991, Ferguson "Fergie" Jenkins became the first and only Canadian-born player ever inducted into the National Baseball Hall of Fame and Museum. As of 2013, there have been 239 Canadian-born players in the major leagues, but Jenkins is the only one in the Hall of Fame. Standing 6'5" with thick shoulders, Jenkins won 20 games or more seven times despite playing in hitter-friendly parks such as Wrigley Field and Fenway Park for 12 of his 19 seasons. He won the National League Cy Young Award in 1971 as a Cub and is the only member of the Hall of Fame with 3,000 strikeouts and fewer than 1,000 walks.

Jenkins' unique stature in baseball history goes beyond those accomplishments, however. He is also the only known ancestor of slaves who used the Underground Railroad to eventually play in the major leagues. According to officials with the National Underground Railroad Freedom Center in Cincinnati, Ohio, approximately 100,000 or more escaped slaves used the Underground Railroad to escape slavery between 1810 and 1850.

Historians will tell you it's no shock to them that Jenkins is Canadian, rather than American. Given the harsh laws the United States had at the time regarding escaped slaves, reaching Canada meant the difference between life and death for many of these brave individuals. The Underground Railroad was a vast network of people, both black and white, who helped fugitive slaves escape to the North and Canada. Many individuals used their knowledge of local terrain to help move slaves from one hideout to the next. Slaves were usually hidden in homes or barns with tunnels and hidden rooms. Laws at that time allowed slave owners to hire slave catchers to track down fugitive slaves. It didn't matter how far away a slave ran—as long as they were still in the United States, slave catchers could pull escapees off the street and return them to their former owners for a reward. Slave hunters also paid rewards to citizens who helped locate runaway slaves, making every person a runaway slave met a potential traitor.

Cincinnati, Ohio, was a major stopping point along the Underground Railroad. This was because Ohio was a free state that did not have slavery while Kentucky, directly south, was a slave state. The only thing separating the two states is the Ohio River. Runaway slaves who found a way to cross the Ohio River and scramble into Cincinnati (or anywhere in Ohio) found that opponents of slavery known as abolitionists were there to help them continue north. Such was the case with Jenkins' great-grandparents on his mother's side, as he explained in his autobiography, *Fergie:*

> My mother . . . her grandparents had come north on the Underground Railroad. Her ancestors were slaves in Kentucky, where her grandfather had worked on a plantation. . . . My ancestors were definitely slaves. They escaped from slavery in the American South before the Civil War, they said. My grandfather Jackson was very old, and I was very young, when he pointed out scars on his wrists and said he had been chained up at night. He recounted stories of how the family had come north with the help of white abolitionists and traveled by night to elude capture. I was young at the time and believed every word he told me, but I figured out later he was born too late to be involved in those events. I think he was telling the stories in the first person to make them more dramatic, but they were true stories that happened to his father or other families like ours.[16]

Jenkins' story about his grandfather underscores the difficulty in researching this material. Slavery is still a very sensitive topic, and many people who have ancestors who were slaves are reluctant to talk about it. Oral histories—stories of family experiences shared by one generation to another—have often been the only way to document the pain and suffering slaves endured. Some of their descendants today are reluctant to admit their family history includes slavery. Others know their family history, but prefer to keep it private.

Officials at the National Underground Railroad Freedom Center support research indicating that Jenkins is the only ancestor of someone who used the Underground Railroad to play in the major leagues. Due to the lack of written evidence, we encourage any other player or manager who knows of a family history of former slaves using the Underground Railroad to share their information with the author of this book and/or the National Underground Railroad Freedom Center.

Cubs fans should take the opportunity to learn about the Underground Railroad the next time they go on the road to see the Cubs play the Reds; the Center is about a long toss from Great American Ball Park a block away. (GeoVerse™056)

You can tell them Fergie sent you.

Chapter 17

Here's Something 'From Out in Left Field'

While This Story May Sound Like It's "From Way Out in Left Field," Many "Cubs Bugs" Are Proud to Know That One of the Nation's Preeminent Medical Districts Would Not Exist Were It Not for the Chicago Cubs.

Illinois medical professionals, students, and patients owe a debt of thanks to the Chicago Cubs. Does this sound like a story "from way out in left field"? Well, that phrase is also the creation of "Cubs bugs" (as Ring Lardner called the team's fans) who flocked to see the World Champion Chicago Cubs play baseball on the future site of the Illinois Medical District (IMD).

If you take the Chicago Transit Authority's Blue Line el train and get off at the Illinois Medical Center stop, it takes only a few minutes to walk to the location where the Chicago Cubs won back-to-back World Series titles in 1907 and 1908 and played in four World Series from 1906 to 1910. Bordered by Polk, Wood, Taylor, and Wolcott (formerly called Lincoln) Streets, West Side Grounds (also called West Side Park II) used to stand at this location. (GeoVerse™063) Home plate was located at the northwest corner of the block (Polk and Wolcott), where the University of Illinois College of Medicine now stands. Almost the entire area where the West Side Grounds' infield stood is now covered by the college, so we're sorry to inform you that there's no chance of "running the bases" today.

The Cubs called this stadium home from 1893 to 1915 after leaving behind the first West Side Park (1885–1891), a venue with laughably small dimensions at barely 200 feet down the lines. The team also played briefly at South Side Park (1891–1893).

For just 25 cents (50 cents for pavilion seating), Cubs Bugs saw the famous double-play combination of Tinker-Evers-Chance back up Mordecai "Three-Finger" Brown as Cap Anson led the best Cubs squad ever to play the game. West

Side Grounds was where Lardner turned sports reporting into an art form. It was where Anson and Albert Spalding ruled as baseball kings over an increasingly rabid kingdom. It was where the first World Series took place. West Side Grounds was where modern baseball history began.

With a seating capacity of 16,000, West Side Grounds was the preeminent baseball stadium in the country in its day. It was also the first to have the dimensions that baseball fans would recognize today (340 feet down the left line, 316 feet down the right, and 560 to center). For the first time, baseball fans put seats on the top of nearby buildings to see the action for free.

West Side Grounds had its eccentricities, as well. Located just on the other side of the left-field fence was the Neuropsychiatric Institute, whose mentally challenged patients would yell strange, obscure, and profane comments at players and fans. Baseball fans grew accustomed to these bizarre comments—hence the term "from way out in left field" came to mean something bizarre or unexpected.

Spalding, who owned the land that housed West Side Grounds, built the stadium for $30,000 in 1892. A smart businessman, Spalding, who relinquished his role as team president in 1891, leased the new stadium to the Cubs for $6,000 per season. The Cubs flourished at West Side Grounds, experiencing the best seasons the organization has ever known. The ballclub may have set a franchise record of 3,300,200 fans in attendance during 2008, but West Side Grounds was where the team won its only World Series championships.

A fire nearly burned down West Side Grounds on August 5, 1894, forcing frantic fans to climb over barbed wire and onto the field to escape death. While nobody died in the conflagration, the scene was horrific, with newspapers reporting that, "The wires were strung with bits of hair and strips of skin and flesh."[17]

On the north side, Charles Weeghman built Weeghman Park in 1914 for $250,000 to house his team, the Whales of the Federal League (the team was also called the ChiFeds, short for Chicago Federals). The 14,000-seat stadium, constructed mostly of steel and brick, was completed in just seven weeks. The park was an instant success, in part because fans were not afraid of it burning down. The Whales prospered during their first season, posting attendance numbers and on-the-field success that rivaled the Cubs and White Sox. For a doubleheader on the final Sunday of the 1914 season, the Whales had an overflow attendance of 34,361 fans who filled every corner of the stadium, even spilling onto the field where they could. On the same day, the Cubs had only roughly 2,000 fans show up at West Side Grounds, and the White Sox had 3,500 at Comiskey Park.[18]

It was clear that there was a whole new ballgame happening in Chicago baseball. The Federal League, National League, and American League went to legal war with each other in 1915. In the end, the Whales owner was welcomed into the NL and allowed to buy the Cubs from Charles Taft, brother of former President William Howard Taft. Weeghman and his group of partner investors (Sinclair, Armour, Wrigley, et. al.) bought the Cubs for $500,000 from Charles Taft and moved the team into the fan-friendly Weeghman Park, which was renamed Cubs Park for the April 20, 1916, home opener.

Abandoned with no team to fill its seats, West Side Grounds was sold to the state of Illinois for $400,000 in 1919. Two medical buildings and a hospital were soon built on the grounds of the former Cubs stadium alongside the Neuropsychiatric Institute. It may seem at first that the psychiatric patients outlasted and beat the Cubs, but it was the sports team that was actually an interloper in this medical district. Prior to the sale of the stadium, the area that is known today as the Illinois Medical Center had founded several research institutions, including the Presbyterian Hospital in 1883 and the College of Physicians and Surgeons in 1881, which became the University of Illinois at Chicago's College of Medicine in 1917.

Today the Illinois Medical District is the nation's largest urban research, education, technology, and health-care district, boasting more than 560 acres of medical and psychological care and training facilities. The nation's largest college of medicine (UIC) is located there. The IMD employs 20,000 workers and has generated an estimated $3.3 billion for the local economy. It has created more than 50,000 direct and indirect jobs and educated countless doctors, nurses, and technicians who help sick patients around the world—whether they are Cubs fans or not.

On April 20, 1916, the day the Cubs played their first game at Cubs Park, Lardner lamented the end of days for West Side Grounds in a poem titled "Elegy in a West Side Ball Park," which went in part as follows:

Now fades the glimmering landscape on the sight.
Save for the chatter of the laboring folk
Returning to their hovels for the night,

All is still at Taylor, Lincoln, Wood and Polk.
Beneath this aged roof, this grandstand's shade,
Where peanut shucks lie in a mold'ring heap,
Where show the stains of pop and lemonade,
The Cub bugs used to cheer and groan and weep.

Chapter 18

A Teenager's Mistake Became Baseball History

West Side Grounds Was the Cubs' Home in 1908, When the Organization Won Its Last World Series. Their Championship Season Hinged on a Teenager's Mistake So Huge That Bars Were Eventually Named for Him, Church Leaders Openly Mocked Him, and Popular Journalists Have Called for the Day of His Error to Be Named a National Holiday.

Since the Cubs last won the World Series, the television and computer were invented, Wrigley Field was built, and Harry Caray was born and died. Chicago won the 1908 World Series, their most recent such victory, thanks to "the most famous [play] in baseball history," according to Cubs historian John Snyder, who calls the moment "one of baseball's most enduring legends."[19] There is even a popular bar in the heart of Wrigleyville, just a home-run's distance from Wrigley Field, honoring the poor teenager who made it all possible: Fred Merkle, whose simple mistake in his very first major league game earned him the nickname "Bonehead." His error is known to this day as "Merkle's Boner."

"I have done a report of some kind on the Fred Merkle story, whether in print, on radio, or on TV, on or about its anniversary, September 23, virtually every year since I was in college," wrote Keith Olbermann in the foreword to David W. Anderson's book, *More Than Merkle*:

> The saga has always seemed to me to be a microcosm not just of baseball, nor of celebrity, but of life. The rules sometimes change while you're playing the game. Those you trust to tell you the changes often don't bother to. That for which history still mocks you, would have gone unnoticed if you had done it a year or a month or a day before. That's who Fred Merkle is. I have often proposed September 23 as a national day of amnesty, in Fred Merkle's memory.[20]

On September 23, 1908, the New York Giants had a half-game lead over the Cubs for the top spot in the NL when the two squared off in New York. Giants first baseman Fred Tenney missed his first game of the season due to a lower back strain, forcing his 19-year-old backup, Merkle, into action despite the fact that the lad had never played a major league game before. Merkle wasn't just a rookie: it was his first game seeing *any* action in the big leagues.

As if scripted by a Hollywood writer, the score was tied 1–1 in the bottom of the ninth with two outs and two men on base. The Giants' Moose McCormick reached third on a single by Merkle, whose clutch hit proved that though he was the youngest player on the field, he could hold his own in the big leagues. Al Bridwell laced a single to center, bringing McCormick home and giving the Giants an apparent 2–1 victory and, more importantly, a 1.5-game lead on the Cubs with only 16 games left in the regular season.

Upon Bridwell's hit, Merkle of course ran for second base. But when McCormick crossed the plate, an estimated 20,000 fans stormed the field. Believing the game was over and seeing a mob scene beginning, Merkle stopped running to second and instead turned toward the Giants clubhouse, behind the center-field wall, to escape the frenzy. In his haste to leave the field, he never touched second base.

Cubs second baseman Johnny Evers was one of the most astute people in baseball, a player who knew every rule of the game better than did most managers and officials. Seeing that Merkle never reached second, Evers screamed for the ball, knowing the rules dictated that the play had to be complete for the run to count. Since Merkle never touched second, the play was still alive despite the thousands of frantic Giants fans on the field. Center fielder Solly Hofman's throw missed Evers and rolled toward third, where Giants pitcher Joe McGinnity had been coaching third base. Seeing shortstop Tinker hustle for the live ball, McGinnity grabbed it and threw it into the crowd to prevent the Cubs from finishing the play. Cubs backup pitcher Rube Kroh, who saw his teammates clamoring for the ball, ran out from the bench and demanded the ball from the Giants fan who had scooped up the souvenir. When the fan refused, Kroh punched him, grabbed the ball, ran through the crowd, and handed the ball to Evers, who stepped on second.

Evers turned to umpire Hank O'Day for the ruling. But O'Day (who was eventually inducted into the National Baseball Hall of Fame in 2013 despite having died in 1935), didn't have time to react as the panicked crowd, clearly sensing that something was happening that they would not like, attacked both him and the Cubs infielders, punching them until New York police officers hustled the officials and players off the field.

Oddly enough, O'Day was prepared for this highly unusual situation calling for an extremely rare ruling. Only 19 days earlier, a nearly identical turn of events had unfolded in another game he had officiated, and he had screwed up the final ruling. In that previous game, like this one, Cubs second baseman Evers proved he knew the rules better than the officials did by tagging the base when an opponent did not complete the final play of the game. On September 4, the Cubs were in the bottom of the tenth inning in a scoreless tie when Pittsburgh won on a single to center field. Pittsburgh had a player on first who never reached second base, but instead left the field assuming the game was over as soon as his teammate on third reached home. Evers, who tagged second for the force out, reminded O'Day that the play had to be completed for the run to count. O'Day flubbed the ruling, calling a 1–0 victory for Pittsburgh. League officials reviewed the game the next day and agreed that O'Day was wrong. O'Day swore he would never get that call wrong again. He just had no idea it would happen less than three weeks later with first place on the line.

Back in New York, while Giants fans celebrated, O'Day filed a report with the league office. Within 24 hours, NL president Harry Pulliam ruled that Evers was right again: the Giants had not won the game because Merkle was actually out at second by a force out, negating McCormick's game-winning run. The game was still tied 1–1. Additionally, Pulliam ruled that the teams would have to replay the game if it turned out that it would determine the outcome of the season for either the Cubs or the Giants.

Unfortunately for Merkle, the two teams finished the regular season with identical records, 98–55. The Cubs won the rescheduled game 4–2 on October 8 and went on to win the World Series in five games against Detroit. Merkle's apparently insignificant blunder directly led to the Cubs' last World Series title more than 100 years ago.

Despite playing for 16 seasons in the major leagues, including four with the Cubs from 1917 to 1920, Merkle was never able to shake the nickname "Bonehead." He was forever known for a mistake he made as a 19-year-old playing his first game in the majors. Merkle was clearly a good player, yet was cursed to appear on the losing side in five World Series during his career (in 1911, 1912, and 1913 with the Giants; 1916 with the Dodgers; and 1918 with the Cubs).

Some historians believe Merkle wasn't just unlucky, but was also a dirty player who agreed to throw games—one of the minor revelations of the infamous "Black Sox" scandal, which is explored later in this book.

"It's not really fair to say that Fred Merkle's mental error cost the New York Giants the 1908 pennant," wrote Dan Gutman author of *Baseball's Biggest Bloopers.* "First of all it was common practice in those days to run right off the field after the winning run had scored. Furthermore, the Giants lost six more games after the 'Merkle game.'"[21]

Unfortunately for Merkle, the overwhelming majority of baseball fans don't remember it that way. Not even church leaders seemed able to forgive Merkle his blunder. In a 2008 *Sports Illustrated* story, Keith Olbermann recounted an anecdote shared by Merkle's daughter, Marianne, which underscored the loneliness her father suffered after that day. The Merkle family was attending church one Sunday during the 1930s—more than 25 years after that fateful game—when a visiting minister introduced himself to the congregation. "You don't know me, but you know where I'm from: Toledo, Ohio," the minister said. "The hometown of Bonehead Fred Merkle."

"Little Marianne knew what would happen next," Olbermann wrote. "'The kindness drained from [my father's] face,' she told me five decades later. Then Fred Merkle rose and wearily told his wife and daughters, 'Let's go.'"[22]

Chapter 19

Oldest Rivalry in Professional Sports

The Oldest Rivalry in Professional Sports Has a Bitter History That Has Drawn Even Former Iraqi Dictator Saddam Hussein and Disgraced U.S. Olympic Figure Skater Tonya Harding into the Fracas.

Sports and bitter rivalries have always gone hand in hand. With all due respect to those teams who wage their wars in football, soccer, and cricket, many believe the Chicago Cubs and the St. Louis Cardinals hold the world's longest-lasting rivalry among professional sports franchises.

San Francisco Giants fan Bryan Stow was brutally beaten into a coma by alleged Dodgers fans on Opening Day 2011 for simply wearing his team's colors. New York and Boston police are forced to raise the numbers of officers on the street every time the Yankees and Red Sox play due to the increase in violence over the years. In the Midwest, however, the Cardinals and Cubs have no such stigma associated with their heated rivalry. But don't let that fool you into thinking the rivalry isn't deep, real, and historic.

Who are the other contenders? The Marylebone Cricket Club was founded in 1787 in England followed by the Calcutta Cricket & Football Club (1792) in India, but those are locations where amateur games are played, not two professional teams competing in action every year. The USA-Canada cricket rivalry would appear to be the world's oldest international sports rivalry. But they are amateur organizations, and the two have had only 33 matches in the last 168 years.

Founded in 1857, England's Sheffield F.C. is the oldest soccer team in the world, followed closely by rival Hallam F.C., founded in 1860. While the teams still play each other, they are amateur organizations and draw little attention. In fact, one of their 2012 matches had only 228 spectators. By contrast, when the Cardinals and the Cubs clash late in the season and both teams have winning records, hundreds of media members report on the series for the millions of fans watching around the globe.

How about the bitter feud between the Boston Red Sox and the New York Yankees? Their first game against each other wasn't until 1903. The Cubs had already established a baseball dynasty by that time, dominating the sport during the 1880s—meaning that the Yankees–Red Sox series isn't even in consideration. Neither modern-day team began playing until the twentieth century.

The National League was founded in 1876 with eight teams located in Boston, Chicago, Cincinnati, Hartford, Louisville, New York, Philadelphia and St. Louis. The Boston Braves moved to Milwaukee and then Atlanta over the decades, changing rivals as they changed geographic locations. Despite the 2,337 games their team has played against the Phillies (after the 2012 season), Braves fans can't seem to agree on whether the Phillies or the New York Mets are their bigger rival—even though the Mets didn't exist until 1962.

The St. Louis Cardinals once left the NL for the American Association for several seasons, and didn't return to the NL until 1892, when the Cubs-Cardinals rivalry began. While the Atlanta Braves and the Cincinnati Reds (a team which also led the NL for a time, in part because they refused to limit the sale of alcohol during games) both have their roots in the NL's creation back in 1876, neither team has been considered a heated rival of the Cubs the way the Cardinals have been. Granted, these things are subjective, but rivalries are born out of proximity and overlapping history, not mere longevity. Cincinnati may be just as close to Chicago as is St. Louis (295 miles from Chicago to Cincinnati, 297 from the Windy City to St. Louis), but following the 2012 season, the Cardinals-Cubs series has had more games (2,306) than the Reds-Cubs history (2,209).

Of course, sheer number of games played isn't the deciding factor, either. After all, the Cubs have played the most games against Pittsburgh (2,401), followed by Philadelphia (2,322), and then finally the Cardinals. Baseball fans would have to be at or near retirement age to remember when the Pittsburgh Pirates last played a meaningful game prior to reaching the 2013 playoffs. The Reds-Cubs rivalry didn't fully begin until the Reds returned to the NL in 1889, seven years after the Cardinals-Cubs rivalry began in 1892.

A look at the Cubs' 2013 schedule against both rivals proves our contention in the financial arena as well. When the 2013 schedule was released, the Cubs were scheduled to play both the Reds and the Cardinals 19 times, but only six of the Cubs-Reds games were scheduled on a Friday, Saturday, or Sunday (when attendance tends to be highest), and none of those games were scheduled after the All-Star break. Meanwhile, the schedule-makers and television networks made sure that twelve of the nineteen Cubs-Cardinals games were played on a Friday, Saturday, or Sunday, including all nine of their scheduled matchups after the All-Star break—while the Cubs' six scheduled games against the Reds after the break all fell on a Monday, Tuesday, or Wednesday. It is no coincidence that the baseball officials and television executives who manage the billion-dollar business of televised games made sure that the Cubs-Cardinals series was given prime weekend dates.

It would be myopic of Cubs fans to think that their team's popularity is the reason why these Cardinals matchups are usually played on weekends. After all, St. Louis has won the World Series 11 times, including as recently as 2011, 2006, and 1982. Meanwhile, the Reds have won the World Series five times, their most recent being in 1990. As popular as the Cubs may be, the Cardinals have had more success in the past several decades than both the Cubs and the Reds combined. Since the Cubs last won the World Series in 1908, the Cardinals have won the World Series eleven times and lost in the championship series eight times. Since 1908, the Cubs have lost the World Series six times and haven't been back to the championship series since 1945. Eleven of the Cardinals' World Series appearances have occurred since 1945.

Further enhancing the rivalry between the Cardinals and the Cubs is the fact that the Cardinals have benefitted repeatedly from poor decisions by Cubs management.

Pitcher Bruce Sutter got his start in Chicago, pitching for five seasons and establishing the role of reliever as legitimate when he won the 1979 Cy Young Award. How did Sutter thank the Cubs after winning his $700,000 arbitration case for the 1980 season? He signed with St. Louis for 1981 and led the Cardinals to the 1982 World Series championship to boot. Sutter's manager in St. Louis was Whitey Herzog, who turned down the Cubs' offer to manage in Chicago because, as discussed earlier, the team played too many day games.

Harry Caray got his start as a St. Louis broadcaster before becoming a Chicago icon. That may be the only acquisition or trade with St. Louis that has gone in the Cubs favor over the decades. In fact, the most infamous, one-sided trade in baseball history—if not in all of professional sports—was between the Cardinals and the Cubs, who, naturally, got the short end of the deal, further escalating this historic rivalry.

On June 15, 1964, the Cubs traded future Hall of Famer Lou Brock to St. Louis for pitcher Ernie Broglio, whose career is only remembered for one reason: the trade for Brock. St. Louis received two forgettable players (Jack Spring and Paul Toth) along with Brock, who immediately led the Cardinals to the World Series title that year. Brock also helped St. Louis win the 1967 World Series, the 1968 NL pennant, and was a first-ballot Hall of Famer who held the record at that time for stolen bases (938) in addition to his 3,023 hits. As for Chicago, the Cubs got Broglio, who won only seven games before his career ended; pitcher Bobby Shantz, who went 0–1 before leaving the team; and outfielder Doug Clemens, who played only 182 games for the Cubs.

The Brock-for-Broglio trade was so disastrous that it actually became a symbol for horrible decisions. For example, the Emil Verban Memorial Society gives out the Brock-for-Broglio Award at club luncheons every other year to the person who has shown the worst lack of judgment. Past recipients of the award include Saddam Hussein (for his disastrous decision to invade Kuwait) and former U.S. skater Tonya Harding (for attacking rival Nancy Kerrigan).

When the most powerful political leaders in the world liken a trade nearly 50 years earlier to a murderous dictator and a disgraced athlete, you know the rivalry is one for the ages.

Chapter 20

Altering Architecture for the World of Sports

The Chicago Cubs Were the First Organization in the World to Take Sports Architecture Seriously, and Every Major Stadium in the World Has Copied One Key Cubs Invention. Additionally, One of the Iconic Pieces of Architecture for Which Wrigley Field Is Known Worldwide Is a Cubs Original, Yet Did Not Begin at Wrigley Field.

The NFL's New England Patriots and Green Bay Packers are trying to copy the Cubs, more than 100 years after the fact. Philadelphia baseball fans have also copied the Cubs, albeit decades before those two football teams. Chicago cannot blame their sports counterparts for mimicking their idea; after all, the Cubs actually copied the idea from *themselves.*

The rooftop bleachers that ring Wrigley Field are a Cubs original, but this idea did not get its start at Wrigley. Fans started the tradition back in 1885, when the White Stockings played at West Side Park (not West Side Park II, later dubbed West Side Grounds, which they called home a few years later). West Side Park was the best stadium in the world at the time, in part because team officials were allowed to experiment with their previous stadium, Lakefront Park, to create architectural innovations so far ahead of their time that every major stadium— whether home to soccer, football, hockey, basketball, auto racing, or really any professional sport—uses them today.

Today, the pride of Chicago is Millennium Park, a mixed-use area that features concert venues, gardens, a skating rink in the winter, and artwork, among other amenities. The history of that location is a true Chicago story: the area is actually reclaimed land filled with the charred debris of the Chicago fire of 1871. City officials covered this wreckage with a public area that included Lakefront Park, home of the Cubs at the time.

Lakefront Park's grandstand was on the southeast corner of Michigan Avenue and Randolph Street, with right field extending along Michigan and left field along Randolph. Chicago's famous "Bean" sculpture (officially named "Cloud Gate"), created by artist Anish Kapoor, sits roughly just outside the former ballpark perimeter in what used to be left-center field. (GeoVerse™077)

In 1882, when Albert Spalding became the principal owner of the team, he set out to make Lakefront Park a jewel. Spalding's efforts paid off immediately. Lakefront became an attraction, just as Wrigley Field would decades later.

With a capacity of roughly 10,000 people, Lakefront became the world's first stadium to have two things: luxury boxes and a telephone. Spalding installed 18 luxury boxes for wealthy fans, providing shelter from the weather with curtains. These were the first luxury box suites in sports history, embracing technology and lavish treatment for those who could afford it. Invented just six years earlier, the telephone was a novelty at the time; Spalding immediately saw the aid it could provide him in delivering commands from the owner's suite (an innovation that managers and players will likely regret forever).

Though Lakefront Park boasted the largest seating capacity ever in a baseball stadium, the field was far from ideal. Since the park sat on a garbage dump, debris from the 1871 cleanup often pushed through the surface; stray bottles, glass, rocks, and other materials sometimes made play difficult.

The Cubs (then called the White Stockings) were forced to leave Lakefront Park after the 1884 season when the land was sold to the Illinois Central railroad company for $800,000 (the U.S. government intervened in the sale, but the team was still forced to relocate). Spalding, however, was unconcerned. After all, thanks to his experience downtown, he knew precisely how to make his new stadium, West Side Park, the best sports arena in the world.

Spalding built the team's new home on a parcel of land bordered by Congress and Throop Streets, roughly where the campus of the University of Illinois–Chicago stands today. West Side Park was the most lavish baseball stadium in the world at the time, boasting luxury suites, plenty of bathrooms, grand entrances, seating for 10,000, and a 12-foot brick wall surrounding the facility.

At the end of their first season in West Side Park, the Cubs were in a heated battle for first place with the New York Giants. The National League pennant was on the line as the Giants rolled into Chicago for a four-game series. Chicagoans were enthralled with the series; it was the talk of the town. Later accounts from reporters said that betting on the game was so heavy (which was most likely the real reason Chicagoans were breathless over the action) that reporters had trouble getting to work in the newsroom, having to push their way through crowds desperate to hear the score and find out whether they had won or lost money.

The first of four games took place on September 30, 1885, making the front page of the *Chicago Daily Tribune*, which described a scene that was captured by only a few photographs:

> By 3 o'clock over 10,000 people had made their way within the enclosure and every available foot of room was occupied, while hundreds witnessed the contest from adjoining house-tops.

It's worth noting that building standards were still being created at that time, so watching the game from a rooftop wasn't the secure venture it is today.

Fans would continue to flock to the rooftops for big games, but it wasn't until the team was sold to Charles Weeghman, who built Wrigley Field in 1914, that the Wrigleyville that fans know today began to grow. The unofficial area around Wrigley Field known as Wrigleyville would become a sports fans' paradise during game days, and is one of the biggest attractions in Chicago today. (Sorry, Cloud Gate, but it's true.)

Wrigleyville's success has spawned numerous copycats around the nation. Philadelphia baseball fans crowded rooftops around Shibe Park after it was built in 1909 to see their team play. Home of the Athletics until 1953, and then the Phillies beginning in 1954, Shibe Park (eventually renamed Connie Mack Stadium) saw fans watching games from rooftops across the street until it was demolished in 1976. Seeking to give their fans some of the charm and fun rooftop fans have enjoyed in Chicago for generations, the Boston Red Sox put seats atop the Green Monster in 2003. Today, nearly every major league venue boasts some form of rooftop seating, bar, or restaurant. The Yankees have the Malibu Rooftop Deck, the Miami Marlins have the Clevelander at Marlins Park, and the Altitude gives patrons willing to pay the price a limited view of San Diego Padres games.

Wrigleyville's rooftop seating has led to a number of legal battles over the years. Rooftop owners and Cubs management have gone to court several times, most notably in 2004 when the Cubs installed tall windscreens to block the view, claiming (laughably) that the screens were actually necessary for security reasons. Rooftop owners reached an agreement with the organization, agreeing to share a portion of ticket sales with the team. When the Ricketts family bought the Cubs in 2009, rooftop owners should have known the issue would come up again. In 2013, the Cubs and rooftop owners entered into another round of legal fighting when the city of Chicago granted the organization approval to add a jumbo electronic scoreboard and other buildings on their current footprint, to the dismay and consternation of rooftop owners.

Sports teams like the Texas Rangers and Houston Astros, among others who have built open-air bars and restaurants into their existing ballparks, are lucky not to have neighboring rooftop owners with whom to contend. Other owners who want their own version of Wrigleyville have been willing to build from scratch. The St. Louis Cardinals have had plans in the works for years to develop a ten-acre plot of land adjacent to Busch Stadium to create a multiuse area that includes residential, retail, entertainment, and office space. According to the Cardinals' website, Ballpark Village, with an estimated cost of $700 million, will be "the country's first fully integrated mixed-use development designed to deliver the excitement and energy of the game day experience to a new neighborhood outside the stadium walls." The first phase of construction on the project is expected to begin in 2014.

Even NFL teams are catching on to the architectural trend started by the Cubs in 1885. In 2011, the Green Bay Packers announced plans to install a rooftop area for fans as part of a proposed $140-million-plus renovation proposal. The New England Patriots have taken the idea of Wrigleyville a step further. Patriots owner Robert Kraft built Gillette Stadium in 2008; the state-of-the-art complex features multiple convention rooms, as well as two massive enclosed clubs atop the stadium that are each larger than a football field and provide fans with views from end zone to end zone while they enjoy food, drink, and fun without worrying about the weather. There's also the construction of a small town, shopping center, and casino under discussion. Nearby Foxboro residents have been fighting the expansion, but Kraft has not tried to hide the fact that he wants to develop the real estate around the stadium into its own small city.

Just like Wrigleyville.

Chapter 21

Wrigley Field: A Holy Place and Final Resting Grounds

Some Fans Call It a Cathedral, But in Truth, They Should Call It a Cemetery—Not Because Hopes of a Championship Have Been Buried There for More Than 100 Years, But Because It Is the Final Resting Place of an Unknown Number of Souls.

Maybe the Cubs are cursed, but not by the goat of 1945 or the black cat of 1969. Maybe, just maybe, the Chicago Cubs are cursed because they destroyed a religious site in order to build Wrigley Field before they were even called the Cubs.

If fans could travel back in time to the 1890s, they would find a much different Friendly Confines at the intersection of Addison Street and Sheffield Avenue. There was no baseball played on the north side of Chicago back then. If you wanted to see Cap Anson and his club, you went to West Side Park, South Side Park, or West Side Grounds. It was an odd, itinerant time for the Cubs, who were forced to leave Lakefront Park, the team's original home, before settling at West Side Grounds. All three ballparks were located near downtown, where both entertainment and employment were centralized. Going all the way up to the intersection of Addison and Sheffield was to spend a day in quiet and serene settings. Back then, families picnicked in the quiet Lakeview neighborhood; the land was undeveloped, open, and—unlike downtown areas—free of the stench of slaughterhouses.

It was also hallowed grounds.

In 1891, the Theological Seminary of the Evangelical Lutheran Church opened on the pastoral land that would eventually become home to Wrigley Field. The seminary, which educated future church leaders, had a relatively small campus of only four buildings: a president's residence located on what would become center field, followed by two office buildings, and St. Mark's Lutheran Church, erected in 1896 approximately where first base is now located.

By the turn of the century, the seminary and church were part of a burgeoning neighborhood that was getting more crowded every year. In 1910, the seminary and church decided to relocate to Maywood, Illinois, selling their land for $175,000 to Milwaukee businessman Charles Havenor, who planned to build a railroad switchyard there. Havenor instead sold the land to Edward Archambault, who agreed to lease the land to restaurant tycoon and prospective baseball team owner Charles Weeghman for $16,000 a year for 99 years. Out of respect for the previous owners of the land—the seminary and church—Archambault placed one condition on the lease: no immoral or illegal business could be built there.

Weeghman razed the seminary in 1914, built Wrigley Field, bought the Cubs, and moved the team north—and a landmark institution was born.

Contrary to myths and rumors, no gravesites were disturbed to build Wrigley Field. However, the ballpark is the final resting spot for some fans. Over the years, several deceased baseball lovers have had their ashes scattered at Wrigley. Beloved former player Ron Santo was the most recent, according to ESPN, after his death from bladder cancer in December 2010.[23] He was the second known Cubs player to be given this honor, as former player and manager Charlie Grimm and his wife both had their ashes spread there as well. Steve Goodman, the songwriter who penned "Go, Cubs, Go!" and "A Dying Cubs Fans Last Request," got his own final request when his brother and friends arranged to scatter his ashes on the field, just as his song had begged.

Cubs executives field requests to have family members' ashes scattered at the Friendly Confines every year. Club officials are tight-lipped about whom they allow to do so, how often, and how it is done. In fact, prior to Santo, only one other person is known to have had his ashes scattered there: Peter J. Goldberg, whose family was given permission in 1981.[24]

Of course, the lack of formal permission doesn't always stop fans from fulfilling the final wishes of friends or family members. In 1995, the Houston Astros were visiting Chicago when Astros outfielder Luis Gonzalez noticed a fan lean over the railing during the seventh-inning stretch and dump a white, powdery substance—the cremated remains of a family member who was a longtime Cubs fan—onto the field. Gonzalez wasn't happy, and said he was reluctant to take the field the next day. Maybe he, too, was cursed: Cubs fans would come to know him as "Gonzo" after he was traded to Chicago weeks later, doomed to patrol the same spot every home game until he happily rejoined the Astros for the 1997 season.

Nobody will ever know how many people have had their ashes scattered in secretive moments as Wrigley Field. But one local cemetery has solved the dilemma for fans denied access by the team. The Bohemian National Cemetery on Chicago's northwest side has a section called "Beyond the Vines" that is a replica of an ivy-covered wall in which the cremated remains of Cubs fan can forever rest in peace. (GeoVerse™084) There's a yellow-painted "400" to emulate Wrigley's center field, along with a small warning track and baseball-style seats on which to rest. The wall is only 24 feet long, so space is limited, just like trying to get into Wrigley Field some days. Nearly a dozen fans have their ashes there, including Russell H. Adams, whose marker states simply: "1911 - 2009. I saw Ruth and Gehrig play at Wrigley."

A true Cubs fan to the end, Adams made no mention of any called shot by Ruth at Wrigley Field.

Chapter 22

The Largest Epidemic in the World

One of the World's Largest Epidemics Was Caused by the Cubs, and All Attempts by Experts to Alleviate It Have Failed.

The Cubs' century-plus losing streak is the longest championship drought in the world for a team at the highest level of competition in its sport (detailed in our final chapter). More than a century of failing to win the World Series has wreaked havoc on the mental state of Cubs fans everywhere, producing epidemic manifestations around the globe.

The Chicago Cubs' streak of championship-free seasons is longer than the existence of any other professional league in baseball and, in fact, of most professional sports leagues in the world. The Cubs' dominated baseball during the 1880s, creating the sport's first dynasty and finishing first in 1880, 1881, 1882, 1885, and 1886 and second in 1883 and 1888. The World Series as we know it didn't begin until 1903, so the Cubs' back-to-back titles in 1907 and 1908 gave fans reason to expect another dynasty was in the works. But the Cubs lost the 1910 World Series. Then they lost the 1918 World Series, and lost again in 1929, 1932, and 1938.

When the team faced the Detroit Tigers in the 1945 World Series, fans were rabid for a championship. Billy Sianis, a fan who had bought the Lincoln Tavern in 1934, bought two tickets to Game 5 of the World Series for himself and Sonovia, a local celebrity. There was only one problem: Sonovia was a goat.

Sianis was a marketing genius. After nursing Sonovia back to health after she suffered a broken leg falling from a passing cart in 1933, he kept her in a pen behind his bar at 1844 W. Madison Street across from the old Chicago Stadium. Sportswriters and athletes got to know both Sianis and Sonovia, even buying the goat drinks. Knowing a good marketing ploy when he saw one, Sianis managed to get Sonovia's picture in the newspapers frequently, each time leading to new patrons. Sianis even grew a long goatee to match his pet/partner; people began calling him "Billy Goat," a nickname he was only too happy to embrace. His sales rose, Sonovia became more and more popular, and by the time Game 5 of the 1945 Series came around, Sianis had only one use in mind for his second ticket. He draped Sonovia in a blanket with a sign pinned to it reading "WE GOT DETROIT'S GOAT" and, despite what has been told in later stories, was allowed to take the goat inside the ballpark.

Other fans, however, were not so happy to be sitting next to a foul-smelling goat, no matter how famous she was. "Ushers asked Sianis to leave," authors Glenn Stout and Richard Johnson wrote in their book *The Cubs*:

> He did, but not until he and an usher staged a faux photo op for the press, Sianis waving his ticket, the goat resting its forelegs on the turnstiles, and a smiling usher blocking Sianis's path into the park. That evening the *Chicago Times* published the picture of Sianis and his goat. . . . All of this coverage, of course, made no mention of a curse. Despite the legend and lore that has since grown to surround the incident, at the time there was no suggestion that Sianis placed any hex on the Cubs.[25]

In fact, there was no talk of Sianis cursing the team until a 1967 story in the *Chicago Tribune* made passing mention of a hex Sianis claimed to have placed, but later removed at the request of Cubs owner Philip Wrigley. Nothing came of the story. But when the Cubs charged for the pennant in 1969, *Tribune* writer David Condon referred repeatedly to the Sianis hex—and this time, the story caught the public's attention even though Sianis still insisted the hex had already been "lifted."

In mid-August, the Cubs were comfortably in first in the pennant race, 9.5 games ahead of the New York Mets. By September, that lead had been whittled down to only four games. Many blamed the team's ensuing collapse on an event that came to be known as "the Black Cat Curse." On September 9, with the Cubs playing at the Mets, a black cat walked in front of the Cubs' dugout while Ron Santo prepared to go to bat. The rest is history: the Cubs collapsed for the rest of the season, sending the Mets on to win the World Series in just their eighth year in existence. Many began to think that the Cubs were indeed cursed.

The New York Yankees, the Boston Red Sox, the Dallas Cowboys, and Manchester United all may have global appeal, but none have greater popularity around the world than Chicago's lovable losers, the Cubs. And no other team suffers from so many alleged curses, either.

The Red Sox were supposedly afflicted with the "Curse of the Bambino" after they let Babe Ruth join the New York Yankees in 1920. But the Red Sox won the World Series in 2004, 2007 and again in 2013. The arrival of these championships clearly indicated that this supposed curse no longer held power over the team's fortunes—if indeed it ever had.

In Japan, the Hanshin Tigers supposedly earned "the Curse of Colonel Sanders" after winning the Nippon Professional Baseball title in 1985. Celebrants jumped into the Dotonbori River from a local bridge, and at one point tossed a statue of Sanders from a nearby Kentucky Fried Chicken franchise into the murky waters. Supporters thought he looked like Randy Bass, the American hero of the Tigers. In an attempt to break this hex, Hanshin fans dragged the Sanders figure from the bottom of the river in 2009. But Hanshin had still not won the NPB championship again as of 2013.

Every sport, every country, every culture has curses and hexes. After all, they make for fun stories and are handed down from generation to generation. But are they just stories?

Bestselling author Malcolm Gladwell investigated word-of-mouth phenomenon in his book *The Tipping Point,* and found that oral stories—like advertising, fads, and diseases—can be contagious. Gladwell calls them, in fact, epidemics.

Viral videos are a perfect contemporary example. Viewers become so addicted to some videos that they watch them over and over again and contaminate their friends' email in-boxes with links to the videos. That is why they are called *viral* videos: because they spread like an epidemic. According to Gladwell, they are actually a form of mass hysteria. "This kind of thing is extremely common," Gladwell wrote. "It's almost natural. It doesn't mean you're mentally ill or crazy."[26]

The 2012 pop hit "Gangnam Style" by Psy was an example of the epidemic or viral video phenomenon. Despite most viewers having no idea what the lyrics were actually saying, the video has had more than one billion hits and became the No. 1 YouTube video of all time. Also in 2012, a more serious mass hysteria broke out in upstate New York, where 15 teenage girls became afflicted with unexplained and uncontrollable spasms, tics, and seizures. No physical explanation was found at their school or after medical exams.

Experts have identified thousands of examples of mass hysteria in history. The Salem Witch Trials in 1692 are now thought to have been the result of mass hysteria among teenage girls who claimed they were witches and/or knew witches possessed by the devil. Interestingly, according to Gladwell, the younger a person is, the more susceptible he or she will be to suggestion.

Meanwhile, the Cubs' curses have continued well into the twenty-first century. In 2003, the Cubs were just five outs away from the World Series when Steve Bartman, probably the most unfortunate fan in Cubs history, reached out instinctively for a ball that seemed to be heading for the stands—an apparent souvenir. Bartman's reach caused Moises Alou to drop the sure out. The Cubs lost the game and the Florida Marlins went on to win the World Series. Months later, Harry Caray's Restaurant bought the infamous "Bartman Ball" for $113,824. Why? In order to demolish it in a public ceremony to break the "curse" on the Cubs. On February 26, 2004, the ball was rigged with explosives and destroyed in a bulletproof tank as fans cheered. But was the Cubs' "curse" lifted?

"There is an illness about being a Cubs fan," said Jim Greanias, a Greek Orthodox priest from Indiana, to the *New York Times* in 2010.[27] And Greanias should know, as he played the central role in what may be the most bizarre spectacle in Cubs curse history: the team asked Greanias to exorcise the team's dugout before the 2008 playoffs. Cubs Chairman Crane Kenney called him after the team made the 2008 playoffs, asking him to come and bless the team dugout.

Why was Greanias, a Greek Orthodox priest in Valparaiso, Indiana, more than 60 miles away from the Friendly Confines, asked to fill this role? "Kenney told me he wanted a Greek Orthodox priest because [Billy] Sianis was Greek," Greanias told the *Chicago Tribune* in 2009.[28]

Sports bring out the child in everyone, allowing adults to enjoy a game like as they did when they were young. And, when in this childish mental state, we, too, can fall victim to the epidemic of suggestion.

Even denying a curse perpetuates the mental epidemic, at least according to the research of University of Michigan social psychologist Norbert Schwarz. His studies, according to a 2007 *Washington Post* article, revealed that merely saying something—even if you say it doesn't exist—reinforces the idea that it *might* exist.[29] In other words, the statement "There is no Cubs curse" becomes nothing more than "Cubs curse" in the dark corners of your mind.

So whether you are a baseball chairman, a Japanese fan idolizing a KFC statue, a Greek Orthodox priest, a secret fan of "Gangnam Style," or someone who believes that the "Curse of the Billy Goat" or the "Curse of the Black Cat" has kept the Chicago Cubs from winning it all, you are merely another one of the millions of people the world over infected with a psychological epidemic.

In the world of sports, some people might just call it being a fan.

Chapter 23

First Cubbie to Pose Naked

The First Cubbie to Pose Nude in a Magazine Was Not the First to Be Fired for Posing Nude in a Magazine—A Distinction That Was Reserved for the Second Cubbie to Pose Nude.

Given the proliferation of sexting and homemade pornography in today's world, it may seem hard to believe that there was a time when people actually shied away from showing their naked bodies to the world. Not so, however, for a couple of former Cubbies, who were apparently ahead of their times.

In 1982, Marla Collins became the first female ballgirl for a National League team. The American League's Oakland A's had been the first team to use female ballgirls, starting in 1969. One of them was Debbi Fields, founder of the Mrs. Fields cookie empire, which has earned her a net worth of nearly $500 million. Collins, on the other hand, earned a different kind of fame.

While working at a White Sox beer stand at the start of the 1982 season, Collins was approached by Cubs executives who knew she had what they were seeking.

"They said, 'We have a job for you.' I would be the first girl ever in the National League," Collins recalled for the *Chicago Tribune's* Cheryl Lavin years later. "It was a new thing. I had no contract, nothing. It was a whole new idea."[30]

Dressed in a skimpy version of the Cubs uniform, Collins retrieved foul balls, provided the umpire with fresh baseballs, and attended public events on behalf of the Cubs. Since the team's games were televised nationally on WGN-TV, Collins received a great deal of public exposure during the four years she held her position as a ballgirl. But it was nothing compared to the exposure she received from *Playboy* magazine, which was headquartered in Chicago. That publication gave her more than $25,000 to pose for the magazine *without* her Cubs uniform. It was an easy choice to make, Collins said, considering the Cubs were only paying her $150 per game (roughly $12,000 for the season).

Draped in furs, a garter belt and nothing else, Collins' appearance in the September 1986 issue of *Playboy* hit the newsstands in late July and had an immediate impact. *Chicago Tribune* columnist Mike Royko wrote about it, and the entire town was buzzing—well, the male half of town, at least. Collins' pictorial was titled "Belle of the Ball Club," and helped the magazine sell out throughout the Midwest. The team, however, was none too pleased—the Cubs immediately fired her for her racy magazine appearance.

"Cub tradition is the issue," Mike Royko wrote in a July 23 column in the *Tribune* the week the magazine appeared, defending the decision. "In the long history of this team, nobody playing for the Cubs has ever appeared nude in public."[31]

Ah, but if only that were true, Royko. Apparently, legendary columnists are not above incorrect reporting. Or maybe he just wanted to forget that Joe Pepitone had posed nude a decade earlier.

The first known major leaguer to pose nude for a magazine was the former Cubs first baseman and center fielder, who had a full frontal spread in the January 1975 issue of *Foxy Lady* magazine. Batting .284 in four years with the Cubs, Pepitone's playing career ended after the 1973 season.

Always flamboyant and outrageous, Pepitone was recalled by former teammates as the first player to ever bring a hair dryer into the clubhouse—which was the cause of the first of many clashes Pepitone had with cantankerous manager Leo Durocher. "I remember the day that Joe came in and ran the hair dryer for the first time," Glenn Beckert said in *Wrigleyville*:

> It was the noisiest thing you ever heard. Leo's office was up two flights of stairs, and he yelled to the clubhouse men, "Yosh, what in the hell is that noise?" There had never been a hair dryer in our clubhouse before, and Yosh yelled up, "Leo, it's Pepitone with his hair dryer." And I remember Leo just scratching his head and closing his office door.[32]

Durocher had reason to be perplexed. Pepitone was nearly bald and wore two different toupees—one during games and another while out on the town.

Pepitone was also the first Cubs player to appear in a *Playboy* publication, years before Collins did so—but not in the way most would expect. *Playboy's* book division published his 1975 autobiography *Joe You Coulda Made Us Proud*.

"Joe was the type of guy who was open with any part of his life," Beckert said. "There wasn't anything he wouldn't discuss."

Or apparently do for money.

To answer the question many men may be wondering about at this point, Collins' likes included "wild and crazy guys." Which was how most people would have described Pepitone.

Chapter 24

The Biggest Con in Baseball History

One of the Biggest Myths in Sports History Turned Three
Cubs Players into Immortals Despite the Fact That
They Held No Individual Records of Greatness.

There are many Cubs apologists who will tell you that the most famous double-play combination in baseball history deserved their 1946 special entry into the Professional Baseball Hall of Fame. But the truth is they were given the honor because of a poem that made them famous—that and the fact that no other players earned induction into the Hall that year.

Shortstop Joe Tinker, second baseman Johnny Evers, and first baseman/manager Frank Chance made up the famous 6-4-3 double-play combination of Tinker-Evers-Chance. They were also the subject of the second most famous poem in baseball history, after "Casey at the Bat." In 1910, Chicago native Franklin Adams was a writer for the *New York Evening Mail* when he wrote his poem "Baseball's Sad Lexicon" about Tinker-Evers-Chance:

These are the saddest possible words,
Tinker to Evers to Chance.
Trio of Bear Cubs fleeter than birds,
Tinker to Evers to Chance.
Ruthlessly pricking our gonfalon bubble.
Making a Giant hit into a double.
Words that are weighty with nothing but trouble,
Tinker to Evers to Chance.

Though short, the poem created a myth so large that it has convinced baseball fans of this threesome's greatness for generations.

Let's answer the first question most fans have after reading the poem: a *gonfalon* is a pennant or flag. The Giants in question were obviously the New York Giants, the Cubs' opponent when Adams covered the game for the newspaper.

Mythmaking is a part of sports, and no players have ever reaped its rewards as fully as Tinker, Evers, and Chance. They were inducted into the National Baseball Hall of Fame after a special, secret meeting called because in 1946, the Baseball Writers Association of America (BBWAA) did not elect any players for induction. A player must be on 75 percent of all BBWAA ballots to be elected; 1946 was the second year during which the writers didn't feel that any of the eligible players met the requirements. (The other seasons in which no players were elected were 1945, 1950, 1958, 1960, 1971, 1996, and 2013.) The number of voters has increased over the years, but in 1946, a player needed to be on 152 ballots to meet the 75 percent requirement. Chance led all candidates with 144, followed by Evers with 130; Tinker was last overall on the list.

"Confronted with the prospect of an empty Cooperstown stage, a six-man Hall of Fame committee responded by anointing nine players, including Tinker, Evers and Chance," MLB historian Jerome Holtzman explained in a *Chicago Tribune* column on May 14, 1992. "In effect, they went in as a unit. Nothing like that ever happened before or since."[33]

Holtzman was one of the most knowledgeable scribes in baseball history. His personal library of baseball books was larger than entire libraries in some small towns. He covered baseball for more than 40 years at the *Chicago Sun-Times* and *Chicago Tribune*. In 1989, Holtzman, known as "the Dean," was elected to the writers' wing of the National Baseball Hall of Fame.

Holtzman's 1992 investigation into the legitimacy of the Tinker-Evers-Chance claim to fame left baseball's most learned scholar with only one conclusion: "They were an above-average double-play combination, but not much more," he wrote, adding, "In baseball, as in life, the pen is stronger than the sword. Because of a press box poet, the Cubs continue to have baseball's most storied double-play combination."

Despite appearing in a New York newspaper, the poem led to the adoption of the phrase "Tinker-Evers-Chance" as Chicago slang for something particularly smooth and effortless. But while this team might have been smooth, were they special? Not so much, according to Holtzman, who found that former BBWAA president Charles Segar had actually researched how good the combo was, with disappointing results for Cubs fans. Between April 15, 1902 (when Tinker-Evers-Chance turned their first double play), and April 12, 1912 (the date of their last twin killing), the Cubs did not lead the league in double plays for even one season. Segar's numbers revealed an average (at best) double-play combination that was simply fortunate enough to have names that sounded optimistic and poetic.

"Segar went through the records from 1906 through 1909, when the legendary trio was at its peak," Holtzman wrote:

> His findings revealed a four-season total of 29 Tinker-to-Evers-to-Chance double plays: eight in 1906; seven in '07, eight in '08, and six in '09.
>
> Segar also checked the reverse, 4-6-3s, started by Evers, not Tinker. The numbers were essentially the same: 25 Evers-to-Tinker-to-Chance double plays. So in these four years, the combined total, both ways, was 54. . . . In 1908, the NL average per team was 75 double plays.

To be fair to Chance and Evers, they each left their mark on baseball history in other ways. Chance was the Cubs' player-manager who led the team to its greatest success in the modern era, winning four pennants in five years from 1906 to 1910 and earning him the nickname "the Peerless Leader." The zenith and nadir of Chance's managing career was 1906, when he led the Cubs to a record-setting 116-win season, but lost the World Series to their crosstown rival, the White Stockings. As a young player, he was called "Husk" due to his thick build and toughness. Chance's ability to take a pitch to the head or body was one of his trademarks; he still holds the Cubs' record for most times hit by pitch in a game (three). In fact, Chance took so many hits to the head by a baseball that he suffered from hearing loss and headaches and underwent surgery in 1912 to relieve a blood clot in his brain. During his 17-year playing career, Chance's lifetime batting average was .296. He led the league in stolen bases twice (with 67 in 1903 and 57 in 1906), and his 103 runs in 1906 also led the league.

Evers was nicknamed "the Crab," both for his tenacity in digging out ground balls and his surly demeanor. In 1913, Evers took over as Cubs manager after Chance left for New York. He managed for only one season, leading the team to a third-place finish (88–65). Despite weighing barely more than 100 pounds, Evers was tenacious and knew the rules better than any other player, as well as most officials. His quick thinking and knowledge of the rules forced the "Merkle

Boner" play in 1908 that eventually led to the Cubs' most recent World Series title. His lifetime batting average was .270 during 18 seasons, and while he never led the league in any category, he was voted the American League Most Valuable Player for the Boston Braves in 1914, his first season playing for a team other than the Cubs.

Tinker clearly gained the most from the notoriety he garnered via "Baseball's Sad Lexicon," earning a Hall of Fame admission for no statistical reason. Scrappy and tough, Tinker was known for getting big hits in key moments, but not much else.

Many fans might be surprised to learn that while this trio has become a part of baseball history, they were not friends. In fact, Tinker and Evers had an open dislike for each other. Tinker played 14 of his 15 years in Chicago, his lone season in Cincinnati coming in 1913—the only season that Evers served as manager. After Evers was relieved of his managing duties at the end of the season, Tinker returned to Chicago for another three seasons.

No players in baseball history have benefitted more from media hype than this Cubs' trio (Sammy Sosa's 1998 home-run season came close, but his induction into the National Baseball Hall of Fame is doubtful). While Adams' poem did not necessarily reach a wide national audience when it was first published in 1910, it was reprinted by the *Tribune* in 1924 when Chance died. The legend then took hold, with fans and reporters recalling from distant memory the greatest double-play combination that never was. The same thing happened in 1947 and 1948, when Evers and Tinker died, respectively, and fans read the poem reprinted in the players' obituaries.

It took a special committee of Hall of Fame voters, embarrassed at another year without any players voted into the Hall, to perpetuate the biggest con in baseball lore: the greatness of Tinkers-to-Evers-to-Chance.

Section III

Race

Chapter 25

Murdered by a Police Officer

The First Puerto Rican Player in MLB History Was a Cubbie Who Achieved More Notoriety for His Mysterious Murder Than for Being a Baseball Pioneer.

The organization that would become the Washington Nationals in 2005 was originally the Montreal Expos; in 2003, they played 22 of their "home" games at Hiram Bithorn Stadium in Puerto Rico. Major League Baseball bought the Expos in 2002 and made the Caribbean stadium the team's part-time home while deciding what to do with the franchise that would eventually go to Washington, DC. With a short field (fences were just 315 feet to left, 313 feet to right, and 399 feet to center), the Puerto Rican ballpark—like hurler Bithorn's career and life—proved to be too short.

Puerto Rico was able to keep their "home" team for only one season, which was barely longer than the 105 games Bithorn played over four seasons in the major leagues. Yet despite a career cut short in part by his service to the United States during World War II, Bithorn made a significant impact on the sport as the first of hundreds of Puerto Rican players to play in the major leagues.

Born in 1916 in Santurce, Puerto Rico, Bithorn was with the New York Yankees' minor league affiliates before the Cubs took him in the 1941 Rule 5 Draft. The son of a Danish mother and a Puerto Rican father, Bithorn was light-skinned enough for entry into the racist ranks of the MLB in those days. The unofficial "eye test" was the one thing that held back dark-skinned players. The term largely used decades ago was "passed"—as in, Bithorn "passed" for being white. Eager to keep the game as white as possible, baseball owners and management would only consider light-skinned ethnic players; even then, Hispanic players usually went by "white" nicknames to mask their true racial identities.

"Segregation also affected Latino baseball players," wrote historian Robin Doak in *Struggling to Become American*:

> Only those with light skin who could pass as white were allowed to play in the major leagues in the United States. Those with darker skin played in the Negro Leagues or in Cuba, Mexico or Venezuela. In all, about 50 Latino ballplayers played in the major leagues before 1947, when Jackie Robinson became the first black player.[1]

Robinson was not the first African American baseball player in the major leagues, but that is the topic of our next chapter. Doak's point was that only light-skinned players such as Bithorn, who were almost entirely of Latino ancestry (though not exclusively, as we learn in the next chapter), passed the unofficial litmus test of bigotry. The league allowed them to play because they looked white.

Bithorn's rookie season in 1942 came five years before Robinson's rookie campaign, but long after the first nonwhite player in the game. Luis "Lou" Castro was the first Latino in the major leagues, playing one season for the Philadelphia A's in 1902. (Cuban Esteban "Steve" Bellan played for the Troy Haymakers and the New York Mutuals of the long-defunct National Association of Professional Baseball Players from 1871 to 1873, but MLB officially considers the NAPBBP to have been a minor league.) The first Latino star player was Cuban-born pitcher Adolpho "Dolf" Luque, who played from 1914 to 1935, primarily with the Cincinnati Reds, and had infamous battles against the Cubs' Charlie Root. Japan-born pitcher Masanori Murakami, the first Asian player, didn't take the field until 1964, for the San Francisco Giants.

Some historians incorrectly called Bithorn the first Latino player in the major leagues. Actually, Bithorn was only the first Latino player to play for the Cubs, which was a tough enough role to fill considering the long-standing racist sentiments within the organization, which was one of the most influential clubs throughout baseball.

Puerto Rico's stature in the Latino baseball community is noteworthy. At the start of the 2013 season, there had been 235 MLB players born in the U.S. territory of Puerto Rico. The only other territories or countries to send more players to the highest ranks of baseball have been the Dominican Republic (566), Venezuela (290), and Canada (239).[2] Following Bithorn's lead were future Baseball Hall of

Famers Roberto Clemente, Orlando Cepeda, and Roberto Alomar, all born in Puerto Rico.

Puerto Rican officials named the island's new stadium in Bithorn's honor after its construction in 1962. In addition to his short—albeit benchmark—career, Bithorn is also known for his early demise. During his rookie year, Bithorn notched just a 9–14 record, but rebounded in 1943 with an impressive 18–12 mark. He missed the 1944 and 1945 seasons due to his service in the navy. By then, age had crept up on Bithorn, who managed just a 6–5 record in 1946 with the Cubs before playing in two games for the White Sox and then bowing out of the MLB early in the 1947 season.

The right-handed pitcher then attempted to rekindle his career in the Mexican winter league. Bithorn was standing in front of a bus station in Almante, Mexico, on December 27, 1951, when Mexican police officer Ambrosio Castillo Cano shot the former Cubs hurler in the stomach. Bithorn died the next day, but officials, sensing that something unscrupulous had happened, didn't file the paperwork until New Year's Day, leading to the popular misconception that Bithorn died on January 1, 1952, rather than December 28, 1951.

Within a week of Bithorn's official death report, Cano was charged with homicide. The story has never been fully explained, but pieces of the incident were revealed before Cano was found guilty of murder in October 1952 and sentenced to eight years in prison. Cano claimed that he and Bithorn were arguing when the pitcher hit the police officer in the face with his suitcase. Cano then shot Bithorn in the stomach, later claiming that he feared for his life. According to Cano, while Bithorn lay in the street dying, he said that he was a Communist spy on a mission and that he only had himself to blame for his death. (No witnesses have ever supported Cano's ludicrous claims.) The argument apparently stemmed from the fact that Bithorn was attempting to sell a 1947 Buick for which he did not have the proper paperwork. Cano was attempting to take Bithorn in to the police station when the fight broke out.

While Cano's supervisor initially supported his story, the local magistrate did not, and on January 7, 1952, Cano was charged with homicide. Details of the case are sketchy. One story claimed Bithorn had as much as $2,000 in American bills on his person at the time, leading Mexican authorities to question Cano's real motive. Although Cano received a serious jail sentence, no one has ever unearthed the real facts of the case.

Despite Bithorn's status as the first Puerto Rican player in MLB history, the media has never investigated the real cause of the disagreement that led Cano to shoot him. The only mention of the incident in the press was a 46-word Associated Press piece published on October 3, 1952, reporting on Cano's sentencing.[3] There was no mention of any motive.

Unfortunately, Bithorn is not the only former MLB player to be murdered under mysterious circumstances. On November 21, 2011, former Seattle Mariners outfielder Gregory Halman was killed by his own brother, Jason, with a knife to the neck when Greg told Jason to turn his music down at 5:00 a.m. On October 31, 2012, former Yankee pitcher Pascual Perez was killed in his Dominican Republic home by repeated blows to the head from a hammer by assailants seeking to rob him of his MLB pension money. The most bizarre death of a major league player was likely on September 17, 1935, when former Dodgers outfielder Len Koenecke chartered a tiny, two-person-crew plane to fly him to Buffalo and then, while drunk, attacked the two pilots, who were forced to hit the ballplayer on the head with a fire extinguisher to stop the assault. Koenecke died from the blunt force trauma; though the pilots were initially charged with manslaughter, they were found not guilty, as Koenecke was believed to be attempting suicide by crashing the plane.

Bithorn remains the only former MLB player to be murdered by police officials.

Chapter 26

Jackie Robinson Was Not the First African American Player

The First African American Player in Major League Baseball Was Not Jackie Robinson. The Truth Is Much Harder for Cubs Fans to Handle.

Only one person in the history of American sports made such an impact on their game—and society overall—that their jersey number has been retired by every team in the game. Baseball fan or not, every American citizen knows Jackie Robinson's legacy as the first African American baseball player, breaking the color barrier in 1947 with the Brooklyn Dodgers. The infielder wore No. 42 for the Dodgers until his retirement in 1956. In 1997, on the 50th anniversary of Robinson's socially significant achievement, commissioner Bud Selig officially retired No. 42 for every team in Major League Baseball.

A leader of social change that went well beyond the boundaries of ballparks, Robinson suffered constant threats, both physical and emotional, from racist fans, players, and executives hell-bent on keeping African Americans out of baseball. Long is the list of Robinson's suffering, from death threats to vicious plays committed by opponents intent on hurting him to hateful insults spewed by players, managers, and executives on a daily basis. Robinson never retaliated during his ten-year career playing first, second, and third base for the Dodgers. He was voted MVP in 1949. In 1962, he became one of the few players ever to be inducted into the National Baseball Hall of Fame on his first ballot.

Robinson was a civic leader who deserves his place in history for helping to desegregate the world; however, he was *not* actually the first African American to play in the major leagues.

Sixty-three years before Robinson's 1947 rookie season, Moses Fleetwood "Fleet" Walker became the first African American to play major league ball.

Walker was a former law student at the University of Michigan, where he was the first African American to play for the Wolverines' baseball team. Few baseball fans outside of Toledo, Ohio, remember Walker's historic place in desegregation history. The accolades heaped upon Robinson should at least be shared with Walker. Cubs fans especially should remember Walker, for were it not for the Chicago Cubs and Cap Anson, Walker would be the player remembered around the world for desegregating baseball, instead of Robinson. Walker's achievements are rarely, if ever, remembered, and today he is treated as little more than a footnote.

Adrian Anson often boasted that he was the first white child born among the American Indian residents of Marshalltown, Iowa. Born in 1852, he later earned the nickname "'Cap" (short for *captain*) in deference to the 27 years he played and managed the franchise we know today as the Cubs (in his time, the franchise was called the White Stockings and the Colts). When Anson retired, local sportswriters took to calling the team the Orphans because the young players were without their longtime leader.

Inducted into the National Baseball Hall of Fame in 1939 for a laundry list of innovations that teams take for granted today, Anson would also be a first-ballot inductee into a Racist Hall of Fame, if one existed. In fact, his racism may have had just as much of an effect on the sport as his numerous contributions to the game. Walker had numerous run-ins with Anson over the years. Unfortunately for history, Anson and his legion of like-minded racist cronies prevailed in the end.

Standing six feet tall and weighing 225 pounds, Anson grew into the well-rounded features of a successful man. As a young athlete, he wore a handlebar mustache waxed into spikes that shot laterally from his face. When his youth faded, so, too, did the mustache. Anson became a linebacker of a player, thick and aggressive. For comparison sake, Sammy Sosa, the Cubs infamous home-run slugger, was also six feet tall and 225 pounds, while prototypical Chicago Bears linebacker Mike Singletary was six feet and 230 pounds.

Walker, on the other hand, was slim with a thick mustache that curled around the corners of his mouth. He weighed only 160 pounds and resembled the comedian Chris Rock in appearance, although Rock probably carries 10 or 20 more pounds. Walker was tough and educated; his father, Dr. Moses W. Walker, was one of the first African American doctors in Ohio, which led to

118

Walker attending Oberlin College before briefly studying law at the University of Michigan. Notwithstanding his slight stature, Walker played catcher at a time when catcher's mitts didn't exist. Broken fingers were commonplace, as were rudimentary facemasks that stuck to the skin in cold conditions. Back then, catchers endured countless spikes-up plays at the plate of the variety that would lead to ejections today, but were merely part of the game in the years just after the Civil War.

In 1882, the separation between major and minor league baseball teams began to blur; stricter rules would soon become necessary. Since its inception in 1876, the NL had been the dominant major league, and its organizations were located predominantly in urban cities (in 1882 the NL teams were in Chicago; Boston; Detroit; Buffalo; Cleveland; Troy, New York; Worcester, Massachusetts; and Providence, Rhode Island). In 1882, the American Association began play (with teams in Cincinnati, Philadelphia, Louisville, Pittsburgh, St. Louis, and Baltimore). This upstart league immediately became a real competitor to the NL due to playing games on Sundays, allowing alcohol sales, and cheaper ticket prices. In 1883, the Northwestern League was created with the idea of taking the game to communities outside of the urban hubs (with teams in Bay City, Michigan; East Saginaw, Michigan; Fort Wayne, Indiana; Grand Rapids, Michigan; Peoria, Illinois; Quincy, Illinois; Springfield, Illinois; and Toledo, Ohio). While the Northwestern League further expanded the sport's popularity, it also forced NL leaders to seek an agreement preventing the various leagues' teams from stealing players from the competition. On March 12, 1883, National League president A.G. Mills convinced the leaders of the American Association and the Northwestern League to agree to respect other leagues' contracts. Known as the "Tripartite Pact" or "National Agreement," this labor agreement also recognized the American Association as a major league on par with the National League, as well as recognizing the Northwestern League as the highest minor league.

Meanwhile, the slight Walker played so well for the University of Michigan in 1882 that the Toledo Blue Stockings of the brand-new Northwestern League signed the catcher for their inaugural 1883 season. On a road trip from Buffalo to Detroit, Chicago stopped in Toledo for an exhibition game against the Blue Stockings on August 10, 1883.

Never one to keep his opinion to himself, Anson made it clear to Toledo manager Charles Morton that his team would not play if an African American player took the field. What Anson did not know was that Walker had hurt his hand in a recent game and wasn't even scheduled to play that day. Morton, eager to calm a potentially explosive scene, explained to Anson and the White Stockings that Walker had been benched to rest his hand.

The White Stockings were the nation's preeminent baseball team at the time, becoming the sport's first dynasty by taking first place in the National League five times and second place twice. Standing atop the baseball world, Anson and his teammates felt entitled to express their feelings for the entire crowded stadium to hear. During pregame warm-ups, White Stocking players loudly and proudly claimed they would not take the field "with no damned nigger," according to Anson biographer David Fleitz in his book *Cap Anson*.

Tolerant only to a point, Morton was enraged at the bigoted antics of his guests, which were enflaming a situation he had doused only moments earlier in a quiet, subtle fashion. Morton immediately changed his lineup for the day, putting Walker in at right field.[4]

When Anson and the rest of the Chicago squad saw Walker warming up for action, they went berserk. Anson threatened to pull his team from the field, to which Morton had a simple reply: do so and your team will forfeit its share of the gate receipts. The ploy worked and Anson relented, but not before snarling at Morton: "We will play this here game, but we won't play never no more with the nigger in."[5]

Chicago, the defending NL champions, squeezed out a 7–6 victory in ten innings against the minor league team. Walker went hitless, drew a walk, scored a run, and made no errors in the field.[6] A spectacular line score was unnecessary that day; merely appearing in the game left Walker's mark on history—and Anson, in particular. It was to be only the first of several battles between Walker and Anson that changed the course of the twentieth century.

Buoyed by their success against the best team in baseball, Toledo went on to win the league's pennant that year, which gave the Blue Stockings the opportunity to move up to the American Association for the 1884 season. That meant the American Association's Toledo squad, with Walker as its catcher, would be a major league team on par with Chicago's White Stockings, led by Anson. (Note that the independent minor league American Association that began play in 1902 shared a name with, but was not the same organization as, the major league American Association, which played from 1882 to 1891.)

On May 1, 1884, Toledo played at Louisville on Opening Day with Walker as starting catcher—the first African American player in major league baseball history. Anson and Walker were now both major league players, but Anson was not finished with Walker, the Blue Stockings, and his passionate racist beliefs.

The second confrontation between Anson and Walker came as part of a rematch between Chicago and Toledo scheduled for July 25, 1884. This time, however, the Chicago squad wanted to make sure that Morton would not be allowed to play his star catcher. According to Walker biographer David W. Zang, Chicago's secretary sent his counterpart in Toledo a letter of terms for the game that was direct and unambiguous:

> No colored man shall play in your nine and if your officers insist on playing him after we are there you forfeit the Guarantee and we refuse to play. Now I think this is fair as we refuse point blank to play colored men.[7]

Defiant again, Toledo refused to meet Chicago's racist demands. The game was cancelled and a second on-field confrontation between Anson and Walker was avoided. But Morton made his stance regarding African American players clear that season, signing Walker's younger brother, Welday, to the Toledo roster for the final five games of the season. Though his tenure was brief, Welday became the second African American player in major league baseball, and the Walker brothers became the first African American siblings to play in the big leagues.

Of course, Anson was hardly the only racist in baseball in 1884; he was simply the most popular. White Stockings owner A.G. Spalding was an infamous racist, as were many fans, who sometimes used baseball as an excuse to flaunt their bigoted opinions. After all, the Civil War had ended only 19 years previously.

During the 1884 season, the Blue Stockings received countless threats, including one sent by supposed fans of the Richmond Virginians to Toledo's office prior to a road trip that brought the team to the former capital of the Confederacy:

> We the undersigned do hereby warn you not to put up Walker, the negro catcher, the evenings that you play in Richmond, as we could mention the names of 75 determined men who have sworn to mob Walker if he comes on the ground in a suit. We hope you will listen to our words of warning, so there will be no trouble; but if you do not there certainly will be. We only write this to prevent much bloodshed, as you alone can prevent.[8]

According to *Sporting Life* magazine, the actual senders of the letter were not even residents of Richmond, and were simply using the game as an excuse to promote their racist feelings.[9] But whether the senders were truly residents—or even fans—didn't really matter; clearly, violence was being threatened if Walker took the field. Fearing for the safety of his catcher, Morton left Walker behind when the team made its road trip to Virginia.

Walker's experience was similar to Robinson's 63 years later, only worse. In 1947, the insults and threats to Robinson came almost entirely from people outside of the Dodgers organization. (While some Brooklyn Dodgers players did sign a petition to ban Robinson from the team, manager Leo Durocher squelched the movement before Robinson came aboard.) For Walker, the worst attacks came from his own teammates rather than opponents, and took the form of physical abuse as well as insults.

During the 1880s, catching was the most dangerous position on the field, and players had little or no added protection. Chest protectors, shin guards, helmets, face masks, and catcher's mitts were either yet to be invented or offered little in actual protection given their novelty at the time. Broken noses, badly bruised eyes, and mangled fingers were common. Furthermore, most catchers communicated freely with their pitchers, using signs so that the catcher knew what kind of pitch was coming. But Toledo pitcher Tony Mullane refused to even communicate with Walker, putting the catcher at risk for injury. "[Walker] was the best catcher I ever worked with, but I disliked a Negro and whenever I had to pitch to him I used to pitch anything I wanted without looking at his signals," Mullane said:

> One day he signaled me for a curve and I shot a fastball at him. He caught it and walked down to me. He said, "I'll catch for you without signals, but I won't catch you if you are going to cross me when I give you signals." And all the rest of the season he caught me and caught anything I pitched without knowing what was coming.[10]

Whether it was his intention or not, Mullane's racist actions led directly to Walker's season ending early. On September 23, 1884, Toledo released Walker because of his sore hands, as well as mounting threats from fans. Weeks later, Toledo dropped out of the American Association, having played only one season as a major league team. It would be another 63 years before Robinson played for the Dodgers.

Walker continued to catch in the minor leagues on the East Coast for the next several seasons, eager to take on any opponent. He would need the experience, as he and Anson had two more battles to fight. This time, more than one man's career and life were on the line. But that is our next story.

Author's note: In 2003, Peter Morris released his findings for the Society of American Baseball Researchers claiming William Edward White was the first African American player in major league history. White played one game for the Providence Grays of the National League on June 21, 1879, with one hit, one run scored, and no errors. But history did not mark White's achievement because nobody thought he was black—White included. White "passed" as a white man, and based on the color of his skin, no one ever questioned his racial identity. Few knew that he was the offspring of Georgia businessman Andrew J. White, a white man, and his mixed-race slave, Hannah White. White claimed he was white in his answers to the 1880 and 1890 U.S. censuses[11]; further, no one who looked at him would question the assertion—he "passed" the eye test. It took researchers more than 100 years of poring through countless records to find a connection to his mixed-race mother, giving White his dubious claim as the first African American in major league history.

What White was able to hide, the Walker brothers could not. Both Fleet and Welday were dark-skinned; there was no question of what race they were to anyone they met. To be fair, however, there are conflicting reports about the Walker ancestry. Many accounts refer to their father as the first African American doctor in Ohio, while other reports claim he, too, was of mixed race, although he was quite dark-skinned. Likewise, their mother, Caroline, was referred to as being either white or a mulatto depending on the source. Given the fact that Caroline Walker was a midwife in Ohio, the most likely scenario is that she was of mixed race.

Regardless of what his DNA tests may yield, it is our opinion that White does not deserve credit as the first African American major league player due to the simple fact that everyone thought of him as a white man. He did not have to face the prejudices of his time, as did the Walker brothers and Robinson.

Chapter 27

How the Cubs Helped Erect the Color Barrier

Segregation in Baseball, as in Society, Was the Work of Countless Individuals. But One Team—The Cubs—And One Player on that Team Have Been Credited with Actively Furthering Racial Divisions in Baseball During the Twentieth Century.

Psychologists, sociologists, and historians have maintained for generations that racism is a learned trait, not an inherited one. So it may seem unfair to point the finger at Cap Anson of the Chicago White Stockings as the reason why baseball (and perhaps society at large) was segregated until Jackie Robinson took the field for the Brooklyn Dodgers in 1947.

There were, after all, more influential bigots in the sport's history. Notable among them was former Cubs player, manager, and owner A.G. Spalding, who insisted on hiring a diminutive African American man named Clarence Duval as the team "mascot." Spalding hired Duval "to dance on the dugout roof in Chicago and degrade himself for the entertainment of his employers."[12] Ironically, Spalding's vast sporting empire became a worldwide name in sports manufacturing thanks to the achievements of African American athletes who excelled at the very sport he tried to keep them from playing.

None other than Kenesaw Mountain Landis, the first commissioner of baseball, has been named repeatedly over the years as the sport's worst racist, as he did nothing to help the cause of African American players. Whatever the truth may be, the fact that baseball was not integrated until after his death in 1944 cannot be denied.

However, while Spalding, Landis, and the rest of the influential decision makers of the time flexed their bigotry quietly behind the scenes, Anson was loud about his feelings, never hesitating to belittle nearly any minority. The problem was, many fans agreed with him, spurring him to spread the poison of his bigotry to others in the game. Wrote Peter Golenbock in his book *Wrigleyville*:

> Since racism ran rampant in all of America at the time, it was certainly easier and more politically correct to go along with Anson, the most popular player in the game, than to stand up to him. Anson did not limit his expressions of bigotry to blacks. . . . The Irish were made comic targets, as were the Jews, but Anson did not revile and shun them the way he did the blacks.[13]

As explained in the previous chapter, Fleet Walker was actually the first African American player in the major leagues, not Robinson. The two previous run-ins that Walker had had with Anson in the Midwest forced Walker to take his game to the East Coast, where he ended up catching for the Newark, New Jersey, Little Giants of the International League (formerly the Eastern League) in 1887.

It was with the Little Giants that Walker made history again, this time teaming up with a 21-year-old African American pitcher named George Stovey to become the first African American battery in major league baseball. As good a catcher as Walker was, Stovey was an even better pitcher, compiling a 33–14 record for Newark. In his 1992 book *Only the Ball Was White*, historian Robert Peterson pronounced Stovey "the first great Negro pitcher."[14] In fact, the 1887 Little Giants boasted not only an all African American battery, but also an Irish battery (pitcher Mickey Hughes and catcher Gene Derby) and a German battery (pitcher Bob Miller and catcher Bart Cantz), giving fans of nearly any ethnicity someone to root for during the season.[15]

But it was the Stovey-Walker battery that caused some ugly trouble when the White Stockings played Newark in an exhibition game on July 14, 1887, leading to changes that would impact professional baseball for years to come. On an East Coast road trip between Washington and New York, Anson and his White Stockings agreed to play the Little Giants. As he had done before when Walker was with the Toledo Blue Stockings, Anson demanded that no African Americans take the field.

After two previous conflicts, Walker appeared to have realized that he wasn't going to get anywhere with Anson. Newark management announced that Walker was not going to play, though no injury was ever cited and Walker was Stovey's battery mate. That left Stovey as the sole African American to take the field.

But Stovey never saw action in the contest. "Take him out or I get off," Anson warned the Newark management.[16] To the surprise of few, Stovey came down with a sudden illness and joined Walker on the bench. "In this encounter, Anson proved the greater force," Walker biographer David W. Zang explained in *Fleet Walker's Divided Heart*:

> The absence of the black battery drew no mention from the press. It was not until the next year that the *Sporting Life* reported that Stovey had not been the victim of illness, but rather of Anson's absolute refusal to share the field with colored players.[17]

Like others in baseball, Newark manager Charley Hackett succumbed to Anson's prejudiced pressure and saw to it that neither Walker nor Stovey took the field.

Newark won the game, 9–4, but the real battle began when the game was over. Stovey was the hottest pitcher in baseball in 1887. He dominated the competition (his 33–14 mark that season was worthy of a career record for some pitchers, and some sources credit him with actually having 34 or 35 wins). The National League's New York Giants considered signing him to their squad, which would have made Stovey the first African American in the NL. John Montgomery Ward, captain of the Giants and a player on Spalding's World Tour in 1888–89, was eager to bring Stovey on board. On April 7, 1887, Ward's New York Giants barely beat the Newark Little Giants, 3–2. Stovey pitched for the Little Giants, prompting Ward, an ardent supporter of players' rights, to urge Giants manager Jim Mutrie to sign both Stovey and Walker to the club. Hackett, however, rebuffed these offers for reasons that were never explained.

The racial biases that had shaped the situation would become clear later. Wrote Golenbock in *Wrigleyville*:

> When John Montgomery Ward made a deal to bring pitcher George Stovey to the New York Giants, Anson drummed up support from other club owners to keep Stovey, and all other blacks, out of baseball. Irish and Jewish players got to compete, but the blacks didn't, not just because of Anson, but because of other powerful bigots, including National League team owners like Al Spalding.[18]

There is no evidence to prove that Anson and Spalding prevented the trade of Walker and Stovey to Chicago's rival, the Giants. Nor is there evidence that

Anson and Spalding talked Mutrie out of pursuing the trade further. Anson, Spalding, Landis, and other executives were careful not to put anything in writing on the subject, mindful to avoid creating any evidence of their behind-the-scenes influence. However, one written account does show how Anson's actions on July 14 (when his Chicago team forced Walker and Stovey off the field) unquestionably led to the first official decision to ban African American players from International League play—the first domino to fall in what became a 63-year blacklisting of African American baseball players.

International League officials met on the night of Chicago's loss to Newark. The *Newark Daily Journal* published an account of the meeting the following day under a headline that screamed what fans had known all along: "THE COLOR LINE DRAWN IN BASEBALL." The ensuing story was simple and damning:

> The International League directors held a secret meeting at the Genesee House yesterday, and the question of colored players was freely discussed. Several representatives declared that many of the best players in the league are anxious to leave on account of the colored element, and the board finally directed Secretary White to approve of no more contracts to colored men.[19]

Emboldened by Anson's ability to get the International League to keep African American players off the field, other teams began to refuse to play against African American players that season as well. On September 10, the St. Louis Browns were forced to cancel an exhibition game scheduled for the following day against the New York Cuban Giants, a popular African American team, when eight Browns players signed a petition saying they refused to play "against negroes . . . [but] will cheerfully play against white people at any time, and think, by refusing to play, we are only doing what is right."[20]

At the end of the 1887 season, the Newark Little Giants released Stovey and Walker. They were fortunate to escape in good health. Previously latent hostilities were now out in the open, and African American players were often targeted for abuse, along with any players who sympathized with them. African American infielder Bud Fowler was forced to invent the game's first shin guards (wooden slats worn under his socks) to prevent the constant damage he received from spikes-up slides into second base while he attempted to turn double plays.

Anson, Spalding, and other contributors to segregation never made mention of their feelings or actions in their autobiographies. There were no recorded minutes of meetings in which baseball leaders made the decision to ban African Americans in baseball. The only "smoking gun" was the *Newark Daily Journal* article, which reported the specific direction to forbid "colored" players in professional baseball. High-ranking officials of Major League Baseball never went on record approving a rule such as the one reported by the *Newark Daily Journal*. They didn't need to: the power behind the rules was obvious. Said Landis in 1943:

> There is no rule, nor to my knowledge, has there ever been, formal or informal, or any understanding, written or unwritten, subterranean or sub-anything, against the hiring of Negroes in the major leagues. Each club is entirely free to employ Negro players to any and all extent it pleases. The matter is solely for each club's decision, without restriction whatsoever.[21]

What Landis didn't say was that no formal rule was necessary to enforce the color lines that everyone now knew were approved by men at the highest levels of the sport.

The fourth confrontation between Anson and Walker came in September 1888, but it was more of a surrender than a battle. After Newark released him in 1887, Walker was given the unique "honor" of remaining in the International League despite the infamous "direction to Secretary White" on July 14, 1887, and allowed to sign with Syracuse. In September 1888, Chicago played at Syracuse, marking the fourth time Anson would refuse to take the field with Walker. But Anson did not need to make the demand, as Walker chose to remain on the bench. By that time he had reached the decision that, in the words of Anson biographer David L. Fleitz, "Blacks and whites should not mix on the field of play."[22] A pioneer in desegregation, years of intolerance with Anson as its mouthpiece had finally worn Walker down.

The Syracuse Stars released Walker during the 1891 season. His baseball days were over. However, his battles against bigotry were far from done.

On April 13, 1891, a group of white men attacked Walker, and he was forced to kill one of them, Patrick Murray, to escape deadly harm to himself. On June 4, 1891, Walker was found not guilty of any crime. Walker went on to become a successful businessman and author. In 1908, he published *Our Home Colony: A Treatise on the Past, Present, and Future of the Negro Race in America*, which called for separation of the races.

In his 1907 book *History of Colored Base Ball*, player, manager, and baseball historian Sol White (who was elected to the National Baseball Hall of Fame in 2006) stated an unequivocal opinion of what happened in 1887 after the Chicago White Stockings played the Newark Little Giants:

> Were it not for this same man Anson, there would have been a colored player in the National League in 1887. John M. Ward, of the New York club, was anxious to secure [George] Stovey and arrangements were about completed for his transfer from the Newark club, when a howl was heard from Chicago to New York. Just why Adrian C. Anson, manager and captain of the Chicago National League Club, was so strongly opposed to colored players on white teams cannot be explained. His repugnant feeling, shown at every opportunity, toward colored ball players, was a source of comment throughout every league in the country, and his opposition, with his great popularity and power in base ball circles, hastened the exclusion of the black man from the white leagues.[23]

The Cubs have changed the world for the better in many ways; unfortunately, race relations are not one of them.

Famous Chicago newspaper columnist Mike Royko once wrote, "Most Chicago whites hate blacks. The only genuine difference between a southern white and a Chicago white was in their accent."[24] Royko would likely have been intrigued to learn that the one man who wanted to change both the future of baseball and racial inequality was lurking within the borders of Chicago for years. His name? Al Capone.

Chapter 28

How Al Capone Planned
to Destroy the Color Barrier

*How (and Why) Al Capone Nearly Bought the
Chicago Cubs, a Purchase That Could Have Changed
the Racial History of the United States.*

"I'm going to make him an offer he can't refuse."

Michael Corleone's line from the 1972 hit movie *The Godfather* has become one of the most popular phrases in American discourse due to the overwhelming international success of Francis Ford Coppola's film adaptation of Mario Puzo's eponymous bestseller. In fact, in 2005 the American Film Institute ranked Corleone's famous words as the No. 2 line in movie history (trailing only Rhett Butler's "Frankly, my dear, I don't give a damn" as portrayed by Clark Gable in *Gone With The Wind*).

However, according to his descendants, Al Capone was actually the first gangster to use that exact same line, in reference to team owner William Wrigley selling him the Cubs. In her 2010 book *Uncle Al Capone*, Deirdre Marie Capone (granddaughter of Capone's brother, Ralph, a known Cubs fan), explained how close the Cubs came to being bought by the man often called Scarface, who wanted to escape the increasingly violent world of bootlegging liquor.

Born in Brooklyn, New York, in 1899, Capone moved to Chicago in 1920 to work in the brothel business. He learned from mentor Frankie Torrio, another New York transplant who had begun looking out for Capone when the future public enemy No. 1 was only a teenager. In 1925, Torrio barely survived an assassination attempt by rival gang members. He decided to put his Windy City crime empire in the hands of his apprentice, Capone. Then in his mid-twenties, Capone was suddenly in charge of a vast illegal empire of bootlegging, prostitution, and gambling.

Along the way, Capone developed an appreciation for the Chicago Cubs. Actually, according to biographer Jonathan Eig in his book *Get Capone*, Capone enjoyed nearly every sport, especially boxing. He even dabbled in boxing promotions for local fighters for a time, and developed a fondness for horse and dog races, gambling heavily and losing often. Capone was known as a "rotten bettor" with a tendency to pick the loser more often than not, leading famed sports writer Damon Runyan to refer to him as the "worst gambler he'd ever met."[25]

Given his affection for gambling and his immigrant background, Capone's fondness for baseball should come as no surprise. After all, according to John Thorn, Major League Baseball's official historian, baseball never would have become the National Pastime without gambling. True, baseball's first commissioner, Judge Kenesaw Mountain Landis, thought of gambling as the scourge of the sport. But in his book *Baseball in the Garden of Eden*, Thorn actually argued that baseball's reliance upon and creation of mountains of statistics and dramatic moments made it a natural sport for gambling—and that gambling gave fans a reason to care about the young sport, providing "the vital spark that in the beginning made it worthy of adult attention and press coverage."[26]

Capone's interest in the game, however, went beyond his passion for gambling. Cheering for a baseball team was a way for many immigrants to assimilate into American culture in a way that few other activities could match, allowing new Italian, German, Irish, and Jewish members of society to join in public conversations that would rarely lead to the conflicts that discussions of religion or politics could cause. In fact, according to Robert Elias's book *Baseball and the American Dream*, baseball is actually based on one of the basic tenets upon which American society was built: the idea that individual success can only be achieved if the team does well, and the team can only do well if the individual gives his all. In short, for immigrants wanting to become a part of American communities, nothing helped one blend in better than cheering for the hometown baseball team. In this respect, Capone and his brother, Ralph, were no different from most children of immigrant parents.

Capone also had personal and professional reasons for siding with the Cubs, rather than the White Sox, when it came time to considering a serious investment of his own funds. "I love Wrigley Field. It's my favorite ballpark," Capone said, according to his grandniece:

I've been associated with the South Side too much. Chicago's my town, and that includes the North Side, which I think will one day become bigger than the South Side. Anyway, Wrigley doesn't know baseball. . . . He knows gum.[27]

Meanwhile, the Cubs players and staff certainly knew Capone. Bill Veeck and other team staff members were well aware that Capone's brother, as well as some of his other "boys," attended baseball games at Wrigley. (In fact, in our next section, on vices, we'll explore how Chicago police rounded up nearly four dozen known bookies in the bleachers at Wrigley Field in an ostensible public crackdown on gambling.) Capone's henchmen also helped protect Hack Wilson's family during his historic season of 1930. And in 1932, Cubs catcher Gabby Hartnett was famously photographed autographing a baseball for Capone. When reporters later asked Hartnett about Capone's attendance at the game, the catcher replied bluntly, "I go to his place of business. Why shouldn't he come to mine?"[28] (GeoVerse™091)

In spite of laws against buying or selling alcohol, the Cubs all-star roster during the 1920s was full of players who never hid their desire to drink in their free time, with Grover Cleveland Alexander, Pat Malone, Wilson, and Hartnett topping the list. But selling alcohol during Prohibition was a dangerous occupation. Raids on speakeasies led to arrests, while battles for ownership of drinking establishments led to gang wars between rival underworld bosses. While the situations produced were sometimes funny (such as the time the portly Wilson got stuck in a window trying to flee from police during a raid on a speakeasy), they were also sometimes lethal.

On September 20, 1926, Capone amazingly survived a drive-by shooting at the Hawthorne Inn when a convoy of more than half a dozen cars (reports vary as to whether there were seven or five) filled with north side gang members shot more than 1,000 rounds into the cafe where the boss was eating. According to mob historian Nate Hendley in his book *American Gangsters: Then and Now,* after learning that north side rival Hymie Weiss was behind the assassination attempt, Capone still wanted to try to reach an accord with Weiss. He believed they could both continue with their lucrative businesses instead of killing each other.[29] Despite Hollywood's portrayal of Capone as a bloodthirsty gangster, Hendley revealed that Scarface was actually pragmatic and businesslike. That being said, he could only put up with so many threats to his interests.

"Capone attempted to convince Weiss that it was pointless for leading gangsters to fight each other," Hendley wrote:

> Weiss wasn't swayed and turned down Capone's offer of friendship. Shortly thereafter, Weiss was shot dead by Capone assassins. [Capone] was 28 years old. Capone was still determined to play peacemaker.[30]

Appearing as the epitome of the calm, confident gangster/businessman to the outside world, only Capone's family knew the emotional toll the battle with his north side rivals was taking on him. Public enemy No. 1 wasn't worried about the government catching up with him, but he did have constant nightmares about harm coming to his wife, Mae, and son, Sonny. "Al had bad dreams almost every night," his wife confided in *Uncle Al Capone.* "He would wake up and the bed sheets would be soaked with sweat. I'd have to change the sheets in the middle of the night."[31]

The nightmare that vexed Capone, Mae revealed, was always the same: in his dreams, he saw the bodies of Mae and Sonny floating in the Chicago River. Both Capone and his wife believed that the gangster had the gift of extra-sensory perception, or ESP, leading them to take the recurring nightmare seriously. For a time, Capone actively considered leaving behind the world of illegal activity and going into legitimate business.

"I've got to get out, Ralph," Capone lamented to his brother:

> I've got enough money. I don't need this insanity. Weiss, [George "Bugs"] Moran and those other assholes are idiots. . . . You can't do business with crazy people. I've been shot at, almost poisoned with prussic acid, and there is an offer of $50,000 to any gunman who can kill me. They don't understand that there's enough for all of us. They don't have to cut in on my territory. What do they expect me to do, let them get away with it? They agree to something, then they break the deal. They're pissed because I run a better business. I make more money than they do. They are jealous bastards. They want what I have. You can't trust' em. Their word doesn't mean shit. I run my outfit like a business. It is a business.[32]

Like Michael Corleone in *The Godfather* trilogy, Capone wanted to "go legit" in his later years and segue his illegally earned fortune into a line of work that would allow his loved ones to live in peace. As with Vito Corleone in *The*

Godfather, Capone was worried about his boy, Sonny, and wanted a better life for him. Also like Corleone, Capone decided to approach a businessman in the world of entertainment with an offer he couldn't refuse. But instead of approaching a movie producer, his focus was on a man in the world of sports: William Wrigley, owner of the Chicago Cubs.

Capone actually hatched several plans to "go legit"—including starting a line of clothing to take advantage of the fact that men across the country were copying his fashion sense—but that idea was dismissed because he was "concerned that getting into fashion would detract from his tough image."[33] Capone also tried to lure Runyan into writing his biography, which Capone then planned to turn into a movie in which he would star as himself. But Runyan (along with several other writers) claimed not to have enough time for the project.[34]

One of the ideas Capone hatched at this time actually took hold—and changed the world for the better. During the Great Depression, Capone began the first soup kitchens, which "created goodwill among the city's less fortunate." His success in helping the needy led Capone's associates to learn that the milk business provided markups as good as, or even better than, bootleg alcohol. Capone's men established Meadowmoor Dairies, then used their political might to get Chicago to pass the first "date-milk ordinance," which forced dairies to put dates on milk containers so that families could ensure the milk they were buying was safe to drink.[35]

Capone's interest in public welfare—along with his desires to be accepted into the legitimate business world and escape organized crime—began to brew in his mind with his love for baseball. He began to hatch a plan to purchase the Cubs. "If I don't take it off his hands, he'll run that team into the ground before long," Capone said of Wrigley's handling of the Cubs. "I could run the organization better than Wrigley can."[36]

Ralph Capone challenged his brother's assertion that he knew enough about baseball to improve the Cubs. And there was also the very real problem of Landis, who would never approve the sale. But Capone had answers for both issues.

First there was the legal matter of buying the team. To deal with that, Capone simply planned to put the deal together with a "beard"—a person who would own the team on paper, but who would be in actuality Capone's handpicked partner. Capone believed he could use his connections in the sports world to get boxer Jack Dempsey or perhaps Hartnett, the Cubs' catcher, to serve as his front man. If neither of them panned out, Capone planned to turn to his Hollywood connections and ask entertainers Al Jolson, George Jessel, or Harry Richman to come in on the plan with him.[37]

As for the Cubs, Capone had even bigger plans for the organization than merely including entertainers in his management. He hoped to undo what Cap Anson and baseball's officials had managed to accomplish decades earlier: the elimination of African American players from the National Pastime. An outsider his entire life in the realms of legal business, Capone disagreed with baseball officials who supported segregation. He even discussed the matter privately with Gus Greenlee, who owned both the Pittsburgh Crawdads and the rights to famed Negro League pitcher Satchel Paige. Capone wanted to buy Paige's contract, as well as the contracts of some other Negro League players, in order to integrate the Cubs—more than a quarter of a century before Jackie Robinson took the field for the Brooklyn Dodgers. Capone also claimed to have talked to Babe Ruth about becoming a player/manager for the Cubs.[38]

And how, Ralph Capone asked, would Capone get Wrigley to sell the Cubs? Wrigley will sell, Capone assured his brother. He would have to, or else. "Because I've got something on Wrigley," Capone said:

> Shit, I've got something on all the big shots in Chicago. Everyone, even the fine upstanding citizens, the pillars of the community—especially them—has something to hide. Something they don't want the public, the law, or their wives to know. Don't worry—he'll sell![39]

Ralph pressed his brother further, pushing him to reveal the details of how he planned to convince Wrigley to sell. If nothing else worked, Capone said, he could always revert to the tactics that had allowed him to eliminate his competition in the world of organized crime: offer a good business deal first, and if that doesn't work, use violence to either get your way or put the cause of the problem in the grave. "I'll pay [Wrigley] a fair price," Capone said. "I'll give him the going rate for a major league team. Maybe even better than the going rate. I'm not hard to do business with."[40]

When Ralph urged for more details on what Capone would offer, Scarface turned to his brother with a wide smile and said, "I'll make him an offer he can't refuse."[41]

Decades later, when the exact same line was spoken in *The Godfather*, Ralph Capone was amazed. "When I heard that line used in *The Godfather*, I nearly fell out of my seat. The same words Al used 40 years before!" said Capone.[42]

No records reveal if Wrigley was ever presented with Capone's "offer he couldn't refuse" before the gangster was convicted of tax evasion in 1931. After his release from prison in 1939, Capone's fortune and mental state were both incapable of seeing through with his lofty baseball plans. Of course, it would have been no small thing for the Wrigley family to find out that Capone had targeted the Cubs.

After his death in 1932, Wrigley's son, Philip, took control of the team, leading the organization into decades of mediocrity. Capone could not have done much worse, and given his plans for racial integration, he might even have made an impact that would have changed the twentieth century for the better. Instead, the highlight of Capone's legacy as a legitimate member of the community was the creation of soup kitchens for the needy and use-by dates on milk containers. Capone's failure to acquire the Cubs meant that Paige never became a member of the Cubs organization and Robinson—not Paige—became internationally known for his role in racial integration.

While Paige didn't become a member of the Cubs, one of his former teammates did—and that Cubs player became a famous baseball ambassador. His name? Nancy.

Chapter 29

Cubs Attempt to Set Racial Coaching History

The Cubs Made Desegregation History in 1962, Hiring the First African American Coach in Major League Baseball History. There's Only One Problem with This Wonderful Story: It Isn't Entirely True.

Even when trying to do the right thing, Cubs executives seem unable to avoid stumbling over themselves—especially when the matter at hand involves race relations.

"I have seen many demonstrations in the south, but I have never seen anything so hostile and so hateful as I've seen here today," said Martin Luther King after being hit in the head with a rock during a peaceful protest in Chicago on August 5, 1966. The same *Chicago Tribune* article[43] that quoted King noted that one protester's sign read "KING WOULD LOOK GOOD WITH A KNIFE IN HIS BACK."

Those events took place more than a decade after the Cubs had desegregated. So the intolerant mood of the citizenry in 1953 when the Cubs signed their first African American players—Gene Baker and Ernie Banks—should come as no surprise to those familiar with the history of race relations in Chicago.

After Jackie Robinson signed with the Brooklyn Dodgers in 1947, teams began rethinking their unofficial segregation policies. But social change is often slow to take hold, and so it was with the Cubs, who waited another six years before signing Baker and Banks, who both mentored under the legendary player/manager John Jordan "Buck" O'Neil of the Negro League's Kansas City Monarchs.

O'Neil was already a living legend in 1953 despite being only in his forties. He was a role model to young African American players due to his combination of baseball skills and eternal optimism. Years later, Banks would credit his famously positive attitude to his tutelage under O'Neil, who joined the Cubs in 1955 as a scout. O'Neil's popularity and baseball smarts were an instant draw for young African American players. Among the many future players O'Neil signed for the Cubs were Hall of Famers Lou Brock, Billy Williams, Banks, and George Altman.

In 1961, Cubs owner Philip Wrigley put his infamous "College of Coaches" idea to work, rotating a group of coaches who shared the role of team manager. Wrigley's idea was to do away with the traditional role of manager and have instead a panel of coaches who would alternate duties every few months, moving from coaching in Chicago to working with and coaching the team's affiliates in the minors. His hope was to create an organization-wide approach to the game that was the same at every level.

In 1961, nine coaches shared the manager role, with horrible results, leading the Cubs to a 64–90 record. The following season, El Tappe, Lou Klein, and Charlie Metro were the three coaches in the rotation. O'Neil was supposed to be the fourth coach, which would have made him the first African American coach in the majors.

However, racial tensions were high in Chicago, and Cubs general manager John Holland was anxious about how fans would react to the team's new employee. The announcement of O'Neil's hiring by Holland was clearly tempered so as not to enflame the public. "O'Neil will serve as an instructor," Holland told reporters when announcing O'Neil's hiring on May 29, 1962.[44] As *Chicago Daily Tribune* writer Richard Dozer made clear in his article, Holland did not intend to treat O'Neil in the same way as the rest of the team's coaches. Instead, the former Negro League player/manager was to be treated as a subordinate:

> O'Neil . . . accompanied the parent team on the last road trip and was in uniform before a number of games, but did not remain in the dugout while the contests were in progress. In announcing the appointment of O'Neil, General Manager John Holland said the new coach will not be a member of the head coaching rotation.

In short, the organization called O'Neil a coach, but only allowed him to work as an instructor.

Always seeking the bright side of negative situations, O'Neil rolled with the insult until July 15 of that season, when the organization's deep-seated racism reared its ugly head. That day, in a doubleheader against the Houston Colt .45s, head coach Metro was ejected and his replacement, Tappe, moved from third-base coach to the head coach spot. Klein took over for Tappe at third until Tappe was also ejected, which automatically promoted Klein to head coach, apparently giving O'Neil the chance to coach third base—a first in major league history.

Then orders came down from team executives to bring in Fred Martin from the bullpen to coach third, rather than having O'Neil do it. The obvious insult came from an unlikely Chicago executive, former manager Charlie "Jolly Cholly" Grimm, who was beloved by the players in the years when the team was monochromatically white. "Cub coaches were told that in the event that one or more of them was thrown out of the game, they were not to give O'Neil the reins," authors Glenn Stout and Richard A. Johnson explained in their book *The Cubs*.[45]

In a *Sports Illustrated* article from September 19, 1994, O'Neil recalled that day in great clarity for writer Steve Wulf:

> After 40 years in baseball and 10 years of managing, I was pretty sure I knew when to wave somebody home and when to have him put on the brakes. . . . Later I found out that Grimm had ordered the other coaches never to let me coach on the lines.[46]

Appearing outwardly content with his subordinate role, O'Neil actually confronted Holland during the season—but not on his own behalf. O'Neil implored Holland to sign more African American players and to let the ones on the roster play more, certain that they could improve the woeful season the team and fans were suffering. (To be fair, one has to wonder how much more playing time the African American players could record considering that Williams played in 159 games, Banks in 154, Altman in 147 and Brock in 123.) But management made it clear that on the north side of Chicago, a baseball team would rather lose with white players than win with black ones.

"I told Mr. Holland we'd have a better ballclub if we played the blacks," O'Neil told author George Castle for his book *The Million-to-One Team: Why the Chicago Cubs Haven't Won the Pennant Since 1945*:

> Then he showed me a basket of letters from fans saying, "What are you trying to do, make the Cubs into the Kansas City Monarchs?" We weren't appealing to black fans anyway, playing on the North Side of Chicago.[47]

Castle summed up the Cubs' treatment of O'Neil succinctly: "Blacks could play for the Cubs, but have no voice in leadership."[48]

The 1962 Cubs team finished with the worst record in team history, 59–103. The team would tie that mark of futility in 1966, but by then O'Neil, despite his cheery outlook, was done with "coaching" the Cubs. He returned to scouting after only one season on the job. Meanwhile, Holland could have done worse than turning his team into the Monarchs, who won the Negro American League pennant seven times in ten seasons (1937–46), with O'Neil as a member of the squad through the whole run.

One of O'Neil's teammates was famed pitcher Leroy "Satchel" Paige, who played for Kansas City from 1941 to 1947 and gave O'Neil the famous nickname "Nancy." The story of the name's origin was emblematic of both his willingness to help a teammate in need and proof of his sense of humor. O'Neil told the anecdote countless times in his playing career, as well as detailing it in his autobiography, *I Was Right on Time*:

> We played this one game on an Indian reservation near Sioux Falls, South Dakota. It was there that Satchel, who had a weakness for a pretty face, and the more of them the better, met this beautiful Indian maiden named Nancy, and since we were going to Chicago to play the Chicago American Giants, he invited Nancy to visit him there. She had some relatives there or something, so she accepted his invitation, and he told her we were staying at the Evans Hotel.
>
> Well, now we were in Chicago, I was sitting in the coffee shop of the Evans Hotel when I saw a cab pull up, and out stepped Nancy. I went out to greet her and tell her that Satchel was upstairs, and the bellhop carried her bags to his room.
>
> A few minutes passed, and another cab pulled up, and this time out stepped Satchel's fiancée, Lahoma, who wasn't supposed to be coming by, as far as Satchel knew. Seeing how this might complicate things just a little bit, I jumped up and greeted her. "Lahoma," I said, "so good to see you. Satchel's not here right now, but he should be along shortly. Why don't you sit here with me, and I'll have the bellman take your bags up to the room."
>
> I went over to the bellman, explained the situation to him, and told him to move Nancy and her bags into the room next to mine, which was also next door to Satchel's, and then to knock on Satchel's door and tell him Lahoma was here. A few minutes later, the bellman came down and gave me the sign that everything was okay. In the meantime, Satchel had climbed down the fire escape, and, lo and behold, there he came walking down the street.

I said, "Look, Lahoma, here comes old Satchel now." Satch gave her a big greeting—"Lahoma, what a surprise!"—and led her upstairs.

That might have ended the trouble, except that later that night, after we had turned in, I heard Satchel's door open and close. Then I heard him knock on Nancy's door. I think he wanted to give her some money and apologize, but while he's whispering kind of loud, "Nancy! Nancy!" I hear his door open again, and I knew it was Lahoma coming out to see what was going on. I jumped out of my bed, opened my door, and said, "Yeah, Satch, what do you want?"

And he said, "Why, Nancy, there you are. I was looking for you. What time is the game tomorrow?" And from that night on, until his dying day, Satchel called me Nancy.

It was the Negro Leagues that gave me an identity, but it was a lot more than just a nickname. I am proud to say it was the Negro Leagues that turned me into a man. That's why this fame that's come my way so late in life is so funny to me. Thanks to Ken Burns, I became an overnight star in my eighties. But as far as I'm concerned, I felt like I was already on top of the world when I got to play with and against some of the best ballplayers who ever lived.[49]

Director Ken Burns featured O'Neil in his seminal 1994 documentary *Baseball*, making the former Negro League player/manager an icon to millions of fans who hadn't previously been familiar with him. The director warned that the constant smile on O'Neil's face should not lead anyone to diminish the racial struggles he had suffered. In fact, in Phil Roger's biography *Ernie Banks*, Burns said:

Race is always there. It's always there, no matter what people want to say. . . . We play a lie to this thing, this belief that we've escaped the specific gravity of race in this country. We haven't escaped it. Chicago certainly didn't escape it in the 1960s. We take advantage of Buck O'Neil, we take advantage of Ernie Banks because we like our progressivism to come with a good nature.[50]

Which is the best explanation for why MLB historians still insist today that the "instructor" Holland hired in 1962 who would "not be a member of the coaching rotation" was actually MLB's first black coach. O'Neil's hiring appears to have been little more than a publicity stunt meant to portray Cubs executives as progressive, when in reality they refused to allow O'Neil to work as a true coach.

The following season, Pittsburgh hired the first African American player to actually lead a team as a true coach. In 1963, Gene Baker, who had been the first African American player signed by the Cubs (as well as Banks' former roommate), was hired by Pirates manager Danny Murtaugh as a member of his full-time coaching staff. Though MLB history regards O'Neil as the first African American coach, the true honor appears to belong to Baker, whom the Pirates hired a year after the Cubs attempted to bestow the "honor" on O'Neil.

To his final days, O'Neil was the subject of unimaginable wrongs. In 2006, at the age of 94, he was shockingly snubbed by the National Baseball Hall of Fame. That year, the Hall held a special one-time election to induct members from the Negro Leagues. The 17 inductees constituted the largest induction class ever and included one woman, two white team owners, and a known gangster—but not O'Neil. Before the vote was tallied, officials asked O'Neil to give an acceptance speech on behalf of all the Negro League inductees, assuming he would be among them. He wasn't, but gave a joyous speech anyway. Less than three months later, he was dead.

"Baseball might as well have told Buck O'Neil to get lost," wrote baseball historian Keith Olbermann after the shocking announcement by the Hall of Fame:

> Just to twist the knife a little further into Buck O'Neil, the special committee elected Alex Pompez, owner of the New York Cubans team. Also an organized crime figure. Part of the mob of the infamous '30s gangster Dutch Schultz. Indicted in this country and Mexico for racketeering. He's in the Hall of Fame. For all time. Buck O'Neil is not. It is not merely indefensible. For all the many stupid things the Baseball Hall of Fame has ever done, this is the worst.[51]

In 2008, the National Baseball Hall of Fame erected a statue of O'Neil inside the museum. That year also marked the creation of the Buck O'Neil Lifetime Achievement Award, which according to the Hall is given "not more than once every three years to honor an individual whose extraordinary efforts enhanced baseball's positive impact on society, broadened the game's appeal, and whose character, integrity and dignity are comparable to the qualities exhibited by O'Neil." In 2011, Roland Hemond, an executive with the Diamondbacks, the White Sox, and the Orioles, became the second person to receive the award.

As Banks said, "The measure of a man is in the lives he's touched."[52]

Chapter 30

First African American Coach and Manager

Frank Robinson Is Credited with Becoming the First African American Manager in Major League Baseball, but in Actuality Not Just One but Two Former Cubbies Can Lay Claim to That Honor.

Some people are destined to have their lives orbit around another person their entire lives. Such was the case for former Cubs players Gene Baker (the first African American signed by the Cubs) and Ernie Banks (the first African American to appear in a game for the Cubs).

On April 1, 1950, the Cubs signed Baker as an undrafted free agent, but he remained in the team's minor league system until late in the 1953 season. Baseball purists have argued that Baker actually needed those years to develop his game, while historians maintain his time in the minors was just another result of the racist attitude abundant in both the game and the Cubs organization at the time. Either way, few would dare argue that Baker was unready for the Big Show when he was called up in the summer of 1953.

But there was still one problem: who would room with Baker on road trips? This concern may sound foolish today, but during the racially turbulent 1950s, the idea of men from two different races sharing such close quarters was unthinkable.

Cubs owner Philip Wrigley and general manager Wid Matthews made a frank assessment of the situation. When Matthews informed his boss that he wanted to sign Banks from the Kansas City Monarchs of the Negro League, their conversation was simple.

"Gee whiz," Wrigley answered, "we are bringing up one Negro player. Why go out and get another one?"

"Well," Matthews replied, "we had to have a roommate for the one we've got."[53]

A rising star in the Negro Leagues, Banks skipped the Cubs farm system completely, making his Cubs debut on September 17, 1953, in a 16–4 loss to the Phillies in Chicago. Five days later, on September 22, 1953, Baker made his Cubs debut in a doubleheader at Cincinnati, and in so doing set a milestone. That day Baker and Banks became the first African American double play combo in MLB history, with Baker on second base and Banks at shortstop.

At the end of their playing careers, both Banks and Baker went into coaching. As a fan favorite, Banks remained with the Cubs. But Baker was traded to the Pirates in 1957 and later began his coaching career with that organization. In fact, Baker became the first African American to manage a minor league affiliate of an MLB team when he took over as manager for the Batavia, New York, Pirates on June 19, 1961, just five months after John F. Kennedy was sworn in as president of the United States. Respected and liked by players and peers alike, Baker was promoted, becoming a member of the Pittsburgh Pirates coaching staff for manager Danny Murtaugh beginning with the 1963 season.

On September 21, 1963, Murtaugh was ejected from a Pirates game against the Los Angeles Dodgers, and Baker took over for the final two innings.[54] Leading his Pirates against the organization that Jackie Robinson had made famous for racial integration, Baker became the first African American to manage an MLB team, albeit for only two innings. The Dodgers rallied in the ninth to win, 5–3.

Banks has his own managerial claim to history, although it is quite similar to Baker's. The Cubs were on a West Coast road trip when they etched a milestone in history. On May 8, 1973, the Cubs were locked in an extra-inning battle at San Diego. Cubs manager Whitey Lockman was ejected in the eleventh inning, and the next in line to take over was Larry Jansen—except that Jansen had been forced to miss the game because his wife was ill. Pete Reiser was next in succession after Jansen to assume the manager role, but he had recently been hurt in a bench-clearing brawl against the San Francisco Giants. That opened the door for Banks to assume the role of manager, which he did handily, leading the Cubs to a 3–2 win in 12 innings. The losing manager for the Padres was Don Zimmer, a former Cub who would later make Cubs history of his own as Chicago's manager.

Some historians incorrectly credit Banks as being the first acting African American manager in history, but he was just the first African American to manage the Cubs. In fact, as had happened before, Baker actually beat Banks to their brief historic moment.

Neither Banks nor Baker was ever hired as a full-time manager for an MLB team. History is often written in small steps, however, and the short-lived success that both Baker and Banks enjoyed when the situations called for them to rise to the task opened the door for others.

Frank Robinson became the first African American manager hired on a permanent basis for an MLB team when the Cleveland Indians named him to the post for the 1975 season. Inducted into the National Baseball Hall of Fame in 1982, Robinson managed four teams (the Indians, the San Francisco Giants, the Baltimore Orioles, and the Washington Nationals) for a combined 16 seasons, guiding his squads to a combined 2,241–1,065 record. He won the American League Manager of the Year award in 1989 and finished in the top five of final voting for that honor on three additional occasions.

Section IV

Vice

Chapter 31

The Chicago Cubs caused The Black Sox Scandal

The "Black Sox" Scandal, Which Forever Tarnished the
Reputation of the Chicago White Sox and Altered How the
Public Viewed Baseball, Was Caused by the Chicago Cubs.

What performance-enhancing drugs have been to baseball in modern times, gambling was to the first quarter of the century. Few are the conversations about baseball in recent years that do not make mention of whether or not a particular player is thought to be "taking any drugs." Likewise, from the late 1800s until World War I, baseball was rife with questions about whether or not players (or even whole teams) were "on the take."

Most fans know that gambling and baseball have a long, dirty history. But it may come as a surprise to learn that a few anonymous tips to Chicago Cubs general manager William Veeck changed the sport forever. While it was the Cubs who initially had everything to lose when the lid was ripped off the scandal that followed, it was actually their crosstown rivals who paid more dearly.

On August 31, 1920, Veeck received six telegrams and two phone calls from anonymous sources in Detroit warning that some very unusual bets were being placed on that day's game in favor of their opponent, the Philadelphia Phillies.[1] The betting was so one-sided, in fact, that the odds swung from 6–5 in favor of the Cubs to 2–1 for the Phillies. The mysterious messages also mentioned Claude Hendrix, the Cubs' starting pitcher for that day's game.[2]

Veeck immediately pulled manager Fred Mitchell into a conference, during which they decided to bench Hendrix and replace him with Grover Cleveland Alexander, who was offered a $500 bonus if the Cubs won the game. The Cubs also benched Fred "Bonehead" Merkle that day with no public explanation, leading to suspicion by some baseball historians that the infamous infielder was in on the fix.[3] Cubs second baseman Buck Herzog played that day, and went hitless in two at-bats, but committed an error that helped give the Phillies a 3–0 win.

That loss and those calls from Detroit would be revealed as only the tip of the proverbial iceberg weeks later when revelations hit the press regarding widespread corruption and game fixing in Major League Baseball—events that would sink both the Chicago White Sox's reputation and its roster.

In hindsight, it seems obvious that Herzog, rather than Merkle, was probably the player that the Cubs needed to watch, considering that players and managers alike knew the Maryland native was crooked. After the 1920 season, Herzog never played again in the major leagues. He was banned for life when multiple stories came to light linking him to gambling over the course of several years. In fact, when the New York Giants lost the 1917 World Series to the Chicago White Sox, Giants manager John McGraw singled out Herzog, his second baseman, as playing out of position so much that it was clear that he was on the take.[4] Herzog was also identified by Giants pitcher Rube Benton as one of the players, along with teammate Hal Chase, who offered him $800 to lose a game in 1919.

If Veeck thought that replacing Hendrix with Alexander against the Phillies was the end of his problems, he was very wrong. In fact, it was revealed two days later that replacing Hendrix with Alexander may have been precisely what shrewd gamblers wanted all along. Veeck, who appeared to be truly trying to keep the game clean, may have inadvertently helped fix the game. Baseball historians have wondered for decades if Alexander was on the take, too, because the same anonymous sources that forced Veeck into action sent a subsequent letter to the *Chicago Herald Examiner* outlining the events of the Cubs-Phillies game, noting that, "Every fellow mixed up with baseball gambling hung around the tickers chuckling over the result of the game."[5]

But there was nothing funny about this revelation—at least not to journalists. Were the gamblers chuckling because the Cubs still lost despite the team pulling Hendrix from the game? Or was it because Alexander was the gamblers' ace in the hole, the pitcher they had wanted on the mound all along? Fortunately for Alexander, his role in the tip-off was soon forgotten in the hubbub over the newspaper stories and government investigations suddenly blowing baseball's dirty little secret wide open. The halcyon days when baseball and casual gambling enjoyed a passing glance from authorities were over. Confronted with this anonymous letter detailing the fix in the Cubs-Phillies game, journalists who had previously turned a blind eye to gambling in sports had to act, as did the government. Baseball would never be the same.

"Had it not been for gambling, there is no way that baseball ever would have become the national pastime," wrote historians Glenn Stout and Richard A. Johnson in their book *The Cubs*:

> While many spectators were true fans, others appreciated the game for its almost limitless gaming possibilities. Most of Chicago's big gambling houses and casinos were concentrated downtown, but many barbershops, saloons, and small neighborhood shops also took bets.[6]

In fact, gamblers didn't even have to leave the Friendly Confines to place bets. On May 23, 1920—weeks before the big bombshell of gambling was to explode on the national scene—undercover Chicago police officers rounded up 47 known gamblers from their customary seats in the bleachers as a public display of cracking down on gambling.[7] But it was all for show, a toothless display of authority meant to make legitimate fans feel more comfortable. After all, if the Chicago Police Department really wanted to do something about gambling on baseball games, they would have looked into the relationship between a certain Cubs staff member and the biggest crime boss in the Midwest, Al Capone, whose presence at Cubs games could be felt even when he was not in attendance.

"I knew [Al Capone] slightly from the ball park and I knew some of his boys even better," wrote Bill Veeck, son of William Veeck, in his autobiography *Veeck as in Wreck*:

> Ralph Capone, Al's brother, was a great Cub fan. We had a ticket man, named Red Thompson, whom the mob guys always dealt with. Whenever I got a $100 bill in Red's bank in later years, I knew Ralph Capone and his boys were at a game.[8]

It was one thing to arrest 47 minnows in a mid-May game, but there was little chance of anyone trying to take on the biggest shark in the Midwest waters. Capone was smarter than that; he was never the focus of the investigation that would engulf the baseball world months later. (Arnold Rothstein, Capone's New York mob rival, was another story—but more on that later.)

After receiving that anonymous letter explaining why gamblers were chuckling about the Cubs game, the *Herald Examiner* commenced its own investigation. On September 4, the newspaper claimed that nefarious characters had claimed as much as $50,000 that day.[9] Smelling blood in the water, rival newspapers pounced on the story as well. Rumors began that the championship had been tampered with just weeks after the final game of the 1919 World Series. Despite having no concrete evidence, journalists such as the *Los Angeles Times'* Barry A. Williams and *New York Evening Mail's* Hugh S. Fullerton began writing about the rumors, digging for the truth. Thanks to the Cubs, they would soon have it.

On September 7, a Cook County grand jury was convened to investigate the topic of gambling and baseball. Over the ensuing weeks, many players and managers were called before the grand jury, but it was the testimony of Benton that began to unravel the sorted story. On September 24, Benton testified that the Cubs' Herzog had fixed the Cubs-Phillies game on August 31, 1920. Herzog had approached Benton, along with Giants first baseman Chase, with an offer of $800 in return for throwing a game against the Cubs. Benton's claim of an $800 bribe supported mysterious back-to-back losses to the Giants the previous season. On September 11, 1919, Benton pitched the Giants to a 7–3 victory at Weeghman Park. The losing pitcher was Alexander, lending more suspicion to the Hall of Famer's involvement in game throwing. The Cubs roster that day included Herzog and Lee Magee, both later proven to have thrown games; Merkle, who was suspected of throwing games, and never played again after the 1920 season; and Hendrix, who pinch hit, and was later suspended from baseball for gambling. Noticeably absent from the game was Giants third baseman Heinie Zimmerman. Why was Zimmerman not in the game? He had been kicked off the Giants team less than 24 hours earlier for attempting to fix the Giant-Cubs game—and never appeared in a game again.

The first of the back-to-back fixed games was the day before Benton's victory, when the Giants claimed a controversial 7–2 victory against the Cubs despite Zimmerman telling starting pitcher Fred Toney it "would be worth his while" to go easy on the Cubs.[10] Toney asked to be removed from the game. Giants manager John McGraw agreed after learning why. Though McGraw let Zimmerman finish the game, it was the last one the crooked third baseman would appear in as a pro. By the way, the losing pitcher for the Cubs that day was Hendrix, and the second baseman was Herzog.

Benton's testimony blew open the grand jury's investigation. Realizing that he was at the end of his playing career, Herzog "sang as loud as he could to save his own skin. He blew the lid off everything, revealing that the World Series of 1919 between the Reds and White Sox had been fixed."[11]

Thanks to Herzog, the grand jury now had the smoking gun it needed. Suddenly, the Cubs-Phillies game that had begun the entire investigation seemed like small potatoes. Journalists, fans, and the grand jury focused on the White Sox, allowing the Cubs' crooked players to slip quietly into the background of the biggest scandal in baseball history.

The rivalry between the Cubs and the White Sox didn't need much to propel it forward, but there cannot be anything more divisive between two organizations than the misdeeds of one team leading directly to the downfall of the other. The 1920 White Sox roster was decimated thanks to the loss of the infamous "eight men out," who were banned from baseball forever due to their involvement in fixing the game. The American League's best team at the time, the White Sox of that era could have become a dynasty for all time. Instead, the New York Yankees won their first World Series in 1923, followed by titles in 1927 and 1928 en route to becoming the most dominant team in baseball history.

Chapter 32

A Con Man and Showgirl Altered 1932 World Series

How a Chicago Con Man and a Showgirl
Altered the 1932 World Series.

The story had everything. Murder. Suicide. Blackmail. Add to that a judge who wanted to see the hometown team win, and you can see why Chicagoans forgot about the baseball scores in 1932 and instead wanted to learn more about who the Cubs players were scoring *with*, not against.

The 1932 season may be remembered as the year the Cubs advanced to their seventh World Series overall, and their second of four in a nine-year span. But real Cubs fans know that 1932 was one of the most gossip-filled years in the history of the organization, with bigger headlines about happenings away from the ballpark than those written about events within the Friendly Confines.

Billy Jurges was a solid infielder in 1931, mostly playing third base, while veteran Woody English anchored the infield at shortstop. But 1932 gave Jurges his chance to prove himself at his natural position, shortstop, when the Cubs gave him the starting spot and moved English to third. A young player with no wife or children, Jurges stayed at the Hotel Carlos, a small establishment less than two blocks from Wrigley Field where several players lived during the season. (GeoVerse™101) For more than a century, young players and players living away from their families have lived in Wrigleyville hotels.

Violet Valli was an attractive 21-year-old woman also living at the Hotel Carlos. She and Jurges, a 24-year-old rising star with the Cubs and one of the city's most eligible bachelors, began a romantic relationship. Born in the Bronx, New York, Jurges ignored any big-city instincts he may have had that warned him about Valli, who was divorced and had had careers as both a showgirl and a model fizzle despite being only 21 years old. Calling Valli a "model" was euphemistic and generous at best. As *Chicago Daily Tribune* reporter Virginia

Gardner wrote: "She modeled in New York for illustrations for confession story magazines."[12] Illustrations such as these were as close as men could get to seeing nude women in print at the time. Marilyn Monroe, Jane Mansfield, and many other famous actresses began their careers with similar "modeling" gigs.

Whether Jurges was aware of Valli's history is unclear, but the young shortstop began seeing her romantically sometime at the start of the 1932 season. But he was not the only man in Valli's life.

Lucius Barnett met and befriended Valli at a west side church around the time when she returned to Chicago from New York City. A known con man despite his claim that he worked in real estate, Barnett learned of Valli's relationship with Jurges and hatched a plan to make money from the young Cubs shortstop.

On July 7, 1932, Valli got drunk on "too much gin," as she confessed to the *Chicago Daily Tribune* the next day in jail, and decided to end her life—but not before taking Jurges' life, too. Drunk and alone, Valli wrote a suicide note addressed to her brother in which she said, in part: "To me life without Billy isn't worth living, but why should I leave this earth alone? I'm going to take Billy with me."

Valli, drunk and armed with a .25 caliber pistol, went to room 509 and knocked. There she confessed the depths of her love to Jurges, revealed she wanted to have a long-term relationship with him, and told him she wished he'd quit the Cubs and go back to working as a bank teller. Jurges, who had only become the team's starting shortstop a few months previously, let her know that he had no intention of having a long-term relationship with her.

While Jurges may not have known (or cared) about Valli's questionable background, team leader Kiki Cuyler did. Known as a teetotaler and a levelheaded guy, the veteran Cuyler had taken his young teammate aside during the days leading up to the incident with Valli and told Jurges he should end his relationship with her. Jurges, a serious young man who did not joke around much with teammates, clearly took the advice to heart, and sought to break off his relationship with the former model.

Emotionally unstable, angry, and intoxicated, Valli entered Jurges' room on July 7 intent on persuading him to marry her. Instead, Jurges told her that their relationship was over. Valli asked Jurges to get her a glass of water from the bathroom. When Jurges turned around, Valli shot the ballplayer twice, one bullet grazing his hand and hitting his ribs, the other hitting him in the buttocks. Jurges wrestled Valli for the gun, which discharged once more, hitting and breaking Valli's wrist.

Jurges was rushed to Illinois Memorial Hospital. He refused to press charges. Valli was taken to Bridewell Hospital and then to jail. Later that week, she was released from jail thanks to a $7,500 bail bond arranged by Barnett.

Chicago buzzed with the story of the incident, although Barnett's involvement was not yet publicly known. All that Chicago knew or cared about was that a showgirl had shot one of the Cubs' young stars in what seemed like a jilted lover scenario. With Jurges refusing to press charges, Judge John A. Sbarbaro dismissed charges against Valli on July 15, saying, "I hope no more Cubs get shot."[13]

"I owe it to my self-respect to consider the entire matter a thing of the past," Valli told reporters. "If I happen to see Bill again, it will be just impersonal."[14]

The story seemed bad enough at that stage. But this strange situation was about to get even stranger. While recuperating from his wounds, Jurges was replaced by Mark Koenig, who hit .353 in the 33 games he played during the rest of the season as Jurges' replacement. Koenig had been acquired from the Detroit Tigers, but had started his career with Babe Ruth, Lou Gehrig, and the New York Yankees, playing on three straight World Series teams (1926–28).

Still healing from his wounds, Jurges could only watch and worry as Koenig replaced him in the starting lineup. The Cubs were doing great in Jurges' absence; suddenly, reaching the World Series seemed possible. To make matters worse, Valli was doing everything she could to capitalize on the notoriety the incident had given her. Even though she had claimed she wanted the shooting to be "a thing of her past," flyers appeared at Wrigley Field on July 24 (less than three weeks after the shooting) announcing that Valli "who shot for love, seeks solace in burlesque after conferring with her pastor."[15] Billed locally as "Violet 'What I Did for Love' Valli, the Most Talked about Girl in Chicago," Valli signed a 22-week contract to dance at nightclubs around town. Jurges, meanwhile, was lucky to be alive. Various newspaper reports stated that the only thing that had saved him from death was the fact that the bullet in his torso had hit a rib, preventing it from doing lethal damage.

During his convalescence, Jurges received a phone call from Valli, who days earlier had claimed publicly that she wanted to move on from her infamy. As soon as Jurges got on the phone, another voice came from the other end of the line: Barnett.

This was the first conversation between the two men in Valli's life, and it wasn't friendly. Barnett, Valli's "friend from church" and most likely the unnamed "pastor" who had convinced her to go back to dancing to capitalize on her newfound infamy, added insult to Jurges' nearly fatal injuries. Barnett threatened to publish Jurges and Valli's love letters unless Jurges and teammate Kiki Cuyler each paid him $50,000. In the days after the shooting, Barnett had offered Valli $5,000 for her love letters, with $2,500 in cash up front. If the blackmail scheme didn't work, Barnett planned to publish the letters as a book tentatively titled *The Love Letters of a Shortstop*.[16]

On August 14, 1932, Barnett was arrested for his blackmail scheme. By that time, Jurges was physically healed and back in the Cubs' lineup. But the sordid incident left psychological scars on Jurges for years to come. Never known as a light-hearted guy to begin with, Jurges bristled at any mention of the injury to his buttocks, and became a loner among his teammates—a guy known for a short temper who did not joke around.

"Billy Jurges had a short fuse. He wasn't the easiest guy to be a friend of," said former teammate Phil Cavarretta years later in Peter Golenbock's book *Wrigleyville*:

> It seemed like he was always mad at something. . . . [Jurges] would never talk about [the Valli shooting]. I wouldn't tease him about it because, to be honest, he would be liable to pop me one. But Billy Herman would. They came up together and were very good friends, and they understood each other pretty well. Bill Herman would kid him about it. When this happened, this young lady shot Billy [Jurges] in the seat, so to speak. Billy [Hernan] would kid him about the two holes in his ass, and Jurges would get so upset he'd be ready to fight.[17]

The final affront to Jurges came from none other than Babe Ruth. As a former teammate of Ruth and Gehrig, Koenig was still a popular player with the Yankees, despite playing against his former squad in the 1932 World Series. Because he had only played in 33 games with the team, Cubs players voted that Koenig was entitled to only a partial share of the team's World Series payout. When Ruth learned of this, he lambasted the Cubs in the press, calling them cheapskates.

The verbal sparring between the Cubs and the Yankees reached its apex on October 1, 1932, during Game 3 of the World Series. In the fifth inning, the portly Ruth stepped to the plate while the players in the Cubs dugout jeered him, lobbing insults and taunts. Those players would forever regret their comments. With the game tied 4–4 and facing a 2–2 count—not to mention the invective of the Chicago crowd—Ruth belted one of the most famous home runs in baseball history.

Ruth's "Called Shot" has gone through more scrutiny over the years than perhaps any other moment in baseball history. Baseball historians love nothing better than to argue over whether Ruth actually called his shot. Reporter Joe Williams, who covered the game for the *New York World-Telegram*, is largely credited with creating the myth of that moment, since his story covering the game claimed that, "Ruth pointed to center and punched a screaming liner to a spot where no ball had ever been hit before."[18]

Many questions remain about the Valli/Jurges incident. Was Barnett the "pastor" who guided Valli into burlesque dancing? How much of the situation was planned by Barnett, who knew the love letters would sell in the wake of the affair's publicity? Would the Cubs have reached the World Series without Koenig as Jurges' backup? Was Ruth's "Called Shot" motivated in part to get back at the Cubs for their shoddy treatment of a former Yankee who was only hired because of Jurges' shooting and their vitriolic attitude toward himself and his current teammates? But former Cub Dick Bartell said at least one thing was clear about Valli: "That young lady triggered all the historic events of the '32 series, including the Babe Ruth called shot that never happened."[19]

Chapter 33

Al Capone Protects Cubs Player Setting History

Many Fans and Players Idolize the Film 'Scarface.' But Only One Player in Baseball History Is Known to Have Used the Protection of the Real-Life Scarface—Al Capone.

It is fitting that the City of Big Shoulders once embraced a fire hydrant of a man as hero. And considering that man stood only 5'6", it's also fitting that the relationship was short-lived.

Everything about Lewis "Hack" Wilson was too short—including his height, his career, and even his life. Everything, that is, except his legacy. Wilson's 191 RBI in 1930 is still the MLB record, and it appears to have little chance of being topped. In fact, since the Great Depression, few players have even come close. Boston's Manny Ramirez had 165 RBI in 1999, tying him for 13th on the all-time list. Sammy Sosa notched 160 in 2001, good enough for 21st on the list. The second man on the list, Lou Gehrig, had 184 RBI in 1931, while the third man on the list, Hank Greenberg, had 183 in 1937.

Wilson's stature, both physically and in the record books, was unique. Standing only 5'6" but weighing a stocky 190 pounds (and getting even heavier in the offseason), Wilson was built like a football player rather than an outfielder. In fact, no other player in the record books had his same proportions. Chicago native and former Minnesota Twins All-Star Kirby Puckett came close at 5'8" and 180 pounds, and relief pitcher Danny Herrera (who lasted only four seasons, finally leaving the majors in 2011) was the same height, but weighed only 165. If trying to imagine Wilson's unusual size is difficult, being his tailor must have been an occupational nightmare. He wore a size 6 shoe but had an 18-inch collar. His hands were so small that he had to sand down his bats in order to get a good grip on them. (The only professional athlete found who matched Wilson's

163

physical measurements was National Football League running back Darren Sproles, who also was 5'6" and 190 pounds.)

Tenacious, powerful, and usually gregarious, Wilson's unusual physique made him a fan favorite with everyone except Cubs fan Edward Young. On June 21, 1928, after heckling Wilson one too many times, Young learned how quick "the human bowling ball" really could be. Young later admitted in court that he had visited one of the city's speakeasies before attending a Cubs doubleheader against the St. Louis Cardinals.

After winning the first game 2–1, the Cubs struggled in a 4–1 loss in the second outing. Fueled with liquid courage, Young berated the Cubs, the center fielder in particular. By the ninth inning, when many fans had already left the park, Young was able to sneak into the box seats close to the field.

With one out in the bottom of the ninth, Wilson grounded out and was returning to the Cubs' dugout when Young called him a string of obscene names. Wilson had had enough from the drunk fan. Wilson lost his cool, broke off his trot to the dugout, and ran at Young, vaulting the low wall and into the stands, where he pummeled Young. Teammates Gabby Hartnett and Joe Kelly joined the fracas, at first appearing to break up the fight. But in reality they, too, were tired of Young's taunts. They pounded on the heckler as well. The melee led to a minor riot, with 5,000 fans scrambling onto the field to escape the fight, which took 12 minutes to quell. Young spent the night in jail, admitted to having been drunk, and was fined one dollar by Judge Francis Allegretti. National League president John Heydler fined Wilson $100.[20]

Two years later, in the middle of his historic 191-RBI season, it was Wilson himself who believed he needed protection. To whom does one of the stockiest players in baseball history turn for help when he needs it? The only guy in Chicago who could pull more weight than Wilson: Al Capone.

Wilson never hid the fact that despite the fact that Prohibition was in full swing, he loved to drink. "I've never played a game drunk," Wilson famously claimed. "Hungover? Yes. But never drunk." And if you liked to drink in Chicago at that time, you were likely a customer at one of Capone's speakeasies. Explained biographer Bill Chastain in his book *Hack's 191*:

> Wilson and his running mate, pitcher Pat Malone, spent considerable time at the speakeasies. Among the clubs they frequented was the Green Mill jazz club on the North Side, run by "Machine Gun" Jack McGurn, who was believed

to be Capone's henchman for the St. Valentine's Day Massacre; and they often patronized Capone's speakeasies.[21]

The infamous St. Valentine's Day Massacre of course changed the culture of violence in America forever. Never before had the country seen such blatant gangland violence; unfortunately, it was just the beginning of a wave of ever more audacious and bolder crimes. (GeoVerse™111) It was this rising tide of violence that brought together Wilson and Capone, ensuring the slugger would have his record season in 1930.

Capone ran speakeasies on Chicago's south and west sides, while rival gang leader George "Bugs" Moran controlled the north side, home to Wrigley Field and the Green Mill. But all that changed on February 14, 1929, when seven of Moran's gang members were gunned down at 2122 N. Clark St. at approximately 10:30 a.m. The assailants were reportedly either dressed as police officers, escorted by police officers, or were actually officers, depending on who you believe. No evidence has ever definitively proven who the attackers were, but what is known is that they pumped 90 bullets[22] from shotguns, machine guns, and revolvers into the defenseless Moran gang members.

Lucky to have overslept that morning, Moran's life was spared, but his influence on the north side was over. Some historians contend that it was not in fact luck that kept Moran safe, but rather that he had been tipped off. Other researchers contend that Moran actually planned the shooting himself. The truth is that nobody knows for sure who masterminded the killing. But public opinion assumed it was the work of Capone's outfit, even though the gangster vehemently denied any involvement.

Always a music fan, Capone soon made himself at home at the Green Mill, where popular jazz musicians always played while in Chicago. Various newspaper articles have claimed that Green Mill insiders frequently witnessed Capone arriving at the cocktail lounge with 10 to 15 bodyguards and that the mob boss often doled out $100 tips. While some of that may be fiction, what is certain is that the Green Mill still has the booth that Capone is reported to have used, and his framed image overlooks patrons enjoying the jazz and poetry slams the venue is known for today. (GeoVerse™122)

There are no eye witness accounts revealing when or how Capone and Wilson got to know each other, but it isn't difficult to make an educated guess. Despite being a south sider, Capone was a Cubs fan who at one point is even reported to have thought of buying the franchise himself; add to that the fact that Wilson and Malone were both celebrities and heavy drinkers who frequented the Green Mill and other Capone speakeasies, and it seems nearly inevitable that they would eventually become acquainted with Capone.

The St. Valentine's Day Massacre was emblematic of Chicago at that time in history. Just five years earlier, Nathan Leopold and Richard Loeb shocked the world by trying to commit the perfect murder, kidnapping 14-year-old Bobby Franks, bludgeoning him to death and leaving him in a culvert. Brash crimes began to become more common. Justice John Paul Stevens was just a child at that time, but recalled the night would-be burglars forced their way into his family's home and held shotguns on his family, threatening to kill them during the home invasion robbery. Commissioner Kenesaw Mountain Landis saw the change in culture and grew concerned about his family being kidnapped.[23] His concern was warranted as fame proved to be no protection in the coming years, evidenced by the kidnapping and murder of aviator Charles Lindberg's son in 1932.

Violent was the world that Wilson saw around him during the 1930 season the rise in violence hit too close to home that summer when a local gang member, Jack Costa, was shot dead in the apartment building where Wilson's family lived. An apparent retaliation for a previous act of violence, Costa's murder proved that being friends with Capone was a dangerous business. Wilson began to fear for the safety of his family (wife Virginia and son Bobby). "Murders and kidnapping were commonplace among gangsters and bootleggers, and even their acquaintances," biographer Clifton Blue Parker explained in his book *Fouled Away: The Baseball Tragedy of Hack Wilson*:

> In fact, Hack Wilson's prominent visibility as the biggest sports star in the city made him a possible target of internecine intrigue. As Hack was on friendly terms with Al Capone, and was making good money himself, concern existed that Bobby might be a target for Capone's enemies—perhaps a kidnapping possibility. And so, a mysterious and silent figure named "T Bone" was assigned to walk Virginia and Bobby to Wrigley Field and sit with them during the games.[24]

No harm ever came to Virginia, Bobby, or Hack.

Wilson was soon traded, his final appearance as a Cub coming on August 30, 1931. Six weeks later, on October 18, Capone was found guilty of tax evasion and given an 11-year sentence that he served first in Atlanta and then at Alcatraz. He

Capone Assists the Cubs

It is probably impossible for twenty-first century fans to fully comprehend what life was like in Chicago during the 1920s. The Cubs were one of the nation's most exciting baseball teams and Prohibition was in place. Thanks to the "Chicago Outfit," which ran illegal bathtub gin bars throughout the city, there was no better place in the nation to get a drink.

One particular anecdote offers a glimpse into the overlapping worlds of baseball and crime during this time. The story was told by Bill Veeck about his dying father, William, and public enemy No. 1, Capone.

Commissioner Landis had made keeping gambling out of the game one of the primary missions of his tenure in baseball management. In his book *Veeck as in Wreck*, Veeck revealed that the commissioner's concern was warranted, at least in Chicago.

In September 1933, doctors told Bill Veeck that his father, William, the former president of the Chicago Cubs during the roaring '20s, had leukemia and did not have long to live. The doctors also said that often, the one thing a dying man can hold down in his stomach is wine. But where could Veeck the younger get it? Prohibition was still enforced at that time, though it was on its last legs (it would be repealed in December 1933).

In Chicago, if you had a problem—especially if you were a Cubs insider—there was always one person who could help. "There was one man in Chicago, I knew, who would know where the best champagne was to be had. Al Capone," Veeck wrote:

> I hurried to Al Capone's headquarters at the Hotel Metropole and told him what I wanted and why.
>
> "Kid," he said, "I'll send a case of champagne right over."
>
> The case was there when I got back. Every morning during those last few days of my father's life, a case of imported champagne was delivered to the door.
>
> The last nourishment that passed between my daddy's lips on this earth was Al Capone's champagne.[26]

Though colorful and entertaining, Veeck's story must be taken with a grain of salt. Capone was convicted of tax evasion in October 1931, at which time he was housed in the Cook County jail. After months of appeals, he was transferred to a penitentiary in Atlanta, which is where he was living in the fall of 1933. Though Veeck likely dealt with the outfit to get champagne for his father, it's highly doubtful that he spoke with Capone directly. His tale does, however, further underscore the connection between Capone and the Cubs, even if parts of it are likely exaggerated.

Landis' campaign to end the connection between underworld figures and baseball almost seems laughable when you realize just how close Capone was to the Cubs. And this connection would only get deeper, as we learn in our next chapter.

was released after seven and a half years. After the 1934 season, having played for Brooklyn and then Philadelphia, Wilson's 12-year baseball career was over. Penniless and estranged from his family, Wilson died in 1948. His body went unclaimed until NL president Ford Frick paid for his funeral. Capone died in 1947 after suffering brain damage due to the effects of syphilis.[25]

Before the lives of these two stocky men came to an early end, Wilson and Capone both ruled Chicago in their own ways, and neither will be forgotten.

Chapter 34

Cubs Manager With
Team-Altering Addiction Problem

Gambling Has Been a Part of Sports Since the First Organized Games Were Played. But Only One Manager Is Known to Have Been Such a Degenerate Gambler That He Was Threatened by the Mob, Had to Borrow Money from His Own Players to Cover His Debts, and Was the Focus of Suspicion Following the Mysterious Death of a Lover Who Left Him a Small Fortune in Her Will.

Gambling, guns, and gals: countless athletes have relished the celebrity lifestyle that attracts the three Gs of potential trouble. But there is only one manager who both drew death threats from the mob and was connected to a suspicious death.

Baseball isn't the only sport to have problems with gambling among managers, coaches, and players. But it has had more than its share of insiders consorting with nefarious characters—the most troubling of them all being a former Cubs player and manager who is in the National Baseball Hall of Fame.

Before delving into this controversial area that connects the dots from Major League Baseball to organized crime during the 1920s and 1930s, it seems only fair to balance the ledger, so to speak, by reminding readers of some of the more recent headline-making gambling scandals in other sports. In the National Football League, for example, the Baltimore Colts' Art Schlichter was banned from the 1983 season for betting on NFL games, a punishment precedent set in 1963 when famous NFL players Paul Hornung (with the Green Bay Packers) and Alex Karras (of the Detroit Lions) were suspended for a season for betting on their own games. In the National Hockey League, Phoenix Coyotes assistant coach Rick Tocchet pled guilty in 2007 to running a gambling ring that included millions of dollars in play and involved Janet Jones, wife of hockey icon Wayne Gretzky. And in January 2010, National Basketball Association commissioner

David Stern suspended Washington Wizards guard Gilbert Arenas for the remainder of the 2010 season after Arenas brought guns into the team's locker room to settle a dispute with a teammate concerning debts owed from card games on the team's chartered flights.

In college basketball, Tulane University shut down its program for three years after a 1985 scandal that revealed players were shaving points; other programs have also been found to have point-shavers on their teams (Arizona State, 1993–94; Northwestern University, 1994–95; and Boston College, 1978–79), but didn't shut down their programs. Boston College was at the center of one of college football's biggest gambling probes, which resulted in the suspension of 13 players during the 1996 season for betting on games, including some players who bet against their own team.[27] In 2013, Europol revealed that an 18-month investigation had produced proof that nearly 700 international matches were fixed beginning in 2008. According to the Associated Press, these fixes resulted in an estimated $10.9 million in profits and included approximately $2.7 million in bribes to players and officials.

Nearly all of the biggest scandals in sports gambling history have involved players rather than coaches or managers. Even the most infamous sports scandal in history, the "Black Sox" ordeal of 1919, involved players, not management. When members of management are involved in gambling, the story becomes highly unusual. Pete Rose's lifetime ban from baseball in 1989 by Commissioner A. Bartlett Giamatti is the easiest example to cite, and arguably the most infamous, since he still had not been reinstated to baseball as of 2013. In 1947, Commissioner Happy Chandler banned Leo Durocher for a year due to his relationships with known gamblers. But Durocher was allowed to return to baseball, leading the New York Giants to the 1954 World Series before taking over the Cubs for seven seasons.

While investigations and public pronouncements have laid the facts behind these example bare, some of the most captivating stories involving sports and gambling have been handled behind the scenes and have taken years for the public to learn about. Even when such cases become public knowledge, there are often many questions that are never answered.

For example, in 1993 NBA legend Michael Jordan retired, ostensibly to grieve for his recently murdered father, James Jordan. Rumors immediately swirled that both Jordan's retirement and his father's murder were related to the star's alleged gambling problem, and that Commissioner Stern had agreed to have Jordan "retire" temporarily instead of enforcing a suspension for gambling on one of the game's greatest players of all time. Evidence has never surfaced proving any aspect of this story, but 21 months after retiring, his "Airness" returned to the NBA, as so many people had predicted he would. Questions still abound about Jordan's brief retirement and his father's murder.

Through all these extreme stories of the overlap between gambling and sports, none hold the unique place in sports history of Rogers Hornsby, who was fired by the Cubs as manager (and technically released as a player, since he was the team's manager/player at the time) due to his gambling problems. Looming even larger was the question of whether Hornsby had ushered in an era of comingling between baseball and the mob, a dark partnership that has been hinted at and feared by baseball purists. While much remains unknown, it seems clear that there was a great deal of overlap between the realms of baseball and organized crime during Hornsby's day.

Hornsby was both one of the game's all-time greats and its all-time jerks. He was a Hall of Famer who captured seven batting titles (including six in a row), hit .400 or better three times, and won the Triple Crown and Most Valuable Player awards twice. He was also an infamous bigot, was sued more than 10 times in his life for failure to pay his taxes or debts—including settlements on car accidents that cost one woman her sight in one eye and a man the use of his arm—and was incredibly unpleasant to be around, according to any and all who knew him.

"Rogers Hornsby was, in my opinion and in that of many others, the most blunt and tactless guy in the world," said Gene Karst in Peter Golenbock's book *The Spirit of St. Louis*. Karst was the public relations manager for the St. Louis Cardinals during Hornsby's tenure with the team prior to joining the Cubs. "Hornsby didn't like Catholics and Jews. He was really prejudiced against blacks and Jews, Catholics and everyone else."[28]

Addiction vexed Hornsby as well—not to alcohol or narcotics, but the ponies. The "Rajah," as he was sometimes called, didn't drink, smoke, or do drugs. He also didn't read or watch movies for fear it would ruin his eyesight. But he did bet on horses, and he didn't care who knew, including Commissioner Landis.

Rajah and Landis locked horns often over the years, usually about betting on horses. Landis despised gambling. Hired to clean up baseball after the 1919 Black Sox scandal, Landis made it his mission to remove gambling of all kinds from the sport. But going to the horse track was not illegal, and Hornsby delighted in reminding Landis of that fact. According to Landis biographer David Pietrusza in his book *Judge and Jury: The Life and Times of Judge Kenesaw Mountain Landis*, the former commissioner once called Hornsby to his office and asked directly about rumors that he had bet on horses:

> "They aren't just rumors," Hornsby said, "I bet on horses. They are my only recreation. . . . I know it's gambling, and baseball and gambling don't mix. That's why I never play cards in the clubhouse with the other players. They're playing for money. I wait till later and maybe pick out a horse. . . . Look at it this way, I don't drink, smoke or go to the movies. Don't even read anything but the baseball box scores. Don't even go to the races over once or twice a year. I can relax by betting a horse now and then."[29]

"Everybody hated Rog," said Marty Marion, a former player-coach on Hornsby's St. Louis Browns. "Rogers was kind of an independent cuss. He would sit down and just be by himself. He never seemed to have any friends to talk to."[30]

Hornsby came into the league at the end of the 1915 season for the St. Louis Cardinals, where he played 12 seasons before finally wearing out his welcome with owner Sam Breadon. Two factors were at the forefront of Hornsby's trade, the same two things that would repeatedly haunt both his personal and professional lives: contemptuous arrogance with anyone who challenged him and an addiction to gambling.

One story tells of an incident in 1925 in which Breadon entered the locker room and began to address the team. Hornsby wheeled on the owner and threw Breadon out of "his" clubhouse. Enraged that an employee would claim the locker room was "his," Breadon began making plans that day with general manager Branch Rickey to get rid of Rajah despite the skills he brought to the team.[31]

Rickey made it clear that he did not like Hornsby. But he knew Rajah made the team better, so he purposefully dragged his feet on trade talks. The gamble paid off. Hornsby won his first MVP award after the 1925 season and Breadon, shockingly, decided to make the second baseman player/manager the following season. It was a horrible decision.

Buoyed by his promotion, Hornsby began bringing Frank Moore, a known bookie, to spring training, and then allowed the underworld figure to sit on the bench during the season. The Cardinals owner told Hornsby to stop bringing

Moore to the ballpark, but Hornsby would not allow anyone, even his boss, to tell him what to do. Moore continued to be a presence around the team all season long.

It was precisely the scenario that Landis predicted would happen if major-league players and/or managers consorted with gamblers. Bad ideas usually start small and end up getting bigger. And so it did with Hornsby. The 1926 St. Louis Cardinals won the World Series led by Hornsby. But when the season ended, the real battles began. Not only did Hornsby demand a three-year/$150,000 contract, but Breadon was also asked to intervene in a growing dispute between Hornsby and Moore, who claimed that Rajah owed him $92,000 in unpaid gambling debts. That was the final straw for the Cardinals owner. Despite having led the Cardinals to the 1926 World Series, where they beat the New York Yankees in seven games, Hornsby was no longer wanted in St. Louis. On December 20, 1926, Breadon traded him to the New York Giants.

The following year, Breadon shared his side of the saga with a reporter for the *Sarasota Herald-Tribune*. Under the headline "HORNSBY WAS SOLD BECAUSE OF HIS DEBTS," the article explained, "Hornsby's friendship with Moore was the real reason for the break in relations between the Cardinal owner and manager."[32]

Knowing that Hornsby had received stock in the Cardinals from Breadon, Moore approached the Cardinals owner to see if he would help settle the debt his player/manager owed. Predictably, Breadon refused to get involved and, wanting to wash his hands of the growing gambling problem, traded Hornsby. "I don't approve of any men who make their money playing baseball [and] gambling it away on horses," Breadon said. "I have nothing to do with Moore collecting his debt from Hornsby."[33]

Hornsby spent just one year with the Giants, who promptly traded him to the Boston Braves, where he spent only one season because the team couldn't afford him. William Wrigley and the Cubs could. Wrigley gave the Braves' $200,000 and five players for Hornsby, who brought all his offense—and offensiveness—with him to Chicago.

The move was particularly stunning given the fact that Hornsby's gambling debts had reached a new low to which no other baseball manager or player had sunk in the sport's history. On February 9, 1928, before Hornsby was traded to Chicago, newspapers ran stories reporting that Chicago mob members were out to either kill or injure Hornsby because he still hadn't paid off his gambling debts to Moore. Wrote David J. Walsh for the *Syracuse Journal* on February 9, 1928, in a front-page column headlined "THREATEN ROGERS' LIFE":

> Certain men in Chicago claim they had to "take the slap" for part of Hornsby's race track "investments" with Frank Moore and that they are out to get the ballplayer the first time he crosses the line into Cook County. Sinister threats of "taking him for a ride" accompanied the tip. In the argot of Gangdom, this means a shooting, mostly fatal.

Rebuffed by both Hornsby and Breadon, in 1927 Moore took the unprecedented step of trying to sue Hornsby in court for his unpaid debts. Moore originally charged that Hornsby owed him $92,000, then lowered the amount to $70,075 and then $45,075. On December 21, 1927, a Missouri grand jury found in favor of Hornsby—which meant, according to Walsh's sources, that Chicago underworld figures who were in turn owed by Moore were not going to get paid.

That made Wrigley's pursuit of Hornsby even more perplexing, given that it would bring the slugger into the city that was home to known powerful underworld figures who were apparently intent on hurting the baseball icon. Unless, of course, having Hornsby playing for the hometown team was exactly what Chicago mobsters wanted.

Walsh's column did not mention Capone specifically—it included only a general reference to "certain men in Chicago"—but it is hard to imagine that any gangland activity involving Chicago would not also include Capone. No evidence is known to exist of any conversation between Capone and Wrigley about bringing Hornsby to Chicago. Wrigley was a shrewd businessman, and there is no evidence to indicate he would compromise himself in such a manner. But if Walsh's story was accurate, why would the mob allow Hornsby, who owed a small fortune to Moore and thus to Chicago mobsters, into their city? "Keep your friends close, but your enemies closer," is one of the most well-known gangster mottos. What better way to keep track of a known gambler than to have him right there on your home turf? That way, if he didn't pay his debts, other forms of compensation could easily be arranged—such as access to knowledge about the team and/or their opponents. It's notable that the time Hornsby spent in Chicago coincided with the most established connections between the mob and the Cubs.

Hornsby's first season in Chicago, 1929, was his best as a player; he batted .380 with 149 RBI and 39 home runs. He won his second MVP award that season for leading the Cubs to the World Series, which they lost to the Philadelphia Athletics in five games. The following season, Hornsby replaced Cubs manager Joe McCarthy late in the campaign, and played himself at second base.

Hornsby's addiction to gambling on horses was as well-known as the fact that teammate Wilson, who set the MLB record for 191 RBI that year, was a favorite at Capone's speakeasies.

"Hornsby used to bet on the horses a lot," said Bill DeWitt Sr., general manager of the St. Louis Browns, one of Hornsby's former bosses, in *The Spirit of St. Louis."* "He was a big bettor. He'd bet $50 across the board or $100 across the board. Sometimes he'd bet $1,500 on a race. He'd bet eight or nine different races. And he was placing bets all over the country."[34]

Meanwhile, This wasn't news to baseball insiders or Landis, who had numerous run-ins with Hornsby over the years about his gambling. Landis was handcuffed by the fact that betting on horses was not illegal, however, the commissioner was eager to make sure that Hornsby didn't consent to allowing bookies on the bench in Chicago as he had in St. Louis, especially considering that Capone's men would likely be the ones in the dugout. Landis' fears came close to reality at the end of Hornsby's only full season as Cubs manager when, on September 30, 1931, newspaper photographers took a photo of Cubs catcher Gabby Hartnett signing a baseball for Capone, who was sitting on in the front row. Technically, the regular season had ended three days earlier, the Cubs finishing third with an 84–70 record. Capone, who would be charged with tax evasion less than three weeks later, was attending the first game of Chicago's City Series between the Cubs and White Sox.

Livid over the photograph, Landis sent Hartnett a telegram reading, "You are not to have your picture taken with Al Capone." Ever the jokester, Hartnett replied with a pragmatic answer: "OK, but if you don't want me to have my picture taken with Al Capone, you tell him."[35]

During spring training before the 1932 season, Hornsby severely hurt his ankle on a slide attempt. He would play in only 19 games that year, his lowest game total since his late-season call up in 1915. Hornsby gave up on the Cubs' chances in late July, telling general manager William Veeck that the team didn't have what it took to overcome the Pirates' 4.5-game lead. Sensing that something was holding his veteran team back, Veeck began investigating the dour attitude of the team. What he found alarmed him and left him with few options.

Not only was Hornsby constantly berating his players and ruining their mental approach to the game, but he was also borrowing money from them to pay off his gambling debts. Upon investigation, it was discovered that Hornsby had borrowed approximately $11,000 from his players despite the fact that Landis had made it clear that he did not want the star to gamble at all.[36] Veeck realized Hornsby's gambling addiction had become a team problem, not just an individual problem.

Cubs third baseman Woody English, who roomed with Hornsby on the road before he became a manager, was quoted in the book *Wrigleyville* as saying, "[Hornsby] borrowed from me, borrowed from Guy Bush . . . Pat Malone was one. [Hornsby] said it was to pay his income tax, but it was gambling debts, and that was the main reason he got fired."[37]

Charlie "Jolly Cholly" Grimm was tapped as Hornsby's replacement. The fun-loving first baseman was just what the Cubs needed. Chicago rallied for the rest of the season and met the New York Yankees in the World Series. So despised was Hornsby by the Cubs at that point that the team voted against the former player/manager getting a share of the 1932 World Series payout. Hornsby pled his case to an unsympathetic Landis, who upheld the players' vote. "That fellow will never learn," Landis said. "His betting has got him into one scrape after another, cost him a fortune and several jobs, and still he hasn't enough sense to stop it."[38]

Hornsby continued playing until 1937, but was a shadow of his former self. And while his playing skills had diminished, his love of the racetrack had not. He continued to manage in the major leagues with the St. Louis Browns and the Cincinnati Reds until 1953, when he was linked to the mysterious death of a woman in Chicago. The scandal helped usher his MLB career to its end and cast another dark shadow over his legacy.

On September 6, 1953, Hornsby's Reds lost 7–2 to the Cubs at Wrigley Field. After the game, he met his mistress, Bernadette Ann Harris, for dinner, bringing along Cubs general manager Jimmy Gallagher and his wife.[39] Harris had occasionally identified herself as "Mrs. Hornsby,"—and even had a driver's license with the name "Bernadette Ann Hornsby"—even though the real Mrs. Hornsby, Jeannette, from whom Rogers had been estranged since 1944, was still his legal wife.[40]

Jeannette (also identified in reports as Jeanette) married Rogers in 1924, filed for divorce briefly in 1934, rescinded the petition, then filed for divorce again nine years later in May 1953. Jeanette's 1953 divorce petition claimed Hornsby was a violent man who had hit her several times before leaving her and their son, Bill, in 1944. Even worse, Jeannette claimed in a wire story that Hornsby had taken and squandered the $25,000 inheritance she had received from her mother.[41] Jeannette sought $600 per month in her divorce papers, but Judge Robert J. Kirkwood lowered it to $400 per month plus $200 for legal fees.

It was four months later that Hornsby, along with the Gallaghers, had dinner after the Reds-Cubs game with Harris. It was the last meal Harris would ever eat. After dinner, Harris returned to her apartment at the Fleetwood Hotel at 6026 Winthrop Avenue. Later that night her body was found on the ground outside the building. A local coroner ruled her death an apparent suicide from jumping off the building brought on by depression. Investigators were called in when it was found that Harris had a card in her purse that read "In case of accident notify Rogers Hornsby" and that she had a safe deposit box and a will that listed only one beneficiary: Hornsby. When authorities opened the box, they found $25,000 in cash.[42] "The Gallaghers probably knew and others close to Hornsby guessed, for some time [Hornsby had] been using Bernadette Harris to hide money from Jeannette Hornsby," Robert C. Alexander explained in his book *Rogers Hornsby: A Biography*.[43]

No newspaper articles linked the $25,000 found in the safe deposit box with the same amount Jeannette claimed was taken from her by Hornsby. The former ballplayer paid his estranged wife $400 per month under the separate maintenance order until her death on May 30, 1956.

As for Harris' death, Hornsby readily agreed with the coroner's ruling of suicide brought on by depression. "She complained she was going blind, that she couldn't talk, that she heard buzzing noises," Hornsby was quoted in the *Chicago Tribune* days later. "I tried to encourage her not to worry."

Cantankerous and callous to others, Hornsby is the only known manager in baseball history to ever be threatened by the mob for unpaid debts and was fired for borrowing money from his players to cover even more gambling debts. Despite sharing his side of the story, Hornsby's connection to the mysterious death and suspicious will of his lover doesn't help his case for being one of the most offensive men ever to play the game.

"He was a cold man," Cubs infielder Billy Herman summarized bluntly.[44] It's doubtful anyone will ever argue with his assessment.

Chapter 35

Banned for Marrying the Wrong Woman

*Some Players Are Able to Cavort with Gangsters and Get
Away With It. But One Former Cubs Manager with Some
Unsavory Connections Instead Received One of Baseball's
Harshest Punishments for Offending the Catholic Church.*

Nothing good can come of it when a member of the United States Supreme
Court denounces your actions in public comments. And when members of the
New York City Diocese of the Catholic Church join the clamor, you can bet that
the final punishment will be bad. Only one person in baseball history has been
banned for his marriage and the fallout that it caused—and, of course, he was a
Cubbie.

Leo Durocher managed the Cubs for seven seasons (1966–72), making his
presence felt from day one. Crusty, quarrelsome, and difficult, Durocher loved
conflict, a trait that made him almost unanimously despised by everyone with
whom he worked. Fergie Jenkins described Durocher's demeanor very simply:
"Tougher than a night in jail."[45]

In his autobiography, *Nice Guys Finish Last*, Durocher wrote:

My baseball career spanned almost five decades . . . and in all that time I never
had a boss call me upstairs so that he could congratulate me for losing like a
gentleman. I believe in rules. . . . I also believe I have a right to test the rules by
seeing how far they can be bent.[46]

As a player, that testing meant doctoring baseballs, stomping on opponents,
and doing anything and everything to gain an advantage. As a manager,
Durocher berated players, cursing them and trying to rile them up so they would
play angry. It didn't always work. In 1971, Durocher accused third baseman Ron
Santo of arranging for the team to have a "Ron Santo Day" at Wrigley Field the

following week. Quite fiery himself, Santo retaliated, going after Durocher. The team was lost to Durocher from that point forward.

"In those early days, he was a son of a bitch," former Cubs announcer Jack Brickhouse said of Durocher. "But he was a sharp son of a bitch. But by the time he was finished in Chicago, he was just an old son of a bitch."[47]

Growing up playing pool and cards, Durocher didn't hide his competitiveness. He tried to win at everything, and that included betting on horses, card games, and any gambling distraction he could find. He was also a man of great contradictions whose aggressiveness often made him both the center of conflicts and the person able to make conflicts disappear. When he learned that his Brooklyn Dodgers teammates had signed a petition against Jackie Robinson joining the team in 1947, Durocher called a midnight meeting and in his blunt fashion told the players that Robinson was a great player, he was going to join the team, and they needed to either get on board or get gone. "Take that petition, you know, wipe your ass with it," Durocher told the Dodgers, before lauding the level of play that Robinson would bring to the team. He ended the meeting in typical Durocher fashion: "I don't want to see your petition. I don't want to hear anything about it. Fuck your petition. Meeting is over. Go back to bed."[48]

Ironically, while Durocher helped pave the way for Robinson's success in that watershed 1947 season, he wasn't the Dodgers' manager when Robinson joined the majors. Instead, Durocher spent the 1947 season banned from the game thanks largely to bigotries by a large group of people who wouldn't accept Durocher.

Truculent and abrasive, Durocher was overly confident due to his status as a national name beyond the baseball field. He was a television personality who appeared on many shows, giving him access to a galaxy of stars such as Frank Sinatra and Danny Kaye, who were friends. He was also a friend of George Raft, a Hollywood actor known for playing gangsters in films.

Raft and Durocher were cut from the same cloth, and they knew it. They both loved gambling, girls, and baseball. During the offseason, Durocher often stayed at Raft's massive Beverly Hills mansion so that they could carouse together at night after Raft returned from work filming at the studio, and Raft stayed at Durocher's apartment in New York when the actor was on the East Coast. The two were close friends, which would have been fine if Raft hadn't also been friends with much more sinister individuals. One such pal was Benjamin "Bugsy" Siegel, a ruthless member of the New York crime syndicate who used his power to open the Flamingo Hotel and Casino in Las Vegas—the start of the mob's presence in the desert. Joe Adonis was another of Raft's friend, as well as a powerful force in Lucky Luciano's crime organization. Memphis Engelberg, a known bookie and racetrack handicapper, was another friend of Raft's, as was Connie Immerman, a white bootlegger in Harlem who ran speakeasies that rivaled the famous Cotton Club.

Durocher claimed in his autobiography that he only met Siegel once, didn't know Adonis except to be able to recognize him when he visited the ballpark, but was friends with Immerman ("I had always liked him") and Engelberg ("Whenever I went to the track, which wasn't that often, I'd have Memphis mark my card").[49]

Beginning in 1944, newspaper stories exposed the friendship between Raft and Durocher after the actor used Durocher's apartment to host a gambling party while in New York on a media junket to promote his latest film, *Follow the Boys*. One wealthy gambler allegedly lost a reported $18,000 that night playing craps with Raft, who was accused of using loaded dice to win 13 straight passes. Newspapers loved the story, but the authorities did not. The Brooklyn district attorney had Durocher's phone tapped. The recordings established a link between Durocher and a check-cashing scandal in Baltimore at the Mergenthaler Linotype Company. Durocher claimed in his autobiography that a few of his checks "had been routinely processed through"[50] the check-cashing house in Baltimore. It was enough to keep newspaper columnists and federal agents watching Durocher.

Gambling influences invading baseball was the personal peccadillo of MLB's first commissioner, Judge Kenesaw Mountain Landis. Happy Chandler, who replaced Landis in 1945, was intent on proving that he was equally hard on criminal influences. Having a man like Raft, whose friends went to the apex of the crime world, as close friends with a manager was precisely the thing that baseball brass wanted to avoid. Having that same manager wire-tapped by the government and connected with a check-cashing crime was even worse. Though Durocher did not apparently profit from the scheme, he was too close to the illegal activity for Chandler to ignore it.

On November 22, 1946, Chandler had a meeting with Durocher at the Claremont Country Club in Berkeley, California. Chandler demanded that Durocher no longer have any contact with Raft and his cronies, Adonis, Siegel,

Engelberg, and Immerman. Durocher agreed, realizing that it was necessary to break ways with his notorious friends in order to stay in baseball.

The matter appeared to be settled until Durocher shared a personal note with Chandler that would prove to be a bigger problem than his associations with underworld figures: he was in love with Hollywood actress Laraine Day, who was married to Ray Hendricks, a band leader and manager of a Santa Monica airport. While neither of them realized it then, that small admission would eventually force Chandler to suspend Durocher for the 1947 season.[51]

The problem was that Day was not yet divorced. Months later, when the story hit newspapers across the country that Durocher, who was twice divorced and 15 years older than Day, was planning to wed the Hollywood actress, reporters and church leaders alike considered his "immoral actions" to be worse than any gambling associations.

On January 20, 1947, California judge George A. Dockweiler issued an interlocutory divorce to Hendricks and Day. This meant that under California law, Day and Hendricks had to wait one year before they could legally marry anyone else. But Day had been around Leo the Lip too long to follow anyone's rules. She gave Hendricks $10,500 and a Ford sedan[52] as settlement and married Durocher in El Paso, Texas, just 24 hours later. By California law, that meant Day could be charged with adultery.

It took months for the legal system to rule on the Durocher-Day marriage, but church leaders needed much less time to offer their own judgments. Justice Frank Murphy, a devout Roman Catholic and member of the Supreme Court, as well as the former mayor of Detroit and governor of Michigan, made his displeasure known to Chandler and the rest of baseball's executives.[53] An influential figure in the church, Murphy turned the pressure up on baseball because of Durocher's actions, which the justice considered immoral.

At the end of the 1946 season, in the wake of stories linking Durocher to Raft and his criminal associates, the Roman Catholic Diocese of Brooklyn had warned the Dodgers that if something wasn't done about the degrading situation in baseball, they would take action. Priest Vincent J. Powell oversaw the Brooklyn Catholic Youth Organization, sponsors of a Dodgers' fan group called The Knothole Gang that allowed young fans into games for free on slow days in order to fill the stands. Estimated to have 50,000 members, the CYO was a massive group of future ticket buyers that the Dodgers could not afford to offend.

The situation was growing worse on the national level as well. Justice Murphy threatened Major League Baseball with a national boycott by CYO members across the country if Durocher wasn't punished.

Meanwhile, Durocher and Day had returned to her 16-bedroom mansion in Santa Monica, worth $200,000[54] (roughly equal to $2.1 million in 2013). Durocher spent his days clearing brush from the six-acre yard and socializing with Hollywood celebrities rather than fretting about the looming threat from the CYO and Justice Murphy. "You'd have thought he would be moody, morose, and sullen," Danny Kaye told *Sports Illustrated*, "but actually he wasn't."[55]

Meanwhile, on the other side of the continent, Durocher's happiness with Day was creating a furor. On March 1, 1947, Father Powell went through with his threat. "The Brooklyn Catholic Youth Organization is withdrawing from the Dodgers' Knothole Club," Powell's press announcement proclaimed, explaining that Durocher was "undermining the moral training of Brooklyn's Roman Catholic youth. The C.Y.O. cannot continue to have our youngsters associated with a man who represents an example in complete contradiction to our moral teachings."[56]

Durocher began to realize the seriousness of the situation after Powell's press release, but years later, he still explained his point of view in a wonderfully sarcastic manner: "I had never claimed to be in any danger of sprouting wings," Durocher wrote in his autobiography. "From a very casual observation of the young men of Brooklyn, I had every confidence that they were quite capable of corrupting themselves without any help from me."[57]

The situation only got worse when Durocher reported to spring training with the Dodgers in Havana, Cuba. Realizing that Cuba was a quick plane ride from Florida, American-based organized crime had begun to infiltrate Cuba during the 1940s. So it should come as no surprise that on one of his first days in Havana, Durocher ran into two of the men with whom he was forbidden to associate: Engelberg and Immerman.

Durocher claimed in his autobiography that when the men came to say hello, he ran the other direction. But he was only leaping from the frying pan into the fire when he tried to hide in the lounge outside. A young stranger asked him to come say hello to a group of men who were playing cards, one of whom was "dying to meet" him. Durocher politely refused. The stranger returned again and again, each time being politely rebuffed by Durocher, who was with Day and Branch Rickey Jr. Finally, Rickey went over to find out who this persistent fan of Durocher's was. It turned out to be none other than Lucky Luciano,[58] the crime kingpin who had been deported from the United States back to Italy months earlier. Between October 1946 and March 1947, Luciano attempted to control his American crime syndicate from Cuba. United States officials pressured Cuban authorities to deport Luciano, whose brief stay in Cuba coincided with Durocher's.

At the same time, tempers flared between the Dodgers' Branch Rickey and the Yankees' Larry MacPhail throughout spring training that year. When Durocher and Rickey saw Engelberg and Immerman enjoying a game in a Yankees' suite, they exploded, claiming to reporters that a double standard existed that forbid the Dodgers manager to speak to the same people who the Yankees general manager entertained as guests. In a newspaper column he ghost wrote with Dodgers traveling secretary Harold Parrott, Durocher claimed that MacPhail had tried to lure him to the Yankees during the offseason, but that he was loyal to Brooklyn. MacPhail was furious about the revelation. Durocher was equally furious about the double standard that forbid him to associate with the same people who enjoyed games in the Yankees' suites. Chandler was furious that the Roman Catholic community was still boycotting baseball games. All of this acrimony seethed around Durocher.

After a brief investigation, Chandler ruled on April 9, 1947, that both the Yankees and the Dodgers would be fined $2,000 apiece for club interference. Durocher's column (which was written by Parrott, and which Durocher rarely actually read) was ceased. And Durocher was suspended for one season for "conduct detrimental to baseball."[59]

Generations of baseball fans still question the extreme punishment Durocher received. Gambling and sports have been in bed since the first days of baseball, but Durocher's relationship with Day was what actually led to his punishment as much as or more than his friendships with Raft and his underworld associates. Dodgers owner Walter O'Malley, who limply defended Durocher during Chandler's investigation, has been suspected for decades of sacrificing his manager as a scapegoat to save the team's relationship with the CYO, the Roman Catholic Church, and all the fans they represented. After all, once Durocher was punished, there was no more mention of any boycotts, something that O'Malley, a "devout Catholic,"[60] undoubtedly had prayed for in the months leading up to Durocher's suspension.

Chapter 36

The Marital Affair That Changed Cubs History

Athletes and Infidelity Seems to Go Hand in Hand All Too Often. But Only One Affair Changed the Course of Cubs History—For the Better.

Beautiful women can make men do crazy things. In recent years, embarrassing truths about extramarital affairs have damaged the reputations of world-famous athletes in nearly every sport. Golfer Tiger Woods and basketball coach Rick Pitino had their careers sullied because of their infamous flings. Football coach Bobby Petrino lost his job at the University of Arkansas because of one. Former National Football League quarterback Steve McNair lost his life over one. But only one person forever linked to the Cubs enjoyed a career renaissance because of an affair.

No, we're not talking about the infamous rumors that Ryne Sandberg's ex-wife was involved with former teammates such as Rafael Palmeiro, Mark Grace, and/or Dave Martinez. Those rumors were never proven, and nobody has ever discussed the matter publicly. However, there was one affair that has been discussed over the years that actually made the Cubs better, not worse.

Harry Caray was so connected with the Chicago Cubs that an image of his face adorns Wrigley Field, a statue of him outside the Friendly Confines welcomes fans, and his Chicago restaurants are a popular attraction. None of that would have happened had he not been caught in an alleged affair with the daughter-in-law of former St. Louis Cardinals owner August "Gussie" Busch.

The Busch family has been synonymous with St. Louis for generations, and Caray had a lucrative endorsement deal with their family business, Budweiser beer. But all of that changed when Caray's contract was dropped after the 1969 season. The reason was clear to baseball insiders: Caray, who was married to his first wife, Marian, at the time, was having an affair with Susan Busch, wife of

August Busch III, son of the Cardinals owner. Susan Busch denied the rumors over the years, though Caray's comments were far from a denial according to authors Peter Hernon and Terry Ganey in their expose on the Busch family, *Under the Influence*: "You couldn't say I did and I wouldn't say I didn't."[61]

According to author Peter Golenbock's book *The Spirit of St. Louis*, the affair began to go public on a rainy night in November 1968 when Caray was crossing the street in St. Louis and was hit by a motorist. Caray's nose and legs were broken and one of his shoulders was separated. Gussie Busch allowed Caray to stay at one of his Florida homes to recuperate after he was released from the hospital. What Caray didn't know was that while he was in the hospital before leaving for Florida, his phone records revealed what neither he nor Susan had. Wrote Golenbock, quoting an anonymous friend of Caray's:

> While Harry was still convalescing, some members of the Busch family began to notice there were a lot of telephone charges on bills linking Harry's room to one of the Busch residences. This rang a bell, and after some checking around, some following by a detective of Harry, it was discovered that Caray was apparently having an affair with the wife of young August Busch [III], Gussie's son. Naturally, this isn't the greatest way to keep your job.[62]

William Knoedelseder, author of *Bitter Brew: The Rise and Fall of Anheuser-Busch and America's Kings of Beer*, was a witness to the affair one night when he was working at a St. Louis restaurant. He discussed what he had seen in an interview years later with *The Riverfront Times* on November 8, 2012:

> I was working the night when the two of them came in together and were seated downstairs. Everyone in the restaurant knew who Harry Caray was, and it quickly flashed around to the staff that the beautiful blonde woman who was with him—and who he was getting along with very well—was Mrs. [Susan] Busch. They were openly affectionate. The conclusion you would jump to is that there was something going on there. No one on the staff had heard any rumors prior to that, so it wasn't like we were making it up. It got to the point that the owner, Vince Bommarito, told people to stop staring.

Gussie Busch, who was married four times and divorced twice himself, wouldn't have batted an eye at this behavior had it not involved his own family. In *Under the Influence*, Hernon and Ganey quoted the conversation Caray and

Gussie had about the rumors when Caray began to worry that his contract would not be renewed:

> Caray decided to confront Gussie about the stories. He told him, "I'm supposed to be breaking up a marriage." The following dialogue, Caray said, then took place.
>
> "You didn't rape anybody, did you?" Gussie asked.
>
> "No."
>
> "If you had a relationship, it was mutual desire, right?"
>
> Caray nodded.
>
> "I've screwed a lot of people because of mutual desire," Gussie said. "So what do you got to worry about?"
>
> Caray was dismissed anyway, prompting the observation, "I guess blood is thicker than water."[63]

Susan and August Busch III were divorced in 1969. Caray remained married to his first wife, Marian, until their divorce in 1974. Caray and his second wife, Dolores, or "Dutchie" to most fans, were married from 1975 until Caray's death in 1998.

After one year calling Oakland A's games and ten years with the Chicago White Sox, Caray began his tenure with the Cubs in 1982, where he became famous worldwide for his enthusiasm and support of the Cubs and, of course, Budweiser beer. Blood may be thicker than water, but business is business, apparently, and nobody was better for Budweiser's business than Caray. In 1980, long after his divorce, August Busch III rehired Caray to help sales in Chicago. In fact, Anheuser-Busch Budweiser took out full-page advertisements across the country praising Caray when the National Baseball Hall of Fame gave him the 1989 Frick Award, which is given to a media member each year.[64]

Caray's huge following in Chicago erased a low moment in his past; in fact, it was because of that low moment that Caray became the most popular announcer in baseball. If the Cardinals hadn't let him go, he would never have resurfaced in Chicago, where he achieved his iconic stature in baseball history and his huge statue outside of the ballpark.

Chapter 37

A Bottle in the Dugout Led to Hall of Fame

A War Hero, Alcoholic, and Victim of an Unusual Illness, This Former Cubs Pitcher Became the First Person with This Disorder to Play in the Major Leagues. He Was Also the Only Known Player Whose Team Kept a Bottle for Him on the Bench.

Grover Cleveland Alexander was such a masterful pitcher that he gave opposing batters fits. What many people didn't know was that Alexander suffered fits too—except his were caused by epilepsy. Sadly, history has remembered him as a drunk who was rumored to keep a liquor bottle in the dugout, rather than as a quiet hero battling demons few people knew about.

As of 2013, five epileptics have reached the major leagues; only one is in the National Baseball Hall of Fame. Alexander's 20-year career spanned from 1911 to 1930. He won 30 games or more three times and was inducted into the Hall of Fame in 1938. As mentioned earlier, Ronald Reagan was proud of his portrayal of Alexander in the film *The Winning Team* (1952) because he liked the perseverance the Cubs pitcher displayed despite numerous setbacks.

Early in his career, Alexander was hit in the head by a baseball while trying to reach second base. The blow knocked him out and he suffered from double vision for months afterward. While this head injury likely contributed to his epilepsy years later, there were other complicating factors.

The Nebraska native pitched only three games for the Cubs before he was drafted into World War I, during which he served on the front lines in France as an artillery sergeant, was gassed by the enemy, and lost hearing in one ear due to exposure to numerous concussive explosions. Upon his return from the war, teammates saw a difference in the pitcher that went beyond his alcoholism. "I don't believe Alex was much of a drinker before he went into the Army," said catcher Bob O'Farrell, Alexander's batterymate in both Chicago and St. Louis. "After he got back from the war, though, he had a real problem."[65]

Alexander's drinking was legendary, not so much for the amount he could consume, but for the myths that grew about him. The most notorious was that the Cubs kept a bottle of liquor in the dugout to help the pitcher steady his hand during games. However, while there was a bottle in the dugout to help Alexander, it didn't contain alcohol.

"Sometimes a fit would strike him while he was out on the mound," said his ex-wife, Aimee (portrayed by Doris Day in *The Winning Team*):

> He always carried a bottle of spirits of ammonia with him. They would have to carry him off the field. Some thought he was drunk. They would take him into the locker room, Alex would whiff the ammonia, fight to get control of himself, and then go right back out and pitch again. . . . I remember once in Pittsburgh, I saw Alex signal the umpire suddenly and call time. I knew what was happening. He went into the locker room for about 15 minutes, came out again, and pitched the entire game.[66]

Sadly, few people understood just how much Alexander was suffering.

In 2012, Major League Baseball helped CURE (Citizens United for Research in Epilepsy) and S4 (Sarah & Southbury Strikeout Seizures) by holding an auction to raise money for these two organizations. The League was partly inspired to take this action due to Buddy Bell, an MLB manager for nine years (three each with the Tigers, the Rockies, and the Royals) after an 18-year playing career, who is also an epileptic. Hal Lanier (who played from 1964 to 1973), Tony Lazzeri (1926–1939), and Greg Walker (1982–1990) are the only other known epileptic players in MLB history.

"There were a couple of times where I wasn't able to play because of a seizure," Bell explained in 2012 for an MLB.com article. "I remember one night in New York, I was taking a shower in the morning, and next thing I know, I woke up in the tub. Obviously, I wasn't able to play that day."[67]

In 1988, Walker was playing for the Chicago White Sox when he nearly died due to a seizure that he suffered in front of his teammates during batting practice. White Sox trainer Herm Schneider was pulled out of the training room to a horrific scene that few sports trainers would be prepared to handle. "It was an ugly, ugly situation," Schneider told *Sports Illustrated* the following year.

Walk was blue, his lips were purple, his eyes had rolled back in his head. Guys were going in to throw up at the sight of it. Some guys just went into the clubhouse probably because they didn't want to see him die. When I got to him, on a scale of one to 10, he was nine-plus dead.[68]

Worried that Walker was choking and unable to breathe, Schneider used a pair of tape-cutting scissors to force the player's mouth open, chipping part of a tooth in the process. As Schneider used a rubber tongue depressor to clear Walker's windpipe, the player bit down on the trainer's finger so hard that it drew blood. Moments later, Walker recovered and was rushed to the hospital. Walker survived, but epilepsy activists were furious, contending that many unnecessary mistakes were made that derailed decades of epilepsy education for the general public.[69] But since few people ever witness a seizure, it's hard to fault a trainer for not knowing how to handle the situation.

Walker's tale only underscores the toughness that made Alexander a Hall of Fame selection. There were times when the right-handed hurler collapsed on the field in much the same way, only to have his teammates save his life. After he recovered moments later, the stoic Alexander would brush off the incident and continue playing the game, to the disbelief of everyone who had seen him collapse moments earlier.

"Sometimes he'd have one of those spells out on the mound and we'd get around him and pull his tongue out," said teammate Pinky Whitney. "And then he'd get up and throw the next ball right through the middle of the plate."[70]

Even more amazing, Alexander was the first epileptic pitcher to throw to an epileptic player (only the second in the history of the game). What's more, it happened in Game 7 of the World Series with the bases loaded. On October 9, 1926, Yankee Stadium was filled with 46,615 fans yearning to see the Yankees win the World Series. Alexander stunned them all, scattering eight hits in a 10–2 spanking that tied the Series with the Cardinals at three games apiece.

Rogers Hornsby, the player/manager of the 1926 Cardinals squad, swore that Alexander never arrived drunk at the ballpark when he was supposed to pitch. On the other days, however, anything could happen. In fact, it was a good bet that if Alexander wasn't scheduled to pitch the next day, he was going to be drunk that night. Once during the regular season, Alexander nearly had his face destroyed taking the field during batting practice because he was so drunk that he couldn't move out of the way of balls hit toward him at third base.[71]

Knowing he would not start in Game 7, Alexander had been drinking the night before. Jessie Haines started Game 7 for the Cardinals, but in the bottom of the seventh inning, he pitched himself into a jam he could not escape. The Cardinals led 3–2 in the seventh when Haines managed to get two outs—but he had also loaded the bases. Hornsby pulled Haines and called for Alexander. Surprised to be called in for relief, Alexander needed to be roused from his slumber (others would later say it was more of a stupor) in the bullpen. Not usually one to need much warm up, this time Alexander took his time getting to the pitcher's mound, first stopping to check with his outfielders and then his infielders.

While it may have seemed that Alexander needed the extra few minutes to shake the pickled cobwebs from his mind, there were other possible reasons for his methodical stroll to the mound. At the plate stood a rookie in the most pressure-packed situation any hitter could imagine: Game 7 of the World Series, losing by one run, bases loaded, two outs. The player at the plate was Lazzeri. The only two epileptics in the game were squared off against each other in a duel that would make one a hero and the other a forgotten footnote to history.

"I wasn't worried about the spot I was in," Alexander said later. "I always had one motto, and it was this: 'I'm a better pitcher than you are a hitter.'"[72]

Lazzeri managed to rip one foul ball that, had it straightened out, would have been a home run. But the wind helped it hook into the left-field stands for a strike instead. Alexander threw two more unhittable pitches, Lazzeri struck out, and the Cardinals went on to win Game 7 by the same margin, 3–2, that they had had when Alexander took the mound.

Alexander's playing career ended following the 1930 season, and with it went his self-control. His drinking became worse than ever while he tried to earn money playing for barnstorming teams that used gimmicks to lure people to the ballfield. One team he played for, the House of David, had their players wear long beards to emulate Orthodox Jewish men for publicity. Ever the contrarian, Alexander remained clean-shaven on his bearded team.

While Alexander may have looked well kempt, his life was falling apart. His wife divorced him, remarried him, then—realizing his drinking would never end—left him again. Drifting from jobs both meaningless and demeaning, Alexander worked as a security guard, a hotel employee, and a sideshow attraction at Hubert's Museum, a flea circus in New York City where he told the story of that famous World Series moment to paying customers. He was working that sideshow in 1939, the year *after* he was inducted into the National Baseball Hall of Fame. Determined to help the troubled pitcher, baseball officials secretly approved a $50 per month pension for Alexander. The pension was then raised to $100.

Sadly, Alexander seems to have been beyond help. Epileptic, alone, and deaf, Alexander continued to drink away the demons that haunted him. On Christmas Eve 1949, Alexander was found unconscious in a Los Angeles alley, near death. When he regained consciousness in the hospital, his ex-wife was by his side; she was forced to scribble notes on paper to help the hurler understand where he was. When the penniless pitcher, who had once been one of the toughest players ever to take the field, realized what had become of his life, he wept into his hands.

Less than a year later, on November 4, 1950, Alexander was dead.

Immortalized in Hollywood films, the National Baseball Hall of Fame, and the minds of fans everywhere, Alexander is the only epileptic to overcome his condition and be inducted into his sport's Hall of Fame. The most notable epileptic athletes outside of baseball are former NFL players and twins Tiki and Ronde Barber, along with retired lineman Alan Faneca. All three were All-Pros during their careers and may one day be inducted into the Pro Football Hall of Fame.

There are several organizations dedicated to educating the public about epilepsy, including the Epilepsy Foundation (EpilepsyFoundation.org), the Alliance for Epilepsy Research (EpilepsyResearch.org), and Citizens United for Research in Epilepsy (CUREepilepsy.org).

Chapter 38

First Overdose in Cubs History

Only One Former Cubs Player Is Known to Have Died of a Drug Overdose and Was Buried in a Cubs Uniform. Despite Spending Only a Short Time with the Cubs, He Is Still a Fan Favorite Who Died Way Too Soon.

How can you not like an overweight, mullet-wearing, Fu Manchu mustache–growing guy who smoked while riding a stationary bike and defended his beer belly by saying: "I've never seen anyone on the DL [disabled list] with pulled fat"?[73]

Rodney Roy Beck, aka Rod Beck, aka "Shooter," was an instant success in Chicago, catapulting the 1998 Cubs to the playoffs thanks to his best season as a closer, during which he notched a career-high 51 saves that earned him an eternal spot in the Cubs' galaxy of stars. However, like Chicago-bred comedians with bulbous proportions and an appetite for drinking and drugs who died too soon, Beck would leave everyone wanting more.

Chicago icons John Belushi and Chris Farley died from drug overdoses, both at the age of 33. Farley's death came in 1998, the year that Beck ignited the town with his large personality and belly. Like Belushi and Farley, Beck died from a drug overdose, his coming in 2007 at the age of 38. Coors Light, Kool cigarettes, and fun times were part of the package when you hung out with Beck, who summed up his no-frills approach to the game simply: "I'm old school. I was taught that ice was for bourbon, not for your arm."[74] Beck never became comfortable with the trappings of stardom—as witnessed by the mobile home trailer he lived in for a season.

Beck proved himself to be a solid closer during seven seasons in San Francisco for the Giants before joining the Cubs in 1998. Chicago showed Beck their confidence in his abilities, giving him a $3.6-million contract for 1998 (the seventh-highest salary on the team). Beck responded with 51 saves.

The team reached the playoffs thanks to a magical game with Shakespearean proportions. Tied at the end of the regular season, the Cubs and Giants were forced to play the famous "163rd Game." This was, in effect, a one-game playoff with the winner advancing to the actual playoffs. Beck's former club and his current one had one night to see which team would continue playing. "It was the first year after Harry Caray had passed," Beck recalled to *Chicago Tribune* columnist Fred Mitchell a few years later:

> Then we had that eerie night of the 163rd game when we had to play the Giants. Then to beat the team that ultimately was still paying me was funny. So they paid me to beat them that night. Dusty [Baker] was in the other dugout, and the Harry Caray balloon was floating in the air. It was eerie.[75]

It would also be the highlight of his career. When Beck was recalling that game to Mitchell in 2003, he was living in his mobile home behind the outfield walls of the AAA Iowa Cubs stadium, hoping for a second chance at the big leagues. What nobody knew at the time was that Beck was already in a gradual decline that would ultimately lead to his death.

The Cubs made Beck their second-highest paid player in 1999 with a $5.5-million contract eclipsed only by Sammy Sosa's $9-million deal. Sadly, it was to be the last year that Beck would entertain fans at the Friendly Confines. He then signed with Boston for three years; from 1999 to 2002, his production declined as he notched only nine saves and a 9–5 record with a 3.46 ERA.

Reconstructive surgery on his right elbow forced Beck to miss the entire 2002 season. In the wake of his surgery, no team offered him a major league contract. The Cubs offered him a minor league contract, which Beck signed. Thinking he would only be in Des Moines (home of the AAA Cubs affiliate) for a few weeks, Beck decided to drive his motor home to Iowa and live in it instead of going through the hassle of renting a short-term apartment. Beck parked his RV approximately 400 feet behind the center-field fence, along the Des Moines River.

The pitcher welcomed anyone to stop by and chat, drink a beer, eat a hot dog, or just hang out. It was an unprecedented move by a legitimate big league star. A blue neon sign in the shape of a martini glass was Beck's signal to the world that he was ready for company. If the light was on, it meant anyone could stop by. "I promise you, that light never goes off," Cubs reliever Phil Norton told Wayne Drehs for a 2003 *ESPN The Magazine* article. "I'm not even sure it has a switch."[76]

All were welcome at Beck's trailer. Some fans brought provisions, but if the beer was anything other than Coors Light, he'd politely refuse, pulling a silver can from the cooler under his RV instead and offering his visitors a can as well. "I didn't want to get a liquor license," Beck joked with Drehs, "so I just give the stuff away for free."

"A fireman stopped by the other night," Beck told Mitchell for his *Chicago Tribune* column while they sat outside his mobile home along the river in 2003:

> A state policeman stopped by. At first I thought I was in trouble. But they would just come by and ask for an autograph and hang out. And I've had some people come by when they weren't on duty and have a beer or whatever. It's been quite the adventure.

Late in the 2003 season, the San Diego Padres gave Beck a chance while reliever Trevor Hoffman was recuperating from a shoulder injury. Shooter notched 20 saves in his limited time with the Padres. They would be the last saves of his professional career. What none of his baseball colleagues realized was that somewhere between Des Moines and San Diego, Beck had developed an addiction to cocaine.[77]

Shooter's life began to unravel. His wife, Stacey, and various friends confronted the pitcher, who resisted at first, but finally admitted to his problem. He went into rehab, then relapsed. Stacey told him he would only be allowed back in the family home if he agreed to get help again.[78] This time the Padres were involved and supportive, placing him in a 30-day rehabilitation program that was followed by six weeks of outpatient therapy. But it didn't stick, and by August, he had pitched only 24 innings in 26 games with a 6.38 ERA. The Padres released Beck, who went back to drugs. Thrown out of his home by his wife, Shooter moved into a nearby house. It was in that home that Beck died on June 23, 2007.

ESPN reporter Amy K. Nelson described the scene that police officers found in Shooter's home:

> Police arrived to a den of cocaine and crack, with pipes in about every feasible place Beck could stash his daily tools of addiction. . . . The baseball player was long gone on that June day, but there were a few remnants of his prolific career,

and reminders of who he once was. Among those was a white ceramic plate in the form of a baseball. Atop it lay a rolled-up dollar bill, Beck's 1993 San Francisco Giants baseball card, and a dusting of cocaine over the plate.[79]

Beck wasn't the first MLB player to die of a drug overdose, but he is the only Cubs player known to have allowed drugs to take his life. Other players who lost their lives due to cocaine include Rod Scurry (1992), Eric Show (1994), Darrell Porter (2002), and Ken Caminiti (2004). Caminiti is the only one whose fame was on the same level as Beck's. None of them was as entertaining.

Shooter's nickname was apt considering the brief, meteoric time during which Cubs fans came to know and love this boisterous pitcher. While we delight in recalling the fun times Beck created and inspired, it would be irresponsible to fail to acknowledge the pain addiction can cause to family and fans alike. Anyone suffering from cocaine addiction can seek help from a number of organizations, including the Coalition against Drug Abuse (DrugAbuse.com) and Cocaine Anonymous (CA.org).

"This is not a game or an occupation; it's a lifestyle," Beck told Drehs in 2003. "So if I give this up, what the hell else am I going to do?" Beck was laid to rest in his casket wearing a full Chicago Cubs uniform, making him forever a Cubs player in more than just fans' memories.

Chapter 39

Greatest Coaching Meltdown
in Recorded History

The Single Greatest Rant by a Professional Coach Is Recited by Diehard Cubs Fans by Heart. Knowing How Inflammatory the Rant Was, It Took This Former Cubs Manager 25 Years Before He Would Listen to It.

We wrap up our examination of memorable moments of vice in Cubs history with the most hilarious, profane, and offensive tirade in sports history.

"The greatest rant in sports history," proclaimed ESPN sports business expert Darren Rovell, was "Chicago Cubs manager Lee Elia's unbelievable tirade."[80]

What separates Chicago Cubs manager Lee Elia's rant on April 29, 1983, from nearly all others in sports history was that Elia's was directed at the Cubs fan base rather than players, coaches, or media members. It is also the only known coaching rant that has been used by politicians for self-motivation. In 2008, ESPN reported that former Illinois Governor Jim Thompson "used to play Elia's rant to psyche himself up before a big political speech."[81]

Before addressing Elia's tirade, we feel an obligation to share some of the other infamous moments of sports lunacy in order to put Elia's bile-spewing, curse-laden rant in proper perspective. Here are some of the most unforgettable rants in sports history, none of which come close to Elia's explosion.

John McEnroe, tennis player, to umpire Edward James at the 1981 Wimbledon final about a questionable call:

> You can't be serious, man. YOU CANNOT be serious! That ball was on the line. Chalk flew up. It was clearly in! How can you possibly call that out? He's walking over. Everybody knows it in the whole stadium and you call it out! You guys are the absolute pits of the world! You know that?

John Chaney, Temple University coach, to John Calipari of the University of Massachusetts during a postgame press conference in 1994 moments after Massachusetts had just beaten Temple 56–55:

I'll kill you! You remember that! When I see you, I'm going to kick your ass!

Allen Iverson, Philadelphia 76ers guard, at a press conference in 2002 when he was asked about missing a recent practice:

I'm supposed to be a franchise player and we in here talking about practice? I mean, listen, we talking about practice! Not a game. Not a game. We talking about practice. . . . We talking about practice? How silly is that? We talking about practice. I know I supposed to be there. I know I supposed to lead by example. I know that. And I'm not shoving it aside, like it don't mean anything. I know it's important. I do. I honestly do. But we talking about practice, man. What are we talking about? Practice? We talking about practice, man.

Jim Mora Sr. of the New Orleans Saints in 1996 after watching his Saints take a 7–6 halftime lead at the Carolina Panthers before losing 16–7; the following day Mora resigned:

That second half we just got our asses totally kicked. We couldn't do diddily poo offensively. We couldn't make a first down. We couldn't run the ball. We didn't try to run the ball. We couldn't complete a pass. We sucked. In the second half, we sucked. We couldn't stop the run. Every time they got the ball, they went down and got points. We got our ass totally kicked in the second half. That's what it boiled down to. It was a horseshit performance in the second half. Horseshit! I'm totally embarrassed. I'm totally ashamed. The coaches did a horrible job. The players did a horrible job. We got our ass kicked in the second half. It sucked! It stunk!

Jim Mora Sr., Indianapolis Colts head coach, on November 25, 2001, couldn't believe a reporter's question about his team reaching the playoffs moments after watching the Colts lose 40–21 to San Francisco, which dropped the team to a 4–6 record (the Colts finished 6–10 and did not make the playoffs):

Playoffs? Wha— Playoffs?! Don't talk about playoffs! Are you kidding me? Playoffs? I just hope we can win a game!

Herm Edwards, New York Jets head coach, in 2002, responding to a mid-week question by a reporter who asked if the coach had to convince his team to not give up on the season after losing to Cleveland days earlier which dropped the team to a 2–5 record overall:

> You play to win the game! Hello? You PLAY to WIN the game. You don't play to just play it. That's the great thing about sports, you play to win it. I don't care if you don't have any wins, you play to win. When you start telling me it doesn't matter, then retire! Get out! Because it matters.

Dennis Green, Arizona Cardinals head coach, on October 16, 2006, after watching his Arizona Cardinals squander a 23–10 lead at start of the fourth quarter to the Chicago Bears, who won 24–23 despite committing six turnovers and accumulating just 168 total yards of offense:

> The Bears are what we thought they were! That's why we took the damn field! If you want to crown them, then crown their ass! But they are who we thought they were! And we let them off the hook!

Mike Gundy, Oklahoma State University head coach, on September 22, 2007, yelling at a newspaper columnist who had written a recent column about the benching of sophomore quarterback Bobby Reid:

> I'm a man! I'm 40! I'm not a kid!

Mike Singletary, San Francisco 49ers head coach, on October 26, 2008, in a post-game press conference about why he banished tight end Vernon Davis to the locker room after the player was flagged for taunting in a 34–13 loss to the Seattle Seahawks:

> I'm from the old school, and I believe this: I would rather play with ten people and get penalized all the way until we got to do something else rather than play with eleven and know, right now, that that person is not sold out to be part of this team. It is more about them, than it is the team. Cannot play with them! Cannot win with them! Cannot coach with them! Can't do it.

With the exception of Green and Mora Sr., the coaches and players quoted above remained in their sport after their infamous comments. For Green and Mora Sr., those meltdowns marked their final season with their respective teams.

In fact, Mora Sr. quit the day after his assessment of the Saints, leaving assistant Rick Venturi to take over for the final eight games of the season.

But none of those verbal explosions was in baseball. Baseball managers are accustomed to blowing off steam, and are thrown out of games on a regular basis. Sometimes they are justifiably upset over a call on the field. Other times, it's a strategic move to inspire their squad. Earl Weaver, Billy Martin, and former Cubs skipper Lou Piniella were masters at the ejection, often providing more entertainment while being thrown out than the game offered the fans that day.

There is one notable rant in baseball history that came close to Elia's, even going so far as to leave one reporter bleeding. In 1993, Kansas City Royals manager Hal McRae, caught up in the moment, began throwing things in his office, eventually hitting *Topeka Capital-Journal* reporter Alan Eskew, cutting the journalist's face as he and his colleagues tried to leave McRae's office. The final line of McRae's diatribe is still often quoted in sports today:

> Don't ask me all these stupid-ass fucking questions. No. I'm sick and fucking tired of all these fucking stupid-ass questions every fucking night. Why in the fuck would I hit Brett for fucking Miller? Miller started the fucking game. He's playing against a left-handed fucking pitcher. Brett is not playing against left-handed pitchers. Why in the fuck would I bat for Miller? You think I'm a goddamn fool? I'm tired of all these stupid-ass questions every night. And stay out of here asking all these dumbass questions. Excuse me. Excuse me. Cocksuckers ask me that stupid-ass shit every motherfucking night. Stupid-ass motherfucking shit! I'm not taking no shit off you guys. And I'm not taking no shit off the fucking players. I'm sick and tired. I'm fed up with every fucking thing. No shit from you guys. No shit from you fucking players. And yet, they can do any motherfucking thing they want to do. I'm sick and tired of all this bullshit. Now, put that in your fucking pipe and smoke it!

Although he wasn't let go immediately following this rant, McRae was fired midway through the next season.

Which brings us to the Cubs' 1983 season, that started off miserably. Elia's reign in Chicago was known for losing. In 1982, Elia's squad finished 73–89, and the first few weeks of 1983 were no better. Friday games at Wrigley Field are usually a festive time for Cubs fans, who find ways to miss work to attend afternoon games. But on April 29, 1983, only 9,391 fans turned out to the ballpark to see the Cubs drop to 5–14 in the standings after a 4–3 loss to Tommy Lasorda's Los Angeles Dodgers. While leaving the field, Cubs players Keith Moreland, Larry Bowa, and Ron Cey allegedly had beer tossed on them.

After the game, Elia let the Cubs fan base know exactly what he thought of them:

> We've got all these so-called fucking fans that come out here and say they're Cub fans that are supposed to be behind you ripping every fucking thing you do. I'll tell you one fucking thing, I hope we get fucking hotter than shit, just to stuff it up them 3,000 fucking people that show up every fucking day, because if they're the real Chicago fucking fans, they can kiss my fucking ass right downtown and PRINT IT!
>
> My fucking ass. What the fuck am I supposed to do, go out there and let my fucking players get destroyed every day and be quiet about it? For the fucking nickel-dime people to show up? The motherfuckers don't even work. That's why they're out at the fucking games. They ought to go out and get a fucking job and find out what it's like to go out and earn a fucking living. Eighty-five percent of the fucking world is working. The other fifteen come out here. A fucking playground for the cocksuckers! Rip them motherfuckers! Rip them fucking cocksuckers like the fucking players! We got guys busting their fucking ass and them fucking people boo? And that's the Cubs? My fucking ass! (GeoVerse™133)

Believe it or not, Elia was allowed to keep his job after his undressing of Cubs fans. However, the bad relationship didn't last long. By August, he was fired for reasons that had nothing to do with his embarrassing and hilarious rant. In less than two seasons, Elia had amassed a .446 managing record (127–158), making his mark in Cubs history one that has more to do with humor than honor.

Said former Cubs public relations executive Bob Ibach, "When we're all dead and gone and they revise the dictionary, under the word *tirade*, it is going to simply say, 'see Elia, Lee.'"[82]

Section V

Innovation

Chapter 40

Cubs' Weeghman
'The First Fast Food Tycoon'

*Fast Food as We Know It Began with the Cubs. Whether
It's Fast Food Chains on the Way to the Ballpark or the
Food Fans Eat While at the Game, Food Made Quickly
for People on the Go Was Invented by a Cubbie
and Quickly Copied Around the World.*

Twenty years before White Castle opened its first restaurant and more than
50 years before McDonald's began franchising its menu, Chicago Cubs owner
Charles Weeghman became one of the founders of the fast food industry, earning
the title "the first fast-food tycoon"[1] and forever changing both the sports we
watch and the food we eat.

Many documents incorrectly cite White Castle, founded in 1921,[2] as the first
fast-food restaurant. It wasn't—that business merely took Weeghman's idea and
expanded on it. Other historians incorrectly cite McDonald's as the first fast-
food restaurant, but that is also wrong. During the 1950s, McDonald's CEO
Ray Kroc merely made the concept of franchising a worldwide success, taking
a single local burger stand restaurant and turning it into a national, and then
global, phenomenon.

Kroc, a native of Oak Park, Illinois, grew up a Cubs fan and even tried to buy
the team in 1972, but was rebuffed by Philip Wrigley and had to settle for buying
the San Diego Padres instead. Wrigley's refusal to sell did not sit well with Kroc.
In his 1992 memoir Grinding It Out, Kroc wrote that, Wrigley's refusal to even
listen to Kroc's offer made him "madder than hell, because Wrigley is just sitting
on that team. He hasn't done a damn thing to improve them, but won't give them
up and let someone else do it. It's idiotic."[3]

It was Weeghman who made fast food popular thanks to his Weeghman's Lunch Room restaurants and Weeghman's bakeries. His 15 restaurants throughout Chicago sought to do one thing and do it well: provide quick food service in a clean environment for hard-working Chicagoans. His first restaurant opened in 1901 on the southeast corner of Adams and Wells Streets in Chicago's downtown Loop neighborhood and was an immediate success. Initially just a luncheonette that catered to working people during the midday rush, Weeghman's restaurants eventually became 24-hour businesses averaging 5,000 customers a location per day—with the exception of his main location, which handled many more.

Outfitted with sparkling white tiles to emphasize their cleanliness, Weeghman's restaurants served only cold food to allow for quick turnaround times on orders. Seating consisted of one-armed school desks in order to squeeze the maximum number of seats into the restaurants. Weeghman also operated bakeries known for their pastries; customers waited in line for his baked goods, as well as his quick sandwiches.

Weeghman often employed new practices that later became standard in the industry. In addition to offering the same food at each location, order tickets were hole-punched to speed up the order-taking and payment processes since customers didn't need to wait for their bill when they finished their meal. This allowed his most popular restaurant, located at Madison and Dearborn Streets, to serve a staggering 35,000 patrons per day.

Weeghman changed food and sports history thanks to his recognition that everybody needs to eat and nobody likes to wait, whether during their lunch break from work or between innings at a game.

"What Charley really wanted was to continue his move up the social ladder and become a gentleman of society, a sportsman," wrote author Stuart Shea in his book *Wrigley Field: The Unauthorized Biography*:

> Handsome, rakish, and sporting dandified outfits, gardenias in his lapel, and bowler hats, Weeghman was enthusiastic enough to win over even the most cynical local reporters.
>
> As the money rolled in from his restaurants, Weeghman began to diversify. He owned a theater at 58 West Madison Street in downtown Chicago and also invested in a pool hall, motion picture houses, and even a film production company. Baseball would be next.[4]

In 1911, Weeghman tried and failed to purchase the St. Louis Cardinals. Undaunted, he turned his sights on a minor league, the Federal League, and began a team in Chicago. The team went by several names, including the ChiFeds and the Buns (in reference to Weeghman's popular pastries), but were officially named the Whales. Always looking to provide the best to his patrons, Weeghman built a new ballpark for the team, then called Weeghman Park but known today as Wrigley Field. It was in this new stadium that Weeghman would continue to change the world.

Having earned his fortune from fast-food eateries, Weeghman installed something new to the game at Weeghman Park: permanent concession stands, an innovation now taken for granted at every stadium in the world. It was Weeghman, the food magnate and visionary, who pioneered the idea.

Weeghman also changed who attended games as much as the amenities they enjoyed when they got there. In 1914, Weeghman was fighting to turn his team and the upstart Federal League into a serious baseball option for fans, competing with the National League's Cubs and the American League's White Stockings in Chicago. It wasn't enough to merely build the best ballpark in baseball; Weeghman had to fill the stands and ensure that fans enjoyed their visit and would return. Pursuing that goal, Weeghman created the promotional idea of Ladies Day, which allowed women to enter free on Fridays. Not only did this expand his fan base and fill seats, it also provided more customers to buy food and drinks at games.

To help ensure fans would enjoy their experience at the game, Weeghman also instituted a new rule that fans take for granted today: they can keep foul balls and home runs that fall in the stands. It was a new and refreshing idea for attendees to be able to keep a souvenir from the game.

The innovations worked. Despite being the third team in a two-league city, Weeghman's Whales proved to be a concern for their competitors. While the Federal League did not release attendance figures, leaving that choice up to individual owners, Weeghman revealed that despite losing approximately $27,000[5] on the 1914 season, the Whales drew an estimated 312,000 fans,[6] the highest attendance figure in the league. That same season the Cubs, who finished fourth in the NL, had only 202,516 in attendance. The White Stockings, playing in a brand-new ballpark (the largest in Chicago), drew 469,290.

First in fast food, concession stands, Ladies Day promotions, and keeping baseballs hit into the stands, the Cubs' Weeghman etched his name in baseball and business history—which is just the way he wanted it. However, success was only part of Weeghman's story. His failures would define the Cubs even more than his restaurants or hyperbolic stories of his success.

Chapter 41

'Billboarding' Baseball Through Radio Broadcasts

The Multibillion-Dollar Baseball Broadcasting Industry Began with the Cubs, Whose Owner Pioneered Contemporary Business Marketing.

"I watch a lot of baseball on the radio," former President Gerald Ford famously once said. His malapropism may be technically incorrect, but sports fans everywhere understood exactly what the Michigan native, who cheered for the Detroit Tigers, meant.

Charles Weeghman may have built the ballpark where the Cubs play, but it was William Wrigley Jr. who made it a home to the millions of fans who flock to the park. Wrigley was a marketing genius whose renegade experiments changed sports forever.

Wrigley came to be a part of the Cubs in large part because Weeghman simply couldn't afford the team. Certainly, sports fans should hold a certain level of respect for Weeghman, but how much is up for debate. After all, had Weeghman been as much of a businessman as he was a showman, he wouldn't have needed Wrigley's help. Overextending himself in an effort to appear more impressive than he truly was would eventually cost Weeghman his ownership of the Cubs.

When he first moved to Chicago at the end of the nineteenth century, Weeghman worked the night shift at King's Restaurant, located in the heart of the Loop at 28 N. Wells Street. King's late night crowd consisted largely of journalists and gamblers, and Weeghman befriended both groups. The journalists were important to Weeghman because, like his eventual partner, Wrigley, he was a masterful marketer who encouraged local newspapers to write exaggerated stories about him (with any errors going uncorrected by the social climber). Nearly every newspaper story from the early part of the twentieth century used the same unchecked, inaccurate narrative when it came to Weeghman's rags-to-riches life: he was a small-town boy from Indiana who earned $10 a week as a waiter when he arrived in Chicago. He saved his money and invested his life savings of $2,800 to open a lunchroom that became an empire, making him a millionaire with a net worth of roughly $8 million—which he spent on building the most beautiful ballpark in the world.

The problem is that this story is not exactly true. Weeghman may have started as a waiter at King's, but the restaurant quickly promoted him to assistant manager, a position in which he earned nearly four times as much per week. After eight years working at King's, Weeghman only had $300 to invest in his first restaurant; the rest of the $2,500 needed was borrowed or came from partners Aaron Field ($700) and Frank Conway ($1,600).[7] However, since the fictionalized story was more appealing, journalists often ignored the truth—and Weeghman never corrected those who left out the accurate details.

As for being a millionaire, Weeghman couldn't actually afford the Cubs when he bought them for $500,000 in 1915. He had already built Weeghman Park for $250,000 in 1914; though it was a beautiful venue, he lost money the first season. And while the man was rich by some measures, his claim of having a net worth of $8 million was based on his own unverified assessment.

Both the exaggerated stories and the need for financial bailouts would become a pattern for Weeghman. But he knew a great deal when he saw one, and buying the Cubs for $500,000, moving them to Weeghman Park, and turning the stadium into the home of the National League Cubs was a no-brainer, even if he didn't have the money to do it himself. Weeghman made a list of the wealthiest businessmen in Chicago and convinced them to join as investors. Wrigley was one of those investors, and his initial minority stake in the organization grew as Weeghman borrowed funds over the following seasons, offering Cubs stock in exchange for cash.

World War I was bad for the restaurant business. The government rationed goods and drafted customers into military service. Decreasing profits soon forced Weeghman to close restaurants across Chicago. By December 1918, he also had to sell his shares in the Cubs to Wrigley and resign as president of the Cubs.

While Cubs fans can thank Weeghman for building the shrine that is Wrigley Field, they should also be thankful that Wrigley was there to save the franchise with his deep pockets and forward thinking. Like Weeghman, Wrigley believed in marketing on a large scale; in fact, he was also one of the pioneers of the direct mail business. Today that means mailboxes stuffed with unwanted advertisements and promotions, but in 1915 it meant free gum. Wrigley mailed four sticks of gum to every address with a phone number in the nation, approximately 1.5 million households. The tactic was enormously successful, and laid the groundwork for even bigger promotions to come.

In 1925, radio station WMAQ's program director Judith Waller approached Wrigley with an intriguing idea: would the Cubs consider broadcasting their regular-season games on the radio?[8] Wrigley, sitting in his office atop the tallest building in Chicago at that time (the famous Wrigley Building), considered the idea.

On August 5, 1921, Pittsburgh's KDKA had become the first station to broadcast a baseball game (between the Pirates and the Phillies). In 1922, postseason games were regularly broadcast, but nobody had considered broadcasting regular-season games on a consistent basis. Nobody, that is, until Wrigley.

The risk was obvious: why give away games for free via radio when there were still empty seats in the ballpark? It wasn't an unreasonable concern. Chicago Blackhawks owner Bill Wirtz infuriated hockey fans for refusing to televise games into the twenty-first century for the very same reason. (After Wirtz's death in 2007, the first thing his son, Rocky, did when he took over the club was to put the Blackhawks back on television. The team's popularity immediately soared and in a four-year span, the Blackhawks won two Stanley Cup championships, twice the number Rocky's father saw the franchise win during his four-decade stewardship of the organization.)

Wrigley knew broadcasting Cubs games would be risky. But sending free gum to more than one million people had been risky as well. In 1915, Wrigley had gambled on the assumption that if someone could afford a phone, he or she could afford a pack of gum. They just needed to try it first to see that they would like it. Wrigley decided to take a chance that the same principal would apply to radio and the Cubs.

On April 14, 1925, both WMAQ's Russell Pratt and WGN's Quin Ryan provided live radio broadcasts of the Cubs' 8–2 win against the Pittsburgh Pirates. It was the first time a professional sports team had embraced the new technology during the regular season. Wrigley's decision would forever change how fans experience sports around the world. WMAQ and WGN continued broadcasting games throughout the 1925 season, though not for every home game. However, both stations provided coverage of the Cubs when they weren't broadcasting games.

Wrigley was thrilled by the impact the broadcasts had on potential customers who executives had always believed were too far away to reach.

Explained Eldon L. Ham in his book *Broadcasting Baseball: The History of the National Pastime on Television and Radio*:

> From 1925 through 1931 teams that featured no radio broadcasting experienced aggregate attendance increases of 27 percent while the Cubs, a team that had been increasing its radio exposure throughout the period, saw its own attendance skyrocket by 117 percent, more than four times the average increase for teams without radio. In the early days, such results seemed counter-intuitive: why go to the game if the game comes to you? But the real phenomenon at work is called "billboarding." Baseball was promoting itself over the airwaves, for radio was everywhere and, thus, so were the Cubs. As a direct result, the public became more and more hooked on baseball. Wrigley was elated. Rather than reducing attendance, the billboarding effect was actually increasing the game's popularity by quantum leaps.
>
> With radio spreading baseball throughout the city and beyond, more fans could follow the team and, more importantly, more non-fans could be reached who were able to follow the Cubs and develop an interest. Broadcasting was even able to reach fans in cars, for manufacturers were installing radio receivers in automobiles as early as 1923. Better yet, the geographic reach of the team had been expanded. Listeners in Iowa, Wisconsin, Indiana and downstate Illinois were able to follow the Cubs, extending the fan base to many states and creating a huge Midwest following for the team. Well into the New Millennium, the Cubs still own a strong fan base in those rural areas, and every summer home game finds thousands of fans from charter buses descending on Wrigley from Des Moines to Peoria and South Bend.[9]

What Weeghman had built, Wrigley improved upon and expanded, creating a legion of Cubs fans upon which the sun never sets—all because of billboarding the Friendly Confines to fans beyond the horizon. Today, fans can hear radio broadcasts of every MLB team and can pay to receive games not broadcast in their area. Each team controls local radio deals, so numbers are difficult to pinpoint for radio revenue. But in 2013, MLB renewed its television rights to ESPN, Turner Broadcasting, and Fox Sports for a combined $12.4 billion.

Chapter 42

The Manager Who Created Modern Baseball

Despite Dying Broke, One Cubbie Was Responsible for Several Innovations in the Game, Including One That Led to a Billion-Dollar Industry in Which Thousands of Fans Participate Annually.

We have already explored the deep-seated racism of former Cubs player/manager Adrian "Cap" Anson. But Anson also had a positive impact on baseball—in fact, the sport would not be the same without him. It may be hard for contemporary fans to realize, but some of the most strategic elements of the game did not always exist. It took the creative minds of baseball innovators such as Anson to develop the game that we know today. Anson was a pioneer when it came to ideas such as pitching rotations, the hit-and-run, hand signals, and team-sponsored spring training. As is the case with much of baseball history, some critics have offered claims that other individuals were responsible for some of these inventions. You can decide for yourself based on the evidence gathered here.

Pitching Rotations: This is the least-debated of Anson's innovations; nearly all baseball historians agree that the Cubs squad of 1880 forever altered the game. In 1880, Chicago's National League team (then called the White Stockings) finished first in the league with a 67–17 record, 15 games ahead of the Providence Grays. (The Grays were led by pitcher/manager John Montgomery Ward, a pioneer himself who was philosophically opposed to Anson—a fact that will be important in our discussion of Anson's place in baseball history.) Chicago's success came after a mediocre season the previous year during which they barely broke .500 (46–33), finishing fourth in the NL. Why the big difference between the two seasons? Two pitchers, Larry Corcoran and Fred Goldsmith, and the way Anson used them to give his team a competitive advantage.

Prior to the 1880 season, baseball teams used pitchers in the same way as most hockey teams use goalies today: employing only one for the majority of games,

215

while also having a backup take the field on occasion. However, Anson had two very good pitchers at his disposal in 1880, and the shrewd manager wanted to get the most out of both of them. For the first time in baseball, two pitchers would share the mound during the season, Corcoran starting 60 games and Goldsmith 24. While two starting pitchers is still a long way from the five that teams usually employ today, this was the first time that multiple pitchers were used in a season as a strategic move, rather than as a necessity due to injury.

The two pitchers also had very different styles, a fact that allowed the team to open the season with a 35–3 mark, including 21 straight wins (still a Cubs record). Wrote Glenn Stout in his book *The Cubs*:

> Corcoran was considered a speed pitcher. Goldsmith, on the other hand, lacked Corcoran's speed but was a pioneer of the curveball. Teams that faced Goldsmith and Corcoran back to back had to adapt to their differing styles, and on occasion Anson even used one man in relief of the other in the same game, making that adaptation even more difficult.[10]

Seeing clear results from using this rotation, Anson evened the balance between the two in 1881, with Corcoran starting 44 games and Goldsmith 39. The result was another first-place finish in the NL. By the end of the century, every team in baseball was using a pitching rotation. Never again would teams rely on only one pitcher to handle nearly all of their games.

The Hit-and-Run: Opinions are split on whether Anson deserves credit for the hit-and-run. Noted baseball historian Bill James wrote in The New Bill James Historical Abstract that credit should go to Boston manager Tommy McCarthy for creating the strategy. However, that assertion appears to be wrong given the evidence of other authors.

James' based his contention on an 1893 interview with Ward, Anson's rival, who credited McCarthy's team with using a new scheme to advance the runner, describing what we would now call the hit-and-run. "It was clear," James surmised, "that Tommy McCarthy and the Boston Beaneaters had developed a new play, the hit-and-run."[11] McCarthy played for the Beaneaters in 1885 and then from 1892 to 1895. It was during his second stint with the organization that McCarthy, according to Ward and later James, created the hit-and-run.

However, by the 1892 season, Ward had reason to refuse to give Anson credit for any innovation that improved the game. In fact, in 1887—six years before his interview denying Anson any credit for the innovation—Ward was thwarted by the bigoted Anson when trying to sign African American players Fleet Walker and George Stovey to the New York Giants. Not only were the Giants a rival of the Cubs, but Ward was an open-minded man who welcomed racial diversity; Anson, on the other hand, was a dyed-in-the-wool racist. While Anson's bigotry was deplorable, it also explains why Ward would want to give credit to anyone other than Anson for any game-improving innovations.

The proof that Anson was actually the first to employ the hit-and-run dates back to an 1877 *Chicago Daily Tribune* article discovered by Anson biographer David L. Fleitz in which the author attempted to explain the new strategy to fans:

> Some chap stated the following conundrum, professing not to understand it: "Why do batsmen strike a ball when a base-runner is half-way to second base on a clever steal?" The answer was found in Thursday's game, when [Cal] McVey started to second base, and Anson hit the ball in the exact spot where [St. Louis' Mike] McGeary had been standing before he ran to his base to catch McVey. It is really a clever batting trick to hit to the right field when it lies all open.[12]

After retiring from baseball, Anson loudly protested that he deserved credit for inventing the hit-and-run. But James dismissed Anson, writing that Anson "was a blowhard and the older he got, the harder he blew. The fact that Cap Anson said, twenty or thirty years after the fact, that his team was using the hit and run play first—that really doesn't mean anything."[13]

James has been a respected baseball authority for decades, but if he had read the *Chicago Daily Tribune* in 1877, he would know that Ward's denial of Anson's invention was biased.

Hand Signals: William "Dummy" Hoy, who lost his hearing as a child, was the first deaf major league baseball player. His rookie season was in 1888 with the Washington Nationals. He played for 14 seasons, pioneering the use of hand signals for balls and strikes along the way. Previously, umpires had only yelled out these calls. However, what few fans know is that this is actually another innovation started by Anson years earlier.

The White Stockings' historic 1880 season was special in many ways, including the fact that it was the first season that a team communicated with hand signals. It began with Anson taking a coaching position in foul territory near third base to help guide his players. (Base coaching was another of Anson's firsts.) While coaching, Anson developed a way to use "hand signals to communicate with players on the field. Pitcher Larry Corcoran picked up on the approach, and after he developed a curveball of his own, he began to signal to his catcher which pitch was coming next by moving around the chaw of tobacco in his cheek."[14]

While Hoy's contribution to the game was significant, the hand signals that he introduced due to his deafness were merely an adaptation of the signs Anson and his players had been using for nearly a decade before Hoy's first game.

Spring Training: Whether Anson actually invented this tradition is among the most debatable of his claims to history. During his early years in baseball, Anson enjoyed drinking as much as any player. But as he grew older, Anson extolled the virtues of good eating, clean living, and abstinence from alcohol, smoking, and womanizing. Yet despite his good example, nearly all of his players reported to the team at the start of the season overweight, out of shape, and in need of several weeks of practice to get into playing condition. In March 1885, Anson took the team to Hot Springs, Arkansas, with the express idea of getting them physically fit and ready to play baseball.

While this idea wasn't entirely new, Anson's intent—namely to have the players lose their excess weight and get in playing shape—was a new approach. Teams had of course played preseason games in the past. For example, in 1870 the White Stockings and the Cincinnati Red Stockings played several exhibition games in New Orleans, while the previous year, the New York Mutuals had played exhibition games against a local team in New Orleans.[15] But between 1869 and 1885, no one took the idea of spring training seriously—in fact, that term didn't even exist then. It was only after Anson, who wanted "to sweat the winter fat off"[16] his players, began going to Hot Springs in 1885 that rivals began to follow suit.

It only made sense that other teams would mimic the White Stockings, who dominated baseball during the 1880s. They finished first in the NL in 1885 and repeated as champs in 1886, thanks in part to being in better shape than their rivals at the start of the season. Finishing first five times in seven seasons, clearly the team was doing something worth copying. "Anson and Spalding may not have invented 'spring training' but they made the concept a viable one," Fleitz wrote, "and all other major league teams followed their lead in subsequent years."[17]

In *Under the March Sun: The Story of Spring Training*, baseball historian Charles Fountain clarified what Anson did differently from anyone else when it came to spring training:

> Cap Anson did two things that his spring-trip predecessors had not. He won championships in his first two seasons after bringing a team south, which convinced him to make spring training a regular affair. And he brought along a newspaper reporter to publicize the trip. Both played no small part in building the legend that he had been first.[18]

Spring training has of course become big business since Anson's time. In fact, the *SportsBusiness Journal* reported in 2012[19] that more than $1 billion was spent between 1988 and 2011 on spring-training facilities in Florida and Arizona. The same report cited figures showing that local cities and counties in Florida and Arizona received approximately $11.5 million in 2011 in revenue generated during spring training. This estimate would be even larger except that the spring-training homes of the Atlanta Braves (Champion Stadium in Florida) and both the Arizona Diamondbacks and Colorado Rockies (Salt River Fields at Talking Stick in Arizona) are privately owned and do not report their revenue figures.

In that same 2012 report, the Cubs' HoHoKam Park was No. 1 in revenue generated by a single team in its own park, creating $1.2 million for the City of Mesa, Arizona. The most revenue generated overall went to the city of Peoria, Arizona, which received an estimated $2.7 million in revenue from the Peoria Sports Complex, spring-training home of both the Seattle Mariners and the San Diego Padres.

Despite his many innovations and the future wealth they would generate, Anson died penniless in 1922. The elaborate tombstone at his grave in Oak Woods Cemetery in Chicago was paid for by a special fund created by the National League to honor one of the most inventive men in baseball history. (GeoVerse™ 144)

Chapter 43

Manufacturing Genius and Global Pioneer

The First Chicago Sports Icon to Walk Away from the Game at the Height of His Career Wasn't Michael Jordan. Rather It Was a Cubs Pitcher Who Became the First to Globalize a Sport.

It seems odd that a company begun by a Cubs pitcher would become the official manufacturer of balls for the National Basketball Association, the Women's National Basketball Association, the Beach Volleyball tour, and the Little League World Series, but not Major League Baseball—well, at least not anymore.

Albert Goodwill Spalding had a short career as a major league player/manager not because his talents were limited, but because his success in the business world led him to end his playing days. What the Cubs (then called the White Stockings) lost when he left would prove to be the rest of the world's gain. Wrote Peter Golenbock in his book Wrigleyville, "Albert Goodwill Spalding was the game's George Washington, the Father of Professional Baseball. Spalding [had] far-reaching, ambitious plans, both for himself and for the game of baseball. . . . Spalding loomed over the game of baseball that he first described as America's Pastime."[20]

After his first five seasons pitching for the Boston Red Stockings (1871–75), Spalding was lured to Chicago by team president William Hulbert, who offered the pitcher the princely sum of $4,000 to become player/manager of the White Stockings. Having notched a record of 204–53 in Boston, the right-handed Spalding had proven his ability to pitch. His managing skills were untested, but Hulbert had faith that the Illinois native who had become Boston's star player would turn the team into a contender.

Hulbert's intuition about both business and baseball were unparalleled. A wealthy coal merchant who loved the game, Hulbert became the White Stocking's first president in 1871. Disappointed at the failures of his team from 1871 to 1875, Hulbert decided that to fix the problems with his team, he would first have to fix even bigger problems in the game.

From 1871 to 1875, the team that would eventually become the Cubs played in the National Association of Professional Base Ball Players, otherwise known as the NA. But in 1876, Hulbert huddled with like-minded executives from teams in Boston, Cincinnati, Hartford, Louisville, New York, Philadelphia, and St. Louis. These men felt that the NA players had too much control of the game and knew nothing about business; they therefore decided to form a new league. On February 2, 1876, they created the National League of Professional Base Ball Clubs, otherwise known as the National League. While it's true that the discord between players and owners dates back to Hulbert and the founding of the NL, it's also true that no other professional sports league has lasted as continuously as has the NL. Hulbert was as much a businessman as he was a baseball fan, and the two traits combined to change history. (GeoVerse™155)

Hulbert's plans for his team, now playing in the NL, hinged on one player: Spalding. Not only did Hulbert offer Spalding a pay raise to leave Boston for Chicago, he also gave the player/manager a cut of all gate receipts. A businessman at heart, Spalding understood that his own earnings would depend on the team's success. Spalding made an immediate impact, leading the White Stockings to the franchise's first NL championship in his first season (1876), going 47–12 with a 1.75 ERA.

But Spalding had business plans of his own beyond playing baseball—and the burgeoning city of Chicago would be the perfect location from which to launch the sporting goods empire of which he dreamed. On February 12, 1876, Spalding and his brother, J. Walter, borrowed $800 from their mother to open a sporting goods store at 118 Randolph Street in Chicago. (GeoVerse™166) Her investment would prove to be a wise one, as Spalding soon convinced NL officials to sign a contract that gave his company, Spalding & Bros., the rights to supply the National League's official baseballs. Spalding's company would hold this right for 100 years, until Rawlings replaced them in 1977. The American League also used Spalding baseballs from 1888 to 1973.

The 1876 season would be Spalding's first and last as a pitcher for Chicago. He moved to first base in 1877—not because his pitching was weak, but because his business was doing so well that he couldn't afford to spend the extra energy, both mental and physical, to pitch every day. But ever the marketer, Spalding wore a special glove manufactured by his company during his last season. Soon Spalding had secured the right to manufacture gloves for major league baseball teams while he was still drawing a paycheck as a player/manager.

Spalding left the playing field after the 1877 season to become secretary of the club, helping Hulbert direct the organization from the front office. Spalding's lasting impact on the game of baseball would prove to be profound. As Glenn Stout wrote in his book *The Cubs*:

> In less than two years, he had not only remade the game but also gained a virtual monopoly over the manufacture and sale of baseball equipment. He retired as an active player at age twenty-seven to run his business and serve as a club official, probably the first professional ballplayer in America to parlay his skill on the diamond into an even more lucrative career in the game off the field. . . . Thus, Spalding inaugurated another grand tradition of Chicago Cubs baseball, one since followed by both later owners, such as Philip K. Wrigley, and the Tribune Company. For much of their history, the Cubs have taken a backseat to the larger business interests of management. Spalding used the White Stockings to position himself to make money regardless of how well the White Stockings played. Wins and losses were less important than profit potential, a circumstance that, over time, Cubs fans would find as recognizable as Wrigley Field's outfield ivy.[21]

By age 28, Spalding had become a millionaire who was getting richer by the month. And his firsts kept coming. In 1878, Spalding & Bros. became the first publisher of the official set of rules for major league baseball. In 1887, the company manufactured the first football for the consumer market. And in 1894, they became the official manufacturer of both the rules book and the ball for professional basketball.

When Hulbert died in 1882, he left a massive void at the top of baseball's hierarchy; his foresight and guidance had changed the landscape of American sports forever. Spalding stepped up to fill the void as owner and president of the team until 1891. During his tenure as secretary and then owner, Spalding proved himself to be one of the smartest men in baseball—as well as the richest. The White Stockings dominated baseball during the last decade of the nineteenth century, taking first in the NL five times and second twice.

Globalization is a common term in the twenty-first century, but Spalding was the first person in sports to attempt to take a national game to the rest of the world. His first attempts at globalizing the sport came in 1874, when he helped organize an attempt to spread the game to England. British tastes didn't take to baseball, however, and the tour "fizzled" because "the aggressive, win-at-all costs attitude of the Americans were too foreign for the British to accept."[22] Building on this experience, Spaulding took baseball on a true global tour between the 1888 and 1889 seasons in order to promote the game in foreign lands (as well as to sell more equipment to untapped markets). As the owner of the first major league dynasty team, Spalding pitted a select group of his White Stockings against handpicked players from other teams. In December 1888, Spalding's All-Star World Tour played exhibition games in Australia, making stops along the way in Hawaii, Sri Lanka, Egypt, Italy, and France, showcasing the sport to would-be fans.

Spalding had a unique influence on the world of professional baseball. What Bill Gates was to computer software, Spalding was to the American Pastime. In fact, it was his vision that actually made baseball the sport of the nation. In 1904, Spalding took it upon himself to establish the story of the birth of baseball. A patriot given to mythmaking and storytelling, Spalding set up a commission of seven sports executives to determine the true origin of the sport. After three years, the commission declared that Abner Doubleday had created baseball in 1839 in Cooperstown, New York. Doubleday was a Union army officer who had overseen the first shot at Fort Sumter at the beginning of the Civil War and later survived the Battle of Gettysburg. It made for a good story (and is the reason why the National Baseball Hall of Fame is located in Cooperstown)—but it was more fiction than fact.

In 1839, Doubleday was a student at West Point, not in Cooperstown, and there is no evidence that he ever played a game like baseball. In fact, he was a serious military officer who would have been surprised to learn that he had supposedly "invented" a sport. What's more, according to John Thorn, Major League Baseball's official historian, the game of baseball was already being played in several big cities during the early part of the eighteenth century, particularly in New York, Massachusetts, and Philadelphia.[23] Each of these areas had large settlements of immigrants from England, where a similar game called Rounders was popular. Spalding wanted to establish the idea that baseball was an American invention, rather than an offshoot of a British sport—and adding a Civil War hero to the story couldn't hurt. Pursuing his dream of creating a national pastime that his countrymen would be proud to play, Spalding created the myth of Doubleday, and had no qualms about bending a few facts in the process.

Like so much in baseball, it was all Spalding's idea.

Chapter 44

Vietnam Protests Changed Security Protocol

*The Cubs Were the First Baseball Team to Install a New
Security Measure That Is Now Used in Every Major
Stadium in the Nation—All Because of a Day When
the Fans Weren't as Friendly as Their Confines.*

During the late 1960s and early 1970s, Chicago became the epicenter of violent demonstrations protesting U.S. involvement in the Vietnam Conflict. (Though it is widely referred to as the Vietnam War, the U.S. military presence in Vietnam from 1955 to 1974 was never actually declared a war by Congress. Only Congress can declare war and it has done so just 11 times in United States history, the last occurring during World War II. Military actions in various locations such as Vietnam, Korea, Bosnia, Iraq and Afghanistan are referred to as wars but they are technically conflicts or military actions, not official wars.) The peak of those protests came during the 1968 Democratic National Convention in August of that year, which sparked five days of violence between police and demonstrators, leading to the trial of seven activists who were the first Americans ever charged with the Civil Rights act, created that year, that made it a federal crime to cross state lines to incite a riot. Known as the Chicago Seven, the activists were indicted on March 20, 1969, and after nearly a year of contentious trial deliberations the group was given a guilty verdict by a jury on Feb. 14, 1970, and sentenced to five years in jail. Even their lawyers were found guilty of contempt of court by the judge. Two months later, on April 14, a riot broke out at Wrigley Field after the first home game of the season.

Cubs officials should have taken more precautions given the ugly atmosphere brewing across the country prior to the game that day. To their credit, team officials did make important changes after the incident—and the security measures that the Cubs put in place after what is known as the Home Opener riot would eventually become customary at every major ballpark and stadium in the world. In fact, even entire cities, including Chicago, have adopted some of the same tactics the Cubs established in April 1970 to deal with unruly behavior.

It's hard for anyone who wasn't alive during the Vietnam era to fully grasp the fervor of the emotional protests that were erupting around the country at that time. Just five months prior to the Cubs' home opener, Washington D.C. had witnessed the largest antiwar demonstrations in the nation's history, with an estimated half million protesters flooding the Mall on November 15, 1969. The Kent State shooting, which left four college students dead after members of the National Guard opened fire on a crowd, occurred just 18 days after the Opening Day riots.

Opinions vary about how the riot at Wrigley started, but what everyone can agree on is that after the Cubs defeated the Phillies 5–4 in the Cubs' home opener, all hell broke loose. Reports regarding the incident clearly state that Wrigley's usual "Bleacher Bums" were not part of the incident. Rather, all witnesses seem to agree that it was young fans described as "out-of-towners" who caused the riot—drunken teenagers and young adults who hurled objects onto the field, specifically trying to hit ushers. That is when things got out of hand. Dan Helpingstine described the incident best in his book *The Cubs and the White Sox: A Baseball Rivalry, 1900 to Present*:

> Fans in the bleachers were cursing and throwing things at the Andy Frain ushers who had stepped out to protect the field at game's end. One seventeen-year-old either fell or jumped from the bleachers down to the field. A group of ushers surrounded the teenager and started kicking him. Fans rushed onto the field from other directions and fights ensued. Another fan tried to rip the cap off Glenn Beckert's head and scratched his forehead. Beckert felt fortunate that no damage had been done to his eye. Reportedly, the Bleacher Bums were in the bar across the street and were disgusted when they saw how things had gone out of control at the ballpark. "These kids are animals," one Bum said. "They dress like us and try to look like us. But they're bums, not Bums."
>
> It is one thing for a few objects to be thrown at opposition outfields. It is another when one of your own players feels threatened, the ushers you employ to keep order beat someone senseless, and the ushers themselves are attacked. The Cubs brass responded quickly.[24]

E.G. "Salty" Saltwell, who was in charge of Wrigley Field operations at the time, talked about that day in Stuart Shea's book *Wrigley Field*:

> The Chicago Police Department said they should have forewarned us [of the anti-war protest group. The protestors] were out-of-towners, not locals, that were gathering for the demonstration. [A police official] told us that they were sports fans, and logic would have said if the Cubs were playing, they would have shown up there.
>
> St. Louis had a problem in controlling the crowds at Busch Stadium. My counterpart, Joe McShane, with the Cardinals, heard about it. He called me [and told me about the baskets in front of the Busch Stadium wall.] He said, "C'mon down here, I'll show you what we did."[25]

The Opening Day Riot forged a cooperative spirit between longstanding rivals the Cubs and the Cardinals. Saltwell, who would later serve as team general manager in 1976, took the advice offered by the Cardinals' McShane. In early May 1970, the Cubs installed wire mesh baskets that still ring Wrigley's outfield wall, preventing anyone from dropping down onto the field.

Interestingly, the baskets also shortened the distance for a home run by three feet. On May 10, 1970, Billy Williams became the first player to benefit from the shortened distance when his long fly ball, which would previously have been able to be caught for an out, landed in one of the baskets for a home run.

In addition to installing these baskets, the Cubs also limited beer sales and stopped selling standing-room-only bleacher tickets. And these changes were only the most visible parts of the Cubs new security measures. The organization also installed security cameras throughout the park to monitor fans' behavior. "It was the first use of cameras at any park in baseball," historian John Snyder chronicled in his book *Cubs Journal*.[26] Today, every ballpark and stadium uses an array of camera systems to monitor crowds—but the Friendly Confines embraced the idea first.

The city of Chicago began to apply the use of video surveillance, pioneered at Wrigley Field, to many parts of the city early in the twenty-first century. In 2003, Chicago began installing highly visible video monitors in high-crime areas. But that was only the beginning for Chicago's video monitoring. "Chicago has gone further than any other U.S. city in merging computer and video technology to police the streets," claimed a *Wall Street Journal* article in 2009:

The networked system is also unusual because of its scope and the integration of nonpolice cameras. The city links the 1,500 cameras that police have placed in trouble spots with thousands more—police won't say how many—that have been installed by other government agencies and the private sector in city buses, businesses, public schools, subway stations, housing projects and elsewhere. Even home owners can contribute camera feeds.

Rajiv Shah, an adjunct professor at the University of Illinois at Chicago who has studied the issue, estimates that 15,000 cameras have been connected in what the city calls Operation Virtual Shield, its fiber-optic video-network loop.[27]

The transformation of Chicago from being the City of Big Shoulders to becoming the City of Big Brother has been a source of contentious debate among citizens and civil rights activists who argue the virtues and drawbacks of this system. But what cannot be ignored is the fact that video surveillance is now a real and omnipresent part of our everyday world—and a major step in the evolution of such practices began with a group of young fans storming the field at the Friendly Confines on April 14, 1970.

Chapter 45

Changing In-Game Entertainment Around the World

*Another Cubs Innovation Changed Ballpark Entertainment
Forever. It Also Led to One of the Most Unusual—and
Hilarious—Ejections Ever from a Baseball Game.*

It would be nearly impossible to find a professional baseball stadium today that doesn't have an organ to entertain the crowd. But prior to April 26, 1941, no stadium had such entertainment. That date, on which Roy Nelson sat behind the newly installed organ at Wrigley Field to lead cheers and entertain the crowd between innings, marked the debut of the grand tradition of organ music at baseball games. The idea caught on instantly—fans loved it and rivals copied the idea.

Since that day, only eight organists have tickled the organ keys at Wrigley Field. After Nelson, the job was held (in chronological order) by Jack Kearney, Frank Pellico, Vance Fothergill, John Henzel, Ed Vodicka, and Bruce Miles before current organist Gary Pressey assumed the job in 1987. By comparison, the Cubs have had 38 managers during the same time period.

Becoming the Cubs' organ player may be more difficult, statistically speaking, than earning a place as starting pitcher or manager. But there is one young man who holds an even more rare distinction. On August 1, 2012, Derek Dye, a 21-year-old intern from the University of Illinois, was ejected from a Class A Cubs affiliate game in Daytona, Florida, for playing the song "Three Blind Mice" after a questionable call at first base. While Dye was not an organist (his role was more that of a deejay, using audio clips to entertain the crowd), his choice of music was an instrumental organ version of the familiar children's song.

Home plate umpire Mario Seneca wasn't amused. Upon hearing the song (which was also the theme for *The Three Stooges* television show), Seneca wheeled around, pointed to the press box, and yelled, "You're done!" He then ordered that no more audio be played through the sound system for the rest of the night.

"I didn't think he'd get angry," said Dye, who admitted he was a Cubs fan. "I just started laughing. I was shocked."[28]

Believe it or not, that wasn't the first time that the song "Three Blind Mice" got someone into trouble at a ballgame. In an MiLB.com article in 1985, Danny Wild described a similar incident that happened during Florida State League action, when Clearwater Phillies organist Wilbur Snapp was ejected for playing the song on the organ.

As for the Dye incident, when the local broadcaster learned that it was the sound system guy who had been ejected rather than a manager or player, he had the same unbridled reaction most Cubs fans would have exhibited. "Derek Dye was just ejected from the game—that is awesome!" the broadcaster enthused. "That is absolutely awesome!"

We agree. It was one of the more unusual ejections from a baseball game with connections to the Cubs. But there is one that beats it, especially since the ejected athlete didn't even play baseball. But that story comes later.

Chapter 46

How 'Casablanca' Altered Baseball

The Film 'Casablanca' and a Ridiculed Idea from
Philip Wrigley Dramatically Changed Baseball's Past—
And May Prove to Change the Cubs' Future.

For generations, Cubs fans and baseball pundits alike have shackled Philip Wrigley with the blame for the Cubs' lousy performance during the decades when he ran the team. But Wrigley's ideas have been rekindled by Cubs president Theo Epstein, who knows that it is role players, rather than big stars, who produce the most success in the long run. Some of Wrigley's ideas, which were blamed for destroying the Cubs chances during the 1960s, have reappeared, and fans are hopeful that they will resurrect the team a half-century—and no championships—later.

In January 1960, Wrigley announced his revolutionary plan to use a rotating roster of coaches to lead the Cubs. The concept was dubbed the "College of Coaches." Explaining his reasoning for having a staff of coaches rather than one individual in charge, Wrigley said, "Our main objective is to standardize our system." Wrigley even went so far as to have the club create a booklet called "The Cubs Way," which explained in detail how everything in the organization was to be taught. As baseball historians Glenn Stout and Richard A. Johnson explained in their book *The Cubs*, Wrigley "wanted the game of baseball taught throughout the Cubs organization exactly the same way so that as a player moved up in the system and then to the major leagues, he would receive consistent instruction and, hoped Wrigley, produce standardized results." [29]

Echoing Wrigley, in 2012 Epstein and his staff finished a 300-page book called *The Cubs Way* to be used by coaches, players, and managers throughout the organization. Epstein intended to cover "everything from what foot you hit the bag with when you're making the turn to how we run bunt plays to what our overall organizational hitting philosophy is," reported Paul Sullivan in the *Chicago Tribune* on February 18, 2012.[30] "Everything about the game, we're going to approach the same way as an organization, from the Dominican Summer League through A-ball, Double-A, Triple-A right up to the big leagues. Playing hard is a big part of it, but playing the game the right way and teaching it consistently is important as well."

Not only were Epstein and Wrigley both trying to create a systematic approach to baseball, they both created manuals on how to teach the game—even using the same name—and wanted the same result: consistency throughout the entire organization. But while Wrigley was considered an eccentric whose newfangled ideas destroyed the team's chances, Epstein was labeled a "boy genius" when he used the same approach to help the Boston Red Sox win the World Series in 2004 and 2007.

During the 50 years that separated Wrigley and Epstein's experiments, the game has been swept by a new approach called "Moneyball" (in reference to the 2003 best-selling book by Michael Lewis, which was made into the second-highest grossing baseball film of all-time in 2011, earning more than $75 million globally).[31] Moneyball introduced the idea of using statistics to determine the best players in baseball, rather than the traditional "eye test," which relied on the consensus of scouts' opinions.

Baseball insiders had known for years about this approach, which is also called *sabremetrics* (in reference to the Society of American Baseball Researchers, or SABR). The approach is also known as *Jamesian baseball* due to Bill James' seminal book *The Bill James Historical Abstract*. First published in 1985, it was this work that first introduced the world of baseball to the kind of in-depth statistical analysis that eventually produced new statistics that twenty-first century fans take for granted. Runs created, game score, and secondary average were some of the new statistics that James created, giving fans a new way to understand the game in greater detail than ever before. Epstein was such a disciple of James that he hired the "sabermetrician" as a senior advisor for the Red Sox in 2002.

But don't be fooled into thinking that Epstein is merely spouting James' approach. A graduate of Yale who later earned a law degree, he became the youngest general manager in baseball history when the Red Sox hired him at the age of 28. Epstein is so gifted that a baseball insider once told him he should "eventually run for president [of the United States]" because he could handle it and had "an extraordinary gift to help people."[32]

Having broken the epic Red Sox World Series drought with not one but two championships, Epstein has helped more people than many U.S. presidents. Now he is working to give Chicago, the only team with a championship drought lasting longer than the one the Red Sox suffered.

Many fans might be surprised to learn that what Epstein took from Bill James' work only supported what he had learned through his family's history in Hollywood decades earlier. Epstein's grandfather, Philip Epstein, and his twin brother Julius wrote the screenplay for the classic 1942 film *Casablanca*, which won the Academy Award for Best Picture, Best Director, and Best Adapted Screenplay. The Epstein brothers worked in Hollywood back when the "contract system" or "studio system" ruled the entertainment world. Everyone in the business of filmmaking, from writers to famous stars, had a contract that bound them to a specific studio—much as baseball players were bound to one team. In a revolutionary move, Epstein has fused together the statistical analysis Wrigley loved with Hollywood's studio system mentality to simultaneously reduce the Cubs' payroll and create consistency throughout the organization, relying on team players rather than big stars to achieve wins.

Of course, the Cubs' transition from a star-laden team to a group of up-and-coming youngsters has been difficult for fans to watch. In 2012, Epstein's second season with the franchise, the Cubs went 61–101—disappointing, to put it mildly. But the team president believes the fans will give Epstein time to enact his plans, saying, "We're being transparent and they're responding by giving back faith, belief and energy."[33] It takes time to build a winner, especially with a franchise that has gone more than 100 years without a championship. But Epstein, wielding his Jamesian approach, has become baseball's version of the Hollywood studio president of the past, preaching that baseball requires many people to work together, each learning their roles and how to do them well, in order for the entire organization to succeed.

"Working at Warner Bros. was a very friendly atmosphere during the days of the studio system," Julius Epstein said in the book *Casablanca: Behind the Scenes*:

> For the writers, it was a club. There were seventy to seventy-five writers at Warners—it wasn't called the motion picture industry for nothing. It was like

an assembly line. . . . But you have to realize that today it's a whole different ball game. The whole contract system is dead. In 1935, I had five released movies in my first year at Warner Bros. . . . Such a thing today would be impossible because in those days, we were under contract, and as soon as you finished one, they shoved another one at you.

The contract system gave you a sense of security, because doing so many pictures, if you batted .500, or even .300, you were in pretty good shape—like a ball player. Today, you more or less live or die on each picture. Instead of five in one year, you're lucky to get one every five years.[34]

During the 1930s and 1940s, studio executives took the approach that if they created dozens of films each year, the odds were in their favor that at least a few of them would turn out to be hits. In short, they had to create more films to improve their chances. The Chicago Cubs have become a twenty-first century version of that system, going out of their way to get rid of stars (and their salaries) in order to create a pool of players all trained in the same way, allowing multiple players to play the same position successfully (in the case of injury, for example). According to Foxsports.com's Greg Couch, the plan is to build a team of role players rather than relying on big stars to achieve victory:[35]

Epstein has focused on scouting and drafting amateur players. He has unloaded as many big contracts as possible at the major league level and put money into amateurs. The Cubs spent a team record $12 million on [the 2011] draft class.

Epstein cut the Cubs' payroll from $125 million in 2011 to $88 million in 2012. Both sabermetricians and Hollywood executives would say it only makes sense: if you can have lower-paid employees generate hits by creating a system that only demands certain requirements of each one, then the overall success of the organization should be inevitable.

According to Epstein biographer John Frascella in his book *Theology*, Epstein looks at players differently than most of his old-fashioned baseball peers, often asking them to do less individually so the team can succeed overall. For example, while fans may love home-run hitters, Epstein has chosen to manufacture runs instead. Where fans love to see a pitcher hit 100 mph on a radar gun, Epstein looks for strong pitchers who can learn control while also achieving longevity over the course of their careers. In short, Epstein has been using the same philosophy as the old film studios, which dictated that lots of small films would yield better results than hiring one big star with a big contract who might fail in a big way.

"Theo wanted to get his players on base in any possible fashion, and score runs without donating outs to the opposition," Frascella wrote in *Theology*, adding that Epstein vehemently eschewed out-producing plays such as the hit-and-run and the sacrifice bunt:

> It was a style more generally known as "station-to-station" baseball. "Station-to-station" meant walks and hits would determine his team's fate. Like a merry-go-round, consecutive walks and hits can move runners fluidly around the bases. . . . His strategy turned every inning into a potential rally. . . . While most other teams were gazing at pitchers' won-lost records, Theo and [Bill] James were taking a good, hard look at strikeout-to-walk ratios.[36]

According to Terry Francona in his book *Francona: The Red Sox Years*, Epstein left the Red Sox for the Cubs after 2011, when upper management forced him to hire more "sexy" players. Francona, who also left after the 2011 season, claimed that the Red Sox hired a consulting firm to investigate the team's diminishing television ratings. The result of the $100,000 study, according to the book, infuriated both Epstein and Francona, who both left the organization as a result. Francona wrote that the report contained marketing notes that suggested more star players were needed to enhance ratings, and that female viewers wanted more "sexy players" like Dustin Pedroia. For Epstein, whose whole approach was built around using role players instead of big stars, it was too much. Wrote Francona, "Epstein was insulted, amused (Pedroia, sexy?) and angry."[37]

Epstein left the Red Sox and joined the Cubs, looking to create a unified organization built around role players who would manufacture runs rather than relying on big plays to save the game. He wanted hurlers who would be able to pitch in the mid-90 mph range for several years, rather than bringing 100-mph heat for only one or two seasons. And he wanted affable players who could "gel and avoid unnecessary friction with teammates,"[38] not prima donnas who would demand the spotlight.

Epstein calls his philosophy "the Cubs Way," just as Wrigley did during the 1960s. Studio executives in the 1930s called it the Hollywood Way. Meanwhile, fans don't care what you call it, as long as Epstein's Cubs are able to achieve what *Casablanca* earned—immortal greatness.

Chapter 47

The First Sports Psychologist

*The Cubs Could Have Reaped the Benefits of a New Field of
Science During the 1930s. Instead, They Ignored the Advice
That Has Since Created Champions in Every Sport.*

Before the confetti had stopped falling from the rafters after the Los Angeles
Lakers won the 2010 NBA championship, forward Ron Artest (who later
changed his name to Metta World Peace), turned to ABC reporter Doris Burke
and gushed for all the world to hear: "I'd like to thank my psychiatrist, Dr.
Santhi. She really helped me relax."

And there it was for the world to hear: sports psychology works. Truth be told,
sports psychology has been a secret weapon among elite athletes in every sport
for years—and one of the pioneers of the field did his best to share his expertise
with the Chicago Cubs.

The use of sports psychology may be widespread today, but during the 1930s,
the notion that athletes, managers, coaches, or executives could benefit from
psychological improvement methods seemed preposterous to nearly everyone in
sports. So when Cubs owner Phillip Wrigley hired Coleman Griffith, the father of
sports psychology, to examine the mental makeup of his team and see if there was
any way it could be improved, it was chalked up by nearly everyone in baseball
as just another one of Wrigley's strange ideas. Cubs manager Charlie Grimm
openly detested Coleman, despite the fact that he might have been able to use his
help—Grimm allegedly fell into a deep depression after his team failed to make
the playoffs in 1937.[39] Grimm's opinion of "headshrinkers," as he called Coleman
and other psychologists, was negative, resentful, and mocking.

Grimm's opinion of Coleman (which reflected the feelings of most athletes
and sports executives toward psychology at the time) was the focus of a key scene
in the classic 1984 baseball film *The Natural*, which starred Robert Redford.

During a scene set in the locker room of the fictitious Knights (based in many ways on the Cubs), a tiny man with an even tinier voice blandly urges the players to success with a speech delivered in a monotone. The psychologist, based on Coleman, tells the team:

> What is losing? Losing is a disease as contagious as polio. Losing is a disease as contagious as syphilis. Losing is a disease as contagious as the bubonic plague. Attacking one, but infecting all. But curable. Now I want you to imagine you are on a ship at sea. . . .

As soon as the bow-tied psychologist begins to use this visualization method, Redford's character rolls his eyes and leaves the locker room in disgust. Such was the attitude of nearly everyone in the athletic world during the 1930s—except for Wrigley.

Unfortunately, having Wrigley as a supporter may have actually hindered the advancement of sports psychology more than it helped it. The world of baseball considered the idiosyncratic Cubs owner to be something of a kook. So if Wrigley supported the idea, how good could it be? At least that was the general opinion held by players, coaches, and managers at the time. Add to that Griffith's frail physical stature, eyeglasses, and mustache, and you have a picture of the type of man most professional athletes were loath to associate with in any way. Yet their reluctance to benefit from his guidance only hurt the Cubs players and coaches in the long run.

History is a peculiar teacher. Nearly everyone in professional sports mocked sports psychology at its inception, but Wrigley and Griffith were actually innovators in a field that would one day become ubiquitous. Founded in 1986, the Association for Applied Sports Psychology now boasts a membership of renowned psychologists around the world who work with athletes to help them overcome their anxiety and stress—something that often reveals itself when an athlete "chokes." The keynote speech at the association's annual conference is named after Coleman Griffith, a man reviled in his time and now honored as the father of sports psychology.

Dr. Christopher D. Green, a professor of psychology at Toronto's York University, wrote a detailed paper about Griffith for the American Psychology Association's *Monitor on Psychology* publication that detailed Griffith's contributions to the world. In 1925 at the University of Illinois, Griffith opened the nation's first research lab focused solely on athletics and psychology. Unfortunately for Griffith, the lab lasted only six years, in large part because Fighting Illini football coach Robert Zupke, much like Grimm years later, didn't want Griffith around his team. The lab was closed and Griffith was doomed to an administrative job until Wrigley asked him to apply his findings to the Cubs following the team's late-season collapse in 1937.

Griffith joined the Cubs at spring training on Catalina Island in 1938 and was with the team throughout the season, filing 16 reports with Wrigley that revealed increasing levels of frustration. Griffith used his own psychological ploys to try to convince Grimm of the benefit of working on his players' mental approach, but the manager refused to take Griffith seriously.

By midseason, Griffith was making specific recommendations to Wrigley that seem almost laughingly obvious by today's standards: for example, Griffith suggested that the Cubs players and coaches weren't taking practice seriously, and that they should approach every practice as if it was a game in order to reduce their stress in real game situations. "Practice makes perfect" is a common aphorism today that all coaches and players accept as if it were a direct message from the Sports Gods. Griffith's 1938 reports to Wrigley echoed this truism, noting that: "[Athletes] should make [the will to win] a necessary feature of every practice period and of every game he plays. He must reduce it to a habit."[40] (Of course, "Practice makes perfect" is a bit more succinct.)

The Cubs ignored Griffith's work. Even Wrigley, the man who had hired Griffith in the first place, failed to employ any of Griffith's suggestions. To make matters more complicated, Wrigley fired Grimm in July 1938 with the team in fourth place and promoted catcher Gabby Hartnett to player/coach. Despite Griffith's assessment that Hartnett "was not at all a smart man" and did not "have the ability to adapt himself to any other style of training and coaching but that with which he had been familiar throughout his playing career,"[41] Hartnett led the Cubs to the postseason thanks to his raw power, most notably evidenced by his famous "Homer in the Gloamin'," now an indelible part of Cubs lore. Hartnett's old-school approach to baseball—see the ball, hit the ball, keep your worries to yourself, and just take the field—resonated with his team because they, too, had been trained that way.

Griffith knew Hartnett and Wrigley were ignoring him. Wrigley reduced Griffith's position to part-time in 1939. He filed only four reports that season, and only one the next. By 1941, Griffith was no longer associated with the Cubs. Wrote Professor Green:

> Most baseball managers saw the project as a failure, and the idea was not picked up by other teams for a long while to come. Griffith returned to the University of Illinois, where he rose to the level of provost. He retired in 1962 and died in 1966, just a year before the founding of the North American Society for the Psychology of Sport and Physical Activity. In 1970, University of Massachusetts professors Walter Kroll and Guy Lewis rediscovered Griffith's work and declared him "America's First Sport Psychologist."[42]

For those athletes who cannot afford to work with a sports psychologist, an article in *Outside* magazine in January 2013 offered some simple approaches to the mental aspect of sports training. Michael Gervais, one of the foremost sports psychologists in the country, outlined five core mental skills that he has taught the U.S. Olympic team, NFL and MLB players, and many extreme sport athletes:

1. visualization (see yourself being successful)
2. self-talk (tell yourself positive messages, not negative)
3. arousal control (learn to calm your inner mind against outside stimuli)
4. goal setting (map out your goals and a plan to get there)
5. preperformance routines (often confused with superstitions, these are specific actions and thoughts athletes use to prepare mentally for competition)

Practice does make perfect. The Cubs proved this, but in the reverse. While the organization reached the 1938 and 1945 World Series, they lost both; and in the 30-year span from 1937 to 1966 they had 24 seasons with a .500 record or worse. The failures of the Cubs—despite their access to psychological help that was years ahead of its time—are a testament to the notion that players become the products of their daily routine. Instead of practicing to be perfect, the Cubs perfected their ability to perpetuate mediocrity.

Chapter 48

Only Team Known to Have
Voodoo Doctor on Payroll

*Only One Sports Team in History Is Known to Have
Hired a Professional Evil Eye to Hex Its Opponents—
And As You Can Probably Guess, It Was the Cubs.*

The Cubs have hired worse—although probably not weirder—advisors than the professional voodoo "expert" supposedly hired by Philip Wrigley.

Wrigley was eccentric, to say the least, and many of his ideas never panned out for the Cubs. Hiring a professional voodoo practitioner to help the Cubs win may have been the nadir of his peculiar approach to the game. Wrigley is the only known owner in American sports to have hired someone to jinx opponents—although one has to suspect that there have probably been others who did something similar and kept it a secret. In fact, that was precisely what Wrigley attempted to do, refusing to discuss this unusual employee for the rest of his life. The world would never have known the story had it not been for Bill Veeck, who included it in his 1962 autobiography *Veeck as in Wreck*. According to Veeck, Wrigley believed in the occult and thought it could influence games for the benefit of the Cubs.

Veeck didn't reveal the name of Wrigley's "voodoo-ologist," but Jerome Holtzman identified him in a *Chicago Tribune* column as Benjamin "Evil Eye" Finkle, who was popular with boxing promoters during the 1930s and 1940s for supposedly jinxing opponents. While Finkle never publicly admitted that Wrigley had hired him, he did claim to be responsible for Adolf Hitler's death.

Reporter Pat Putnam tracked down Finkle in a Miami bar for a 1978 *Sports Illustrated* article. The Evil Eye proved to be worth the bar tab he would likely stick you with if you stayed still long enough. "Two parts voodoo, one part fraud,"

243

was how Putnam described Finkle.[43] Drafted by the military in 1942, the army transferred Finkle to Europe in 1945. There the army "stationed Finkle on the top floor of a hotel in Paris and pointed him toward Germany," Putnam wrote:

> Each day Finkle rode the elevator to the top floor and from there he cast his hex toward Berlin. Two weeks after he began, word came that Hitler had killed himself.
>
> "If they had thought of that sooner," Finkle said, "I probably could've ended the war in '43. I figured the least I'd get was a Silver Star. I never even got a good-conduct ribbon."

Growing up in St. Louis, Finkle became a boxing manager by the age of 14 and sold newspapers in bars, a dangerous job if you didn't have the right friends:

> I sold papers all over the country; there ain't a hallway or an alley anywhere I didn't work in. I got the scars to prove it. You could get killed if them circulation goons caught you peddling the wrong sheet. In Chicago I get [sic] lucky. A killer named Dion O'Bannion took a liking to me. He was out on parole for murder. The *Chicago Examiner* got him out cause they needed a tough street guy. He put out the word that the corner of State and Van Buren was mine. He stayed my good friend until Al Capone shot him full of holes.

After O'Bannion was shot dead at his florist shop in 1924, Finkle returned to the "safer" world of boxing, horse racing, and professional wrestling, where he began to hone his craft of "Jewish voodoo" (as he called it) with three signature hexes: "the Slobodka Stare," "the Zinger," and "the Whammie."[44] Finkle claimed his "optical infrared ray" was responsible for Secretariat's famous win against War Admiral on November 1, 1938. It was around this time that Wrigley evidently took notice of Finkle. According to Veeck, Wrigley hired the Evil Eye for $5,000 with a $25,000 bonus if the Cubs won the pennant.[45] Veeck did not specify during which season the Evil Eye was hired, nor did he mention him by name in his autobiography. But he did make it clear that Wrigley took the entire matter seriously, although Veeck did not.

"There's nothing funny about this," Wrigley warned Veeck. "This man may help us. And don't go talking to your newspaper friends about this. Or anybody else, either." Veeck didn't until more than 20 years later, when he thankfully wrote his life story, published in 1962.

"For the rest of the year we carried our Evil Eye around the league with us," Veeck wrote:

> At home, he sat directly behind the plate, gesturing furiously at opposing pitchers, none of whom seemed disposed to enter into the spirit of the thing at all. . . . Our man operated under a severe handicap for such a chancy profession. He could not stand cold weather. . . . On cold days, he would go up to the office, stand over the Western Union ticker and put the whammy on the tape as the play-by-play came in.
>
> Let me make it clear that I don't want this to be taken as a blanket indictment of all Evil Eyes. Most Evil Eyes, I'm sure, are honest, tax-paying, respectable citizens. It's only that rotten three percent who don't give you an honest day's work for an honest day's pay who give the whole profession a bad name.[46]

Wrigley was the only one who took the entire thing seriously. To put the Evil Eye's $5,000 salary in perspective, the highest salary on the 1939 Cubs roster was the $20,000 paid to both Gabby Hartnett and Dizzy Dean. In 2012, the two highest salaries on the Cubs' roster were Alfonso Soriano's $18-million contract and Ryan Dempster's $14-million one. If an Evil Eye's going rate was one-quarter of the best salary on the team, then he would have earned between $3.5 million to $4.5 million in 2012. That may sound expensive for a little voodoo, but had it helped the Cubs win the World Series, most Cubs fans would have seen it as worthwhile—which is exactly what Wrigley was hoping for.

While we have had some fun at Wrigley's expense in this section, we have to give the former owner credit as a man who "left no stone unturned," as Holtzman wrote in a 1990 *Chicago Tribune* column[47] that claimed Finkle was a "certified hypnotist." While there is no indication that Finkle was a certified anything, Holtzman's claim gives Wrigley yet another first in sports history. Sports hypnosis has gained popularity over the decades, and today there are firms that specialize in this form of mental training. To his credit, Wrigley had the foresight to recognize sports psychology as a legitimate field decades before the rest of the world saw its value. If the Evil Eye was indeed a sports hypnotist (assuming hypnosis is real), Wrigley has yet another claim to being one of the founders of sports psychology.

Our bet is that Holtzman, for all his good intentions, was wrong about Finkle being a certified hypnotist; what's more, although sports psychology is a recognized field, most people still consider hypnotism little more than a parlor trick. But if nothing else, it makes for a good story.

"It was like I found a gold mine in my eyeballs," Finkle said of his supposed voodoo powers.[48] And Wrigley Field was a goldmine for him, too, thanks to baseball's most superstitious owner.

Chapter 49

First Physical Trainer in Baseball

One of Philip Wrigley's More Creative Ideas Was Also Called His Worst by Many Critics. But as Usual, Wrigley Was Ahead of His Time. Every Team in Every Sport Now Employs Someone in the Role That Wrigley Tinkered with in 1963.

Philip Wrigley has often been misunderstood. He loved working on engines and mechanical parts, but when he tried to apply that knowledge to human beings, everything fell apart. Such was the case with yet another first in sports history pioneered by Wrigley.

Today, every sports team has vast weight rooms filled with special training equipment and staffed by strength professionals who oversee players' workouts. There are now entire companies specializing in workouts for certain positions. But it wasn't always that way. In fact, the first team to attempt such tactics—which was also the first to hire someone to oversee this area—found its players and coaches alike were simply too entrenched in old-fashioned methods to give this new approach a fair shake.

"I was ahead of my time," said Colonel Robert Whitlow, whom Wrigley hired as the Cubs' athletic director on January 10, 1963, becoming the first person to hold that position in Major League Baseball. "None of the ballclubs had special training rooms. Now they have as many as two and three rooms filled with the latest machines," continued Whitlow.[49] Whitlow was accustomed to being first. He was also the first athletic director at the Air Force Academy. This 6'5", 230-pound colonel quickly turned his cadets into peerless physical specimens. But doing the same thing with a group of professional baseball players proved to be a different kettle of fish. It didn't help that Whitlow had no professional baseball experience (although he did pitch for UCLA during his college years). Major league players had their own traditional ways of doing things, and they were not interested in changing.

It also didn't help that Whitlow's responsibilities were vague from the beginning. He became a fourth layer of management with unspecified duties. Whitlow was technically under only Wrigley in the management structure, overseeing both general manager John Holland and team manager Bob Kennedy. But Whitlow's only discernible accomplishment during the two years he was with the Cubs abolishing Wrigley's "College of Coaches" and installing Kennedy as the team's manager. (It's little wonder that as a student of military hierarchy management structures, Whitlow saw the need for one voice in charge in the dugout.) At the announcement of his hiring, Wrigley said Whitlow would be "responsible for the conduct of the club on the field."[50] But what did that mean? Nobody was sure.

The fit and trim Whitlow knew that the Cubs would not be successful if they were not in shape. He took his role as athletic director seriously, audaciously requiring the team to work out, eat better, and avoid alcohol and late night partying. Today, teams spend hundreds of thousands of dollars each year on personnel and equipment to do the same thing. Recalled Ron Santo in *Wrigleyville*:[51]

> [Whitlow] would run spring training, and they ran it like a military camp. The only thing we didn't have was army uniforms. You couldn't believe it. We never did things like this . . . jumping jacks, this, that, you had to be in a straight line, you had to be in formation. It was something. An army colonel was running spring training!

Formation? Exercise? Special foods? Baseball players were not ready for that kind of regimentation. In fact, the widespread opinion in the baseball world was that players got in playing shape by playing actual games during spring training, not by following a strict workout regimen and dietary restrictions.

"The players were eating too many hot dogs," Whitlow told Jerome Holtzman for a *Chicago Tribune* column in 1994. "I was trying to come up with an energy food. I found a company that was into that sort of thing. They were patterned after chocolate milk balls, but they had a lot of vitamin C. The players liked them, but after a while they sort of lost interest."[52]

Actually, the players didn't lose interest so much as they hated taking orders from a non-baseball guy, and a military man, to boot. Said Don Elston in *Wrigleyville*:

We didn't like what he was doing at all. He came out in the morning with calisthenics, jumping jacks, and all that jazz. . . . "This is the way we did it in the army. This is what we're doing here." And we resented that. There was *a lot* of resentment about the Colonel. He was a nice man, but we didn't like that concept. He was the athletic director? In college maybe. Not in the major leagues.[53]

Today, Whitlow's ideas are an integral part of professional sports of all kinds, not just baseball. In fact, strength trainers are indebted to Whitlow for helping to create their field. The Professional Baseball Strength & Conditioning Coaches Association was founded in 1993—30 years after Whitlow became the first and only known athletic director in pro sports—with only five professional strength trainers registered during its first year. According to the nonprofit organization's website, the PBSCCA now has strength coaches from every MLB team, as well as many minor league squads.

As historian John Snyder explained in his book *Cubs Journal*:

Whitlow had many ideas about conditioning, diet, and use of a computer to spot trends and formulate strategy that later became common in baseball, but his lack of experience in the sport gave him no credibility. Whitlow was ignored by general manager John Holland and head coach Bob Kennedy. The colonel resigned in January 1965, and the position of athletic director was abolished.[54]

Many historians have called the Whitlow experiment a failure or worse. "A terrible idea"[55] wrote one historian, while another said, "Had it not been so sad, it would have been funny."[56] But Wrigley and Whitlow have had the last laugh: while the title of athletic director no longer exists in professional baseball, the specific strength and nutrition guidelines that Whitlow tried to instill in the Cubs are alive and well today. They are simply handled by many more people, including nutritionists, strength trainers, and team trainers. In fact, the ideas of healthy eating, workouts, and discipline are very much a part of teams in every sport, whether professional or amateur, and have been for decades thanks to pioneers like Whitlow.

"Baseball simply was not ready for an athletic director," Wrigley said after Whitlow quit. "Maybe in the years ahead baseball will accept one. Whitlow was ahead of his time." That quote came from Jimmy Greenfield's book *100 Things Every Cubs Fan Should Know & Do Before They Die*, and the author followed up the quote with one observation: "That time still hasn't come."

We respectfully but vehemently disagree. In fact, the financial market analysis company IBIS World estimated in a February 2013 report[57] that the health and fitness club market in the United States alone generates roughly $26 billion annually, and that "demand for gyms and health and fitness clubs will continue to rise over the next five years, as the general public becomes more health-conscious and the aging population places a greater emphasis on staying fit."

Whitlow and Wrigley cannot claim credit for the creation of fitness clubs, of course, but they certainly were the first to make health, fitness, and strength a priority in baseball specifically and in professional sports in general.

Wrigley was only partially correct when he said that Whitlow was ahead of his time. Wrigley was too.

Chapter 50

Uniforms Alterations That Changed the Game for Worse

One of the Worst Ideas in Baseball History Was Conceived by a Cubs Player and Owner.

One of the most pivotal figures in the history of both baseball and business was former Cubs pitcher, manager, president, and owner A.G. Spalding, whose legend as a great pitcher and an even better team manager have been eclipsed by the company he started, which still manufactures baseball equipment today, nearly 100 years after the death of its founder. Baseball fans of all ages are familiar with the sporting equipment brand Spalding, which manufactures baseballs, gloves, uniforms, and equipment for leagues all over the world. His importance to the game of baseball was so noteworthy that the Society for American Baseball Research (SABR) ranked Spalding as the No. 2 contributor to the game from the nineteenth century. The only man to play every role in the theater of baseball—from star player to successful manager to club executive to manufacturing mogul—Spalding was one of the most powerful men in sports, a fact he used to his advantage.

What many fans don't know is that Spalding was also responsible for the worst idea in baseball history—and the fact that it was implemented, albeit only on a short-term basis, only attests to the influence he had over the game.

Born in 1850 and raised in the Rockford, Illinois, area, Spalding fought off loneliness in the farmland by playing baseball. By his early teens, Spalding was described by the *Rockford Register* as "undoubtedly the best pitcher in the West."[58] The Chicago Excelsiors signed him at the age of 17. The team folded after Spalding's first and only game, but the boy's passion for baseball was far from diminished. The teenager dropped out of high school and focused on baseball, playing for the local Forest City team.

Standing 6'1" and 170 pounds, Spalding blossomed into a talented pitcher and was soon signed by the Boston Red Stockings. He was an immediate success, posting a 204–53 record during his five years with the team. In 1874, Spalding became the star player for the first overseas baseball tour, for which players went to England to play exhibition games. The experience gave him the idea for a World Tour of his own in 1888–89.

Always looking for a new challenge in baseball (as well as a way to make more money), Spalding traded in his star player status in Boston in 1876 for a chance to become a player/manager for the Chicago White Stockings. Spalding had another reason for wanting to play for his "hometown" Chicago team: he and his brother had started a new business there that same year manufacturing baseball equipment. He and his brother, Walter, started A.G. Spalding & Bros., the precursor to the international Spalding manufacturing empire, with an $800 loan from their mother, Harriet. The plan was simple: A.G. would use his baseball popularity to secure contracts and help develop product while Walter would manage the company. This was truly a family business: their sister, Mary, balanced the books, and they even asked their mother to help sew uniforms on occasion.

A.G. Spalding & Bros. secured the contract to supply the official baseball for the National League beginning in 1876, and was the only supplier for the next 100 years. Hardly limited to just baseballs, however, Spalding also debuted many other products that sports fans take for granted today. Spalding began selling the first major league baseball glove in 1877, and in 1878, he published the first official rules of baseball. Spalding was still a powerful figure within the sport, as well; in fact, due to the sudden death of Cubs owner and NL founder William Hulbert, Spalding became president of the Cubs in April 1882.

Unfortunately, not all of Spaulding's innovations turned out well. Spalding was able to convince NL officials to alter its uniform rules at the annual meeting on December 9, 1881. As supplier of uniforms to the league, Spalding used this rule change to benefit his company—with grave results. The 1882 season marked the first and only time in professional sports history that an entire league took the field with players wearing uniforms color-coded based on their position, rather than their team affiliation. All players wore the same white pants, belts, and ties, but the shirt and cap for each player differed depending on what position they played:

Pitcher: Baby blue
Catcher: Scarlet
First baseman: Scarlet and white
Second baseman: Orange and black
Third baseman: Blue and white
Shortstop: Maroon
Left fielder: White
Center fielder: Red and black
Right fielder: Gray

The only way fans and players could tell which team each player was on was by the color of his socks (or stockings):

Buffalo Bisons: Gray
Cleveland Blues: Navy blue
Chicago: White
Boston: Red
Providence Grays: Light blue
Detroit Wolverines: Gold
Troy Trojans: Green
Worcester Ruby Legs: Brown

Mass confusion ensued. Players and fans alike referred to the uniforms as "clown costumes" or "monkey uniforms." (GeoVerse™177) While players said it was insulting to have to wear such ridiculous uniforms, media members had fun with the flamboyant outfits, as evidenced by this quote from the book *Orator O'Rourke: The Life of a Baseball Radical*:

> The umpire seems to have been entirely overlooked. Serpentine pantaloons, in imitation of a barber's pole, harlequin jacket and a circus clown's wool hat would give them a neat and not particularly gaudy suit, and afford a kaleidoscopic effect as they skipped towards first-base along with a batsman. A log-cabin quilt, worn as a toga, would heighten the effect and add dignity to the office.[59]

The consequences of these new uniforms were both predictable and instantaneous. Confusion reigned on the field, especially when a first baseman singled or was walked. Pitchers repeatedly threw to first to hold the base runner on, only to find (after the ball went sailing past first base) that he had thrown to the wrong player because he was wearing a scarlet and white uniform. The surprised base runner would take off for second (and maybe third) while the first baseman ran off to retrieve the ball. The same thing happened when a second baseman reached second, a third baseman reached third, or a catcher ran home.

The league ended Spalding's uniform "experiment" by the second month of the season. Teams went back to their old uniforms for the rest of the year: home teams wore white uniforms and visitors wore gray or colored uniforms (a rule that still holds true today).

The fact that Spalding was able to convince NL officials to go along with his idea for nearly two months was only proof of how much power he had over the game. After all, the only real benefactor of the change was his manufacturing company, which essentially made the same "uniform" for every team (except for the socks), reducing costs for a product that the league was contractually obligated to purchase. It made life easier for the company, forced the NL to purchase new uniforms for every player, and assured that A.G. Spalding & Bros. would have a healthy bottom line. It was not the first time a Cubs executive had altered the game for his own benefit, and it surely was not the last.

Section VI

Entertainment

Chapter 51

First Pop Song in American Music History

The Crossover Between Baseball and Pop Culture Began with a Chicago Player Who Set Milestones in Music and Publishing and Who Is Also Credited with Inventing the Hobby of Autograph Collecting.

Nearly 100 years before Bob Uecker, Jim Brown, Wilt Chamberlain, Michael Jordan, Shaquille O'Neal, Merlin Olsen, or any of the other sports stars who became as famous (or infamous) for their acting roles as they were for their athletic careers, former Chicago baseball star Mike "King" Kelly beat them to the punch. Kelly, who performed in vaudeville shows at the end of his career, would undoubtedly have added films to his list of accomplishments had movies existed in the latter part of the nineteenth century. In addition to his performances on the stage, King Kelly was the inspiration for the first pop song in recorded history, wrote the first player autobiography, was quite possibly the inspiration for the most famous sports poem in history, and launched the pastime of autograph collecting.

Fans couldn't seem to get enough of Kelly. Standing 5'10" and weighing 170 pounds, he was defiant and handsome, a hard drinker and a known womanizer who loved the attention of the crowd. As Glenn Stout wrote in his book *The Cubs*:

> He [Kelly] found a way to exploit every possible advantage during a game, such as cutting corners when he ran the bases if he noticed the umpire looking the other direction. In one particularly notable act of tactical brilliance, Kelly was sitting on the bench when the opposition lofted a foul ball in his direction. The King sprang to his feet, called out, "Now catching, Kelly," and caught the ball. The out stood, for there was no rule against making a substitution in the middle of a play.[1]

Called "the Babe Ruth of the nineteenth century,"[2] Kelly's immense popularity was largely due to his daring on the base paths, where he pioneered the "hook" slide that fans loved to see—and which became the basis for a famous song years later. The hard-partying player was known for his exploits with women and his disdain for authority figures, two traits that seemed to make him more popular than any other player. Kelly may not have lived to be very old, but he had a life that many young men dream of living.

After two seasons in Cincinnati to start his career, Kelly signed with the White Stockings as a free agent before the 1880 season, sparking the first dynasty in professional baseball history. During the next seven seasons (1880–86), Kelly led Chicago to five first-place finishes in the National League, as well as one second-place finish.

Despite his great talent, however, Kelly was a problem for the team. Owner A.G. Spalding and player/manager Cap Anson both preached restraint when it came to alcohol and womanizing. Kelly laughed off their demands and did as he pleased, taking full advantage of his reputation as arguably the greatest player in the game. Wrote Stout:

> Not only was Kelly a drunk, a gambler, and a womanizer, but even worse, his behavior seemed to have little effect on his play, which made discipline impossible to enforce. In fact, although Kelly had spent most of the 1886 season drinking more often and harder than ever, he had responded with his greatest season ever, hitting .388, scoring 155 runs in 118 games, and knocking out 175 hits. A performance like that led others on the team to follow his example and excuse their own behavior and ignore Anson's admonitions to hew to the straight and narrow.[3]

Spalding had had enough of Kelly's antics, and on February 14, 1887, sold his rights for $10,000—a staggering amount at the time—to Boston, who welcomed the colorful Irishman to town. Chicago's dynasty ended with the departure of Kelly, who became an even bigger legend during his tenure in Boston thanks to artists who gave the ballplayer immortality in poetry and song.

Ernest Thayer's famous poem "Casey at the Bat" first appeared in the *San Francisco Examiner* on June 3, 1888. Later that summer, East Coast newspapers reprinted the poem, switching "Kelly" for "Casey"—one of the reasons historians cite Kelly as the inspiration for the poem. Another reason was that Kelly, who had parlayed his outrageous personality into a vaudeville act, appropriated the poem, reciting it as if he had written it himself. Thayer, however, never confirmed that Kelly was the inspiration for the poem, contending rather that "Casey" was an amalgam of several different players.

While Kelly's claim to being the inspiration for "Casey" is questionable, what isn't is the effect he had on popular music, according to biographer Marty Appel, author of *Slide, Kelly, Slide: The Wild Times and Life of Mike King Kelly*. In 1889, well-known vaudeville actor, singer, and comedian John W. Kelly (no relation) published the song "Slide, Kelly, Slide"; his costar, Maggie "the Irish Queen" Cline, then made it famous by using it in her stage performances. Two years later, on August 3, 1891, popular singer George J. Gaskin recorded the song on a wax cylinder, a new invention that allowed multiple recordings to be made at once. The cylinders were sold in the marketplace beginning in 1892. This time period also marked the beginning of tracking music sales, and the first song that topped the charts, according to Appel, was "Slide, Kelly, Slide" (GeoVerse™188), with its catchy refrain:

Slide, Kelly, slide!
Your running's a disgrace!
Slide, Kelly, slide!
Stay there, hold your base!
If someone doesn't steal you,
And your batting doesn't fail you,
They'll take you to Australia!
Slide, Kelly, slide!

The line about Australia refers to Spalding's offseason baseball tour of 1888–89, which took an all-star team of players to games in Australia, along with other stops around the world, in an effort to popularize the game internationally. Spalding, a teetotaler, despised Kelly's drunkenness and refused to allow him on the team despite the fact that he was one of the best players in the game.

Wrote Appel:

By January 9, 1892, the song had become America's first "pop hit record"—a song that was neither classical nor opera, patriotic nor religious. It was just a silly song that captivated the nation and helped make baseball more mainstream than it had been. . . . [Kelly] was full of innovation in his short life. The very practice of signing random autographs for strangers on the street began with Kelly—not just for ballplayers, but for all celebrities.[4]

In addition to becoming the first hit pop song, "Slide, Kelly, Slide" also became the inspiration for two movies of the same name. Chicago-based Essanay Studios produced a silent film in 1910, which was followed by a 1927 talking film "talkie" starring William Haines as Tom Kelly, the ace pitcher of the New York Yankees. While the movie changed Kelly's affiliation to the Yankees, it did feature two other actors with connections to the White Stockings/Cubs. The father of Kelly's love interest in the film was played by actor Harry Carey, who was the inspiration for the pseudonym chosen years later by announcer Harry Christopher Carabina, known to the world as Harry Caray. And Tony Lazzeri, who played for the Cubs in 1938 but was more-well known for striking out against Grover Cleveland Alexander in during the 1926 World Series, appeared in the film as Tony Lazzen.

Between signing autographs, writing his 1888 autobiography *Play Ball: Stories of the Ball Field,* and the popularity of both "Casey at the Bat" and "Slide, Kelly, Slide," Kelly was the first true crossover celebrity in American sports and entertainment. However, by the time "Slide, Kelly, Slide" hit the charts, the ballplayer was near death due to his hard drinking. Kelly was hospitalized during the fall of 1894. Entertaining to the end, while there he slipped on the floor, prompting him to utter, "This is my last slide."[5]

Sadly, that would be no joke. Kelly died on November 8, 1894, at the age of 36.

A 1945 veteran's committee selected Kelly for induction into the National Baseball Hall of Fame, which credited him with writing the first autobiography of a baseball player, but made no mention of his contributions to American music culture or his connection with "Casey at the Bat."

Chapter 52

Child Actor Hit President in Head

One Cubs Hustler and Child Movie Star Managed to Hit the President of the United States in the Head with a Baseball and Get Away with It.

Standing just 5'8", center fielder Henry Lee "Peanuts" Lowrey was always getting players (and coaches) to gamble in whatever form possible, usually cards games and shooting dice. The diminutive player learned his hustling skills growing up in California, where his grandfather's ranch was used as one of the settings for the *Our Gang* films, featuring beloved characters Alfalfa, Buckwheat, and Spanky.[6] His family used that fact to get Lowrey into several of the films.

The acting bug never left Lowrey. After earning a discharge from military service during World War II, he returned to his two loves: baseball and the movies. Lowrey's baseball fame (he played from 1942 to 1955, while his tenure with the Cubs lasted between 1942 and 1949) and acting background would give him the chance to continue his movie career. He had minor roles in three baseball movies: *The Pride of the Yankees* (1942), *The Stratton Story* (1948), and *The Winning Team* (1952).

As we've already discussed, *The Winning Team* was a biopic about Grover Cleveland Alexander starring actor Ronald Reagan as the Cubs pitcher. One scene in the film depicts Alexander trying to run to second base on an infield hit. In the course of trying to turn the double play, the opposing second baseman drills Alexander in the head so hard that the pitcher is bedridden for days. Lowrey was the actor given the role of throwing a white beanbag shaped like a ball at Reagan's head during the scene.

In his autobiography *An American Life*, Reagan, a lifelong Cubs fan, wrote that he as particularly proud of his six of his movies. Of those films, Reagan screened only one for several private audiences at the White House: *The Winning Team.*

Lowery may also have been the first player to introduce incentive-clause contracts in baseball. Realizing that he was far from the best player on the Cubs roster (Stan Hack, Bill Nicholson, and Claude Passeau claimed that honor at that time), Lowrey never signed the contract that Cubs general manager Jim Gallagher offered him in the offseason before spring training. Instead, Lowrey waited until he had a chance to see the competition and guess how the team would use him that season, then requested new clauses in his contract before signing.

Lowrey's size allowed him to play nearly any position on the field, from third to short to the entire outfield. Using this to his advantage, Lowrey had management insert a clause in his contract dictating that the team would pay him extra for games in which he played more than one position.[7] This and other clauses allowed Lowrey to make as much, if not more than, star players combining their own contractual incentives and base salaries. Instead of resenting these unusual negotiating skills, Gallagher had respect for Lowrey's confidence. "Let me tell you about that little son of a bitch," Gallagher said in Peter Golenbock's book *Wrigleyville*. "[Lowrey] made more money on that ball club than Stan Hack, Bill Nicholson and Claude Passeau."[8]

Of course, Lowrey had other ways of earning money as well. Whether it was poker, dice, or pool, Lowrey always seemed to come out on top. Recalled teammate Lennie Merullo:

> He could con you, he was sharp. If he had to cheat to beat you, he would do it. That was Peanuts Lowrey. . . . When Gallagher told me Peanuts was making more than [Hack, Nicholson, or Passeau], I believed him, knowing Peanuts. My own son was around the ballpark. He didn't idolize me. He idolized Peanuts.[9]

In 1949, the Cubs traded Lowrey to Cincinnati. He would also play in St. Louis and Philadelphia before his playing days ended in 1955. He then began a career as a coach, eventually coaching for the Cubs, the Phillies, the San Francisco Giants, the Montreal Expos, and the California Angels. But no matter where he played or coached, Lowrey said his heart was always with the Cubs.

"Even when I played and coached against them. I always wanted to see them win," Lowrey said.[10]

Chapter 53

Cantankerous Comedy Changes Television

*One of the Most Despised Men in Baseball Moonlighted as
One of Television's Favorite Comedy Guest Stars Despite Being
Thrown Out of the Game for a Season for His Behavior.*

Abrasive, combative, defiant, and loud, Leo Durocher was an unlikely candidate to become one of the first crossover television stars in baseball history, especially in comedy programming. This was the same man who received the longest penalty in baseball (outside of a lifetime ban) when he was banned from the game for a season in 1947 due to "conduct detrimental to baseball." He also angered nearly every person he worked with in the sport, including the biggest names in the game.

Anecdotes about how hated Durocher was are nearly endless. In Cubs circles, Ron Santo wanted to fight him, Fergie Jenkins likened him to a bad night in jail, and Jack Brickhouse called him an "old son of a bitch." Ty Cobb once waited after a game near the locker room to fight the young ballplayer, who had the audacity to ridicule Cobb mercilessly despite being new to the big leagues. Luckily for Durocher, Babe Ruth talked Cobb out of it. Ruth later tangled with this famous curmudgeon himself, dubbing Durocher "the All-American out" when the Yankees traded Durocher to the Reds in large part due to his surly disposition. Durocher's constant jabber and hounding of opponents (as well as teammates and officials) earned him the well-earned nickname "Lippy" or "the Lip." Even mild-mannered Dodgers announcer Vin Scully had a caustic comment about "the Lip": asked about Durocher's 1976 decision to take a job with Japan's Yokohama Whales, Scully reportedly said, "It took the U.S. 35 years to get revenge for Pearl Harbor."

So how did a mean-spirited, abrasive S.O.B. like Durocher manage to achieve a career in television comedies? It helped that he had influential friends, but it helped even more that his wife was a beautiful Hollywood actress. After Laraine Day and Durocher's controversial marriage in 1947 (and subsequent remarriage in 1948), Day became known as "the First Lady of Baseball." When her husband became manager of the New York Giants in 1948, she was hired to host a 15-minute pregame show called *Day with the Giants* (also the title of her 1952 autobiography). Though the network had hoped that having a beautiful starlet hosting a baseball show would entice more women to follow the sport, the real byproduct of the show was that male fans tuned in 15 minutes before the first pitch.

Many of Hollywood's biggest stars had roots in New York, and thus rooted for the Giants. With Day hosting a television show about the team, the connection between Hollywood and Durocher became even stronger. In his autobiography *Nice Guys Finish Last*, Durocher underscored his many friendships with the most popular people in entertainment. Durocher claimed that NBC vice president Manny Sachs had been offering him a job for years; Sachs saw the gruff baseball man as a perfect character for Hollywood. Durocher finally signed with NBC in 1956 as the host of a weekly television show called *Game of the Week*. In addition to his weekly baseball show, Durocher appeared on 15 NBC shows in nonsports roles from 1954 to 1959, including *The Bob Hope Show*, the pilot for *The Dinah Shore Chevy Show*, and three appearances on *The NBC Comedy Hour*.

Durocher's ties to the entertainment world had begun years earlier when he went overseas to entertain the troops after World War II, singing and dancing with his friend entertainer Danny Kaye to the cheers of soldiers who all seemed, Durocher said, to be from New York. Describing his attempts to sing and dance, Durocher joked in his autobiography, "You cannot believe how revolting I was, but I loved every minute of it."[11]

After the New York Giants won the 1954 World Series, sweeping the Cleveland Indians, Durocher's connections to Hollywood were cemented by a roast at the Hillcrest Country Club. Few actors, much less a baseball lifer, have ever been feted the way Durocher was. He set the scene in his autobiography:

> The dais was the most glittering I have ever seen: Danny Kaye, Frank Sinatra, Bob Hope, Danny Thomas, George Burns, Milton Berle, Dean Martin . . . you name him, he was there. Ten million dollars worth of talent.[12]

All of these celebrities were either born in New York or had worked their way to Hollywood through New York. As skipper of the World Champion New York

Giants, Durocher was more than just a friend to these entertainers; he was a hero who, better yet, loved to gamble, curse, and have a good time.

When the Los Angeles Dodgers brought Durocher on as a coach from 1961 to 1964, the confluence of television stars, baseball, and the cranky Durocher was too much for producers to pass up. During the 1960s, Durocher appeared on ten more shows, including some of the most popular programs of the time: *The Beverly Hillbillies* (on which he tried to sign Jethro to pitch); *Mister Ed* (the horse offered Durocher hitting tips); *The Munsters* (Herman Munster got a tryout after hitting Durocher in the head with a baseball from eight blocks away); *The Joey Bishop Show; The Donna Reed Show;* and *The Judy Garland Show.*

From 1940 until his death in 1991, Durocher appeared in more than 40 television shows in addition to his work with NBC's *Game of the Week* and All-Star Game broadcasts.

The players who had endured Durocher's ugly behavior must have felt some vindication watching him taking pointers from a talking horse. After all, many players felt that they, too, had been forced to talk to a horse for years when dealing with Durocher—or, more accurately, the hind end of one.

Chapter 54

First Television Character Named for Cubbie

One Former Cubs Player Was Immortalized as the Inspiration for the Name of a Famous Television Sitcom Character.

Don't be surprised if you don't remember former Cubs first baseman Steve Bilko. After all, he played only 47 of his 600 major league games for Chicago in 1954. Even so, his name may very well sound familiar, as he was the inspiration for the character known as Sgt. Ernest G. Bilko on the half-hour television comedy *The Phil Silvers Show*, which aired on CBS from 1955 to 1959.

Silvers played the main character, Sgt. Bilko, a con man in the army's motor pool and a hustler who was constantly trying to make a little extra money on the side. The show was a critical success, but only lasted 142 episodes. What many may not realize is that the comedy material mined by Sgt. Bilko led to one of the most successful television comedies of all time, *M.A.S.H.*

In his autobiography *The Laugh Is On Me*, Silvers explained why he and his partner, Nat Hiken, picked Steve Bilko as their inspiration for Sgt. Bilko: "Since [Nat and I] were both sports fans, especially baseball, we used familiar names. Nat came up with Bilko, after a minor league player, Steve Bilko. It also had the welcome connotation of a man 'bilking' you."[13] The writers based other characters on the show on real sports figures as well, including Private Paparelli (based on umpire Joe Paparella) and Corporal Barbella (based on Rocky Graziano's real name, Thomas Barbella).

In 1954, the Cubs bought Bilko's rights from the St. Louis Cardinals for $12,500. Bilko hit just .239 with 22 hits in 103 at-bats, and had a mere four home runs scattered over his 47 with Chicago. At the end of the season, the team sent him back down to the minors, where he spent the bulk of his 13-year career.

Other television characters have mythical connections to baseball players, but they came long after Bilko's documented inspiration of Sgt. Bilko. Former

Yankees catcher Yogi Berra claimed to be the inspiration for the cartoon character Yogi Bear, and nearly every Red Sox pitcher from the 1970s would like to think that he was the inspiration for handsome chick magnet Sam "Mayday" Malone on the popular show *Cheers*.

Chapter 55

A Wild Thing Happened on Way to Playoffs

The Best Example in Sports History of Life Imitating Art Forever Joined the Reputations of a Pitcher and An Actor Who Wished He Was One.

Long before Charlie Sheen became known for his "tiger blood," he was "winning" as the lead actor in the No. 1 movie in the nation, in which he played a role he seemed born to portray. It was also a role one Cubs reliever seemed born to copy.

Sheen's character was Ricky "Wild Thing" Vaughn, a fastball-throwing, mullet-wearing relief pitcher for the Cleveland Indians in the movie *Major League*. The film debuted during the first week of April 1989 and immediately took the lead in the box office rankings. Meanwhile, real-life player Mitch "Wild Thing" Williams—a fastball-throwing, mullet-wearing reliever who debuted with the Chicago Cubs during the first week of April 1989—immediately took the team to first place in the standings. Williams started the season saving his first five opportunities, giving the Cubs their best start in 14 years, as well as first place in the National League East. The year 1989 would be the apex of both Williams' playing career (a career-high 36 saves earned him his only All-Star selection) and Sheen's lead-acting career in films.

Williams was an erratic pitcher whose aim was unpredictable—as with Sheen's film character. Despite Vaughn playing for the Indians in the movie, the connection between the two pitchers was obvious. Author Rob Neyer described Williams as "The living embodiment of Charlie Sheen's character in *Major League*. Problem was, Mitch wasn't acting."[14]

Prior to joining the Cubs, Williams pitched for three years with the Texas Rangers, issuing 220 walks, 18 intentional walks, and 14 wild pitches in 274.2 combined innings, as well as hitting 24 batters and balking 13 times. In Williams' autobiography, *Straight Talk from Wild Thing*, former teammate John Kruk told a story about how the young pitcher admitted he couldn't pitch to lefties. Williams also said he felt sorry for some batters, particularly Larry Walker, saying, "His head is like a magnet for my fastball. I feel sorry for the guy."[15] One of the best scenes in *Major League* involves Vaughn knocking the head off a wooden cutout of a batter. It would be understandable if Walker didn't find the scene very funny.

On May 10, 1989, life imitated art when Williams took the field during the eighth inning with The Troggs' song "Wild Thing" blaring over the Wrigley Field speakers. It was the same song that had played when the fictional character of Vaughn came on the field. Williams adopted the nickname "Wild Thing" from that point forward in his career—which only lasted two seasons in Chicago. In 1990, Williams' saves dropped from 36 to 16, while his ERA went up from 2.76 to 3.93. The Cubs traded him to the Philadelphia Phillies at the start of the 1991 season; there he changed his jersey number from 28 to 99, Vaughn's jersey number in *Major League*.

"Mitch Williams, that f----- guy never gave me credit," Sheen told *Sports Illustrated* [which edited out the actor's choice of adjective].[16] "Come on, dude; you're coming out to the Wild Thing song. . . . You changed your number. . . . Can I get a little nod?"

Sheen may be happy to know that more than two decades after appropriating his character's moniker, appearance, and jersey number, Williams finally came clean. "Yes, I got my nickname from the pitcher that Charlie Sheen played," Williams confessed in his autobiography. "He didn't get the nickname from me."

Chapter 56

Jay-Z Immortalizes Cubbie

Life Imitates Art, Part II: One Cubs Player Finds Himself the Subject of One of the Biggest Songs and Albums of 2006.

The Cubs' connection to the movie *Major League* doesn't end with Mitch "Wild Thing" Williams. In fact, life soon imitated art when the Cubs benefitted from another team with management woes that chose to follow the plot of the movie.

Major League tells the story of an unscrupulous team owner intent on moving her franchise from Cleveland to Miami. She assembles a team of misfits whom she believes will play so horribly that no fans will show up, and that the resulting poor attendance will allow her to move the team.

Back when the movie was made, there was no baseball team in Miami. But the Florida Marlins began to play in South Florida in 1993 (and were renamed the Miami Marlins in 2012). The Marlins won the World Series in 1997 and 2003, but team management copied the selfish actions of the owner from *Major League* when, following their second championship, they began to dump players (and their costly salaries) in order to squeeze more money out of the franchise. The Marlins cut nearly all of their productive players after the 2005 season, lowering the team's salary from $60.4 million in 2005 to just $14.6 million in 2006. One of the players traded was outfielder Juan Pierre, a fleet-footed base stealer who bagged 65 steals during the 2003 championship season. Pierre went to the Cubs in exchange for Sergio Mitre, Ricky Nolasco, and Renyel Pinto. Pierre became an instant spark plug for the Cubs, playing in all 162 games and bagging 58 stolen bases and a .292 batting average.

Chicagoans weren't the only ones to take notice of Pierre's skills. Jay-Z, one of the most famous hip-hop entertainers in the world, included a line about Pierre in a duet he sang with his wife, Beyoncé Knowles, called "Deja Vu":

I used to run base like Juan Pierre,
now I run the bass, high-hat and the snare

"Deja Vu" reached No. 4 on the Billboard singles chart and helped Beyoncé's album, *B'Day,* debut at No. 1 on the Billboard 200 chart with 541,000 units sold the first week.

It had been 114 years since the last time a Cubs player was the topic of a song that topped the charts—back when Mike "King" Kelly was the subject of "Slide, Kelly, Slide."

Pop is not always a lasting art form, however, as exemplified by the fact that Beyoncé's album spent only one week atop the Billboard 200 and Pierre spent only the 2006 season with the Cubs before signing with the Los Angeles Dodgers as a free agent for the 2007 season.

Other Cubs songs have had more staying power than Pierre's tenure with the Cubs. Steve Goodman wrote his song "Go, Cubs, Go"—which WGN-TV often uses as the theme music for Cubs broadcasts—in 1984. Goodman, a Chicago native and lifelong Cubs fan who died of leukemia in 1984 at the age of 36, also wrote the second most famous Cubs song, "A Dying Cub Fan's Last Request." This touching song is about a Cubs fan asking that his ashes be scattered at Wrigley Field. After several years of Cubs officials denying the family from scattering Goodman's ashes the singer's brother, David, convinced a member of ballpark security to let him complete the singer's final request and release his ashes in the outfield bleachers before the start of the 1988 season.

Musician Eddie Vedder may very well have written the most enduring Cubs song ever, his 2008 tune "All the Way." An Evanston native and lifelong Cubs fan, Vedder was able to do what no other songwriter has ever accomplished: play his Cubs ode before a packed audience at Wrigley Field. Vedder and his band, Pearl Jam, played a sold out Wrigley Field in July 2013. Only time will tell if Vedder's ode has the lasting effect of Goodman's. But given the poetry of his lyrics (and Pearl Jam's immense popularity), we're willing to bet it will. Here's a sample of Vedder's lyrics:

Yeah, don't let them say that it's just a game.
Well, I've seen other teams and it is never the same.

When you go to Chicago, you're blessed and you're healed,
The first time you walk into Wrigley Field.

Heroes with pinstripes and heroes in blue,
Give us the chance to feel like heroes do.
Whether we'll win and if we should lose, we know
Someday we'll go all the way.
Yeah, someday we'll go all the way.

Chapter 57

Highest Grossing Movie of All-Time Was Cubs Invention

The Highest-Grossing Baseball Movie of All Time Told the Story of a Team Created by Cubs Owner Philip Wrigley.

There may be no crying in baseball, but there sure is a lot of money to be made from films about the sport.

The 1992 movie *A League of Their Own*, directed by Penny Marshall, changed the world of entertainment in several ways. Cubs owner Philip Wrigley created the real women's baseball league that the movie was based on, the All-American Girls Professional Baseball League, which existed from 1943 to 1954. While the league was relatively short-lived, Marshall's film will live forever in the minds of future generations of baseball fans and in the record books. *A League of Their Own* is the highest-grossing baseball film of all time, with a lifetime gross of $107 million as of 2013.[17] *Moneyball* (2012) and *The Rookie* (2002) tie for a distant second at $75 million each.

The Chicago Cubs also have a direct connection to yet another top grossing baseball film. Daniel Stern's 1993 directorial debut, *Rookie of the Year* (about a young boy who pitches for the Cubs), claims sixth place with $53 million in gross receipts. The other top 10 grossing baseball films are *Field of Dreams* (1989), with $64 million; *The Benchwarmers* (2006), with $59 million; *Bull Durham* (1988), with $50 million; *Angels in the Outfield* (1994), with $50 million; *Major League* (1989), with $49 million; and *The Natural* (1984), with $47 million. In case you're wondering, the highest-grossing sports film overall was *Forrest Gump"* (1994), with $329 million, followed by *The Blind Side* (2009), which raked in $256 million. (For the record, *Forrest Gump* is classified as a football film.)

Tom Hanks has another claim to sports immortality other than starring in the film with the top sales. "There's no crying in baseball!" was the famous line from Hanks' character, baseball coach Jimmy Dugan, in *A League of Their Own*. When the American Film Institute released its list of the top 100 movie quotes of all time,[18] Dugan's famous admonishment to ballplayer Evelyn Gardner (played by Bitty Schram) was No. 54 on the list.

Hanks' character Dugan was loosely based on former Cub Jimmie Foxx who, like Dugan, allowed a drinking problem to shorten his career. Wrigley hired Foxx to manage in the AAGPBL as a way to help Foxx stay in baseball and pay his bills. At the end of *A League of Their Own*, Geena Davis' character, Dottie Hinson, comes across the Hall of Fame plaque for Dugan, which states that he hit 58 home runs in 1936 for the Chicago Cubs. In real life, Foxx hit 58 home runs for the Philadelphia Athletics in 1932. He played only two seasons for the Cubs at the end of his career (1942 and 1944), during which time he hit only three home runs. Foxx was inducted into the National Baseball Hall of Fame in 1951.

Chapter 58

Cubs Pitcher Who Helped Change Hollywood History

One Former Cubs Pitcher Turned His Back on Baseball and Went to Hollywood, Where He Helped Break the Color Barrier.

If you saw *Jurassic Park* or *Speed*, then you saw former Cubs pitcher Jophery Brown at work, though you almost certainly didn't know it. A pitcher with the Cubs from 1966 to 1969, Brown left the game for Hollywood, where he spent the next 30 years working on hundreds of films and television shows as a pioneer stuntman.

The scene in the film *Speed* in which a bus jumps across a break in the freeway had Brown at the wheel. The opening scene in *Jurassic Park* begins with a dinosaur eating a worker played by Brown ("Jophery, raise the gate!"). He also orchestrated the gunfights in *Scarface*, as well as the car stunts on the television show *The A-Team*. He was the body double for Morgan Freeman in many of his movies—and his brother, Calvin, served the same role for Bill Cosby for much of his career.

Jophery (also listed as Jophrey in many baseball guides) and Calvin were two of the first African American stuntmen in Hollywood. Cosby, the first African American television star of a primetime show (*I Spy*), insisted that the show's production company hire African American stuntmen rather than white ones in black face (referred to as "painting down" in Hollywood lingo).

Scouted by Buck O'Neil when he played for Grambling University, Brown was drafted in 1966 and worked his way through the Cubs' minor league system until he was called up at the end of the 1968 season. He appeared in only one major league game, taking the mound for two innings on September 21, 1968, and surrendering one run and one hit. The Cubs didn't use him for the rest of 1968, and sent him back down to the minors at the end of the season.

After going 9–10 during the 1969 season for the San Antonio Missions (an AA affiliate of the Cubs), Brown decided to go into show business. He had an "in" thanks to his brother, who, along with Willie Harris, had founded the Black Stuntman's Association in 1967. It was the first organization of its type, forcing Hollywood to hire minorities to do stunt work or act as body doubles for African American actors instead of using white ones in makeup. Jophery, Calvin, and Harris became the first three African American stuntmen in Hollywood.

Being a former athlete proved to be a huge advantage for Jophery. His athleticism allowed him to work on nearly 400 films and television shows during his career, more than twice that of his brother and Harris combined. Despite being part of the small fraternity of players who only played in one major league game, Brown was honored in 2010 with the Taurus Lifetime Achievement Award for his 30-plus years of stunt work in Hollywood.

Chapter 59

First Permanent Baseball Crossover Star to Television

Brown Was Not the Only Former Cub to Transition to Hollywood. Another Former Cub Starred on ABC's No. 1 Show and Earned a Star on the Hollywood Walk of Fame—Not Bad for a Former Philosophy Student.

A star on the basketball court, the baseball diamond, and the television screen, Kevin Joseph Aloysius "Chuck" Connors did it all and set milestones along the way that few philosophy students could ever imagine attaining.

Connors' most widespread fame came from his role as Lucas McCain, the lead character of *The Rifleman*—ABC's No. 1 show during its first season in 1958,[19] and No. 4 overall, trailing three other westerns (CBS's *Gunsmoke*, NBC's *Wagon Train*, and CBS's *Have Gun — Will Travel*, respectively). *The Rifleman* was the first show on television to feature a widowed parent (Connors) raising a child.

But sports fans will likely be more impressed by Connors' athletic achievements than his acting ones. The 6'5", 200-pound Connors was a well-rounded athlete who played basketball and baseball at Seton Hall, where he studied philosophy and literature. The New York native signed as a free agent with the Brooklyn Dodgers for the 1940 season, then signed with the New York Yankees for 1941 before being drafted into the army. After his tour of duty (during which he served at West Point), Connors re-signed with the Dodgers in 1946, remaining in their minor league system until he was traded to the Chicago Cubs in 1950.

While Connors made athletic history in 1946, it wasn't with Brooklyn. That year he signed to play with a new professional basketball team, the Boston Celtics. On November 5, 1946, Connors made NBA history by becoming the first player in league history to shatter a backboard. It happened during pregame warm-ups before a game against the visiting Chicago Stags. The feat wasn't as entertaining as the mighty dunks that Shaquille O'Neal and Darryl Dawkins became known for years later. The backboard in question was missing a key part, causing the rim to rip away from it when Connors took a simple set shot. It took an hour to fix.

Connors averaged 4.6 points per game during his only full season with the Celtics. After playing four games in the 1947–48 campaign, he turned his attention to baseball full-time.

On October 10, 1950, Connors and Dee Fondy were traded to the Cubs for Hank Edwards and cash. In 1951, Connors earned only two home runs, 18 RBI, and a .239 batting average in 66 games before the Cubs relegated him to their AAA affiliate in Los Angeles. After spending the 1952 season there, Connors left baseball to pursue a career in acting. His screen debut came in the 1952 film *Pat and Mike* starring Spencer Tracy and Katharine Hepburn. "They paid me 500 dollars for my week's work in that movie," said Connors according to former colleague David Fury.[20] "I figured they'd made some mistake on the adding machine, but I stuck the check in my pocket and shut up. Baseball, I told myself, just lost a first baseman."

Connors appeared in more than 120 movies and television shows during his acting career, including classics like *Old Yeller, Geronimo,* and cult favorite *Soylent Green.* In 1984, Connors became the only former Cubs player or coach to earn a star on the Hollywood Walk of Fame (former Cubs announcer Ronald Reagan also has a star, and, with their mutual connection to the Cubs, was also a personal friend of Connors). In 1991, the former first baseman was inducted into the Cowboy Hall of Fame in Oklahoma City.[21] In 1977, he earned an Emmy nomination for his role in the television miniseries *Roots.*

A scholar with a sense of humor, Connors used his intelligence to befuddle and entertain teammates and fellow actors throughout his life. As a young baseball player, he memorized Shakespearean passages for use when the time was right. According to Fury, Connors scolded umpires after a bad call by saying, "The slings and arrows of outrageous fortune I can take, but your blindness is ridiculous!"

The umpires still ejected him.

Connors was not the only Cubs player with a noteworthy basketball background. Pitcher Fergie Jenkins played for the Harlem Globetrotters in 1967 and 1968, touring with the team throughout the United States and Canada.

Jenkins conceded that the Globetrotters wanted him mostly because he was Canadian and his celebrity status would boost their attendance on tour through the Great White North. After Jenkins proved himself as a basketball player, the Globetrotters brought him back in 1968. Though he had fun playing with Meadowlark Lemon and Curly Neal, Jenkins was perplexed (albeit thankful) that the Cubs let one of their star players participate in another sport. "The funny thing is the Cubs gave me their blessing to play basketball," Jenkins wrote in his autobiography *Fergie*, "but they went ballistic when I went horseback riding."[22]

Jenkins was the fourth in a string of baseball players hired by the Globetrotters as celebrity participants. The others were Satchel Paige (1954), Bob Gibson (1957), and Lou Brock (1961). Jenkins, however, was the only Canadian ever to suit up for the team.

Chapter 60

Cubs First to Record Team "Shuffle"

*The Cubs Began a Tradition That Is Nothing to
be Proud of—Unless You're a Bad Singer.*

Though many athletes have tried, few have been able to make a successful crossover
into the music industry. Sure, former New York Yankee Bernie Williams can brag
that he was nominated for a 2009 Latin Grammy for his instrumental album
Moving Forward. But Carl Lewis' botched national anthem in 1993 was both
a low point in musical history and a high point in unintentional comedy. John
McEnroe, Pele, Shaquille O'Neal, Kobe Bryant, Deion Sanders, Bronson Arroyo,
Barry Zito, Ozzie Smith, Coco Crisp, and Chris Webber are only a few of the
athletes who have attempted to make their mark in music history, with dubious
results.

The Cubs have had several players try their hand at music. Former player/
manager Charlie Grimm often played his banjo and sang in the clubhouse, and he
spent his off-seasons on theater stages throughout the Midwest entertaining crowds.
Back at the turn of the twentieth century, former Cubs Mike Kelly, Cap Anson,
and Rabbit Maranville all took to the vaudeville stage. And even gruff manager Leo
Durocher sang and danced for the troops overseas after World War II.

In 1908, Joe Tinker and Johnny Evers lent their name to a ghostwritten song
called "Between You and Me" (a love song, strangely enough).[23] The song's real
writer, Chicago music publisher Will Rossiter, simply thought he would sell
more records with the Cubs players' names attached and was apparently unaware
that Evers and Tinker had an infamous feud that lasted decades. But the two
apparently squelched their bitter feelings when the opportunity to make some
money arose—although neither player sang in the recording.

The history between baseball and music goes back even further, to before the
Civil War. In 1858, J. Randolph Blodgett wrote "The Base Ball Polka" while he

was playing for the Niagara Baseball Club from Buffalo, New York.[24] So, no, the Cubs cannot claim to have been the first team to have players who were singers. They cannot even claim to have the first teammates to form a band. The St. Louis Cardinals' Gashouse Gang of the 1930s had a group of players led by outfielder/first baseman Pepper Martin who started a band called the Mississippi Mudcats. The group played popular country tunes in the clubhouse and occasionally on the radio.

All of these players turned musicians of the past played popular songs of the day rather than original pieces of their own. That all changed in 1969. That year Detroit Tigers pitcher Denny McLain, who played the electric organ, toured the country, even playing in Las Vegas. Soon after, he began an unfortunate string of run-ins with the law that ruined his career and overshadowed his athletic and musical accomplishments.

That same year several Cubs players recorded the first song sung by teammates bragging about how good they were. The song was a folksy tune that appeared on an album called *Cub Power*. Entitled "Hey Hey Holy Mackerel" (GeoVerse™ 199), it featured utility player Willie Smith, second baseman Nate Oliver, and catcher Gene Oliver singing:

> *Hey! Hey! Holy mackerel! No doubt about it!*
> *The Cubs are on their way.*
> *The Cubs are gonna hit today,*
> *They're gonna pitch today,*
> *They're gonna field today.*
> *Come on, man, the Cubs are gonna win today*
>
> *Hey! Hey! Holy mackerel! No doubt about it!*
> *The Cubs are on their way.*
> *They've got the hustle.*
> *They've got the muscle.*
> *The Chicago Cubs are on their way.*

Sure, the lyrics are tame by today's standard, but history must begin somewhere. The title of the song referred to the home-run calls of announcers Jack Brickhouse ("Hey! Hey!") and Vince Lloyd ("Holy mackerel!"). The same trio of Cubbies sang another tune called "Baseball Baseball" on the album, and Nate Oliver and Smith did a number called "Pennant Feeling." It was a feel-good album that even featured the Bleacher Bums singing versions of "Hey Hey Holy Mackerel" and "Take Me Out to the Ballgame."

In 1984, the Cubs once again found themselves bragging about their team in song. That was the first year since 1969 that the North Siders were any good, clinching the National League East division. Before the season ended, five Cubs recorded the song "Men in Blue" (GeoVerse™200), sharing their self-confidence with the world. Pitcher Rick Sutcliffe, catcher Jody Davis, first baseman Leon Durham, and outfielders Keith Moreland and Gary Woods appeared on this country tune that included lyrics similar to "Hey Hey Holy Mackerel," but with a modern edge:

> *It's been a long time since 1945,*
> *But the Wrigley Field faithful always kept the spirit alive,*
> *And now's the time and here's the place we even up the score,*
> *The hopes are high the pennant will fly,*
> *Over Wrigley Field in '84,*
> *And as sure as there's ivy on the center-field wall,*
> *The men in blue are going to win it all*

At the same time the Cubs were singing "Men in Blue," the National Football League's San Francisco 49ers were taking advantage of a new technology—videotape—to record a rap song titled "We're the 49ers." Of course, this team had a right to brag: the 49ers went 15–1 in the regular season and crushed the Miami Dolphins 38–16 in the Super Bowl. Sadly, the Cubs did not fare as well that year, losing the National League Championship Series to San Diego in five games.

The 49ers' song was a regional hit that didn't get any national play. "Men in Blue" started out that way, with a local distributor expecting merely tepid regional sales, but orders soon poured in from across the country. The original pressing of 10,000 singles sold out almost instantly.[25]

As most sports fans (and even many nonsports fans) know, the following year the Chicago Bears recorded "The Super Bowl Shuffle"—a song that would eventually hit No. 41 on the Billboard charts and garner an Emmy nomination in rhythm and blues. What the Cubs had begun, the Bears improved upon.

Soon there was no stopping teams in every sport from recording their own songs bragging about how good they were. In 1986, the New York Mets recorded "Get Metsmerized," the Los Angeles Dodgers sang "Baseball Boogie," the Los Angeles Rams had "Let's Ram It," and the Los Angeles Raiders made "Silver and Black Attack." In 1987, the Calgary Flames recorded "Red Hot." In 1988, the Philadelphia Eagles made "Buddy's Watching You." In 1990, the US World Cup soccer team helped record "Victory," and the Miami Dolphins made "Can't Touch Us." In 1993, the New York Knicks made "Go NY Go." In 2005, the Cincinnati Bengals and Bootsy Collins recorded "Fear Da Tiger."

This list obviously doesn't even touch on all the high school and college sports teams who have recorded songs since the start of the twenty-first century, particularly doing covers of the teen hit "Call Me Maybe" by Carly Rae Jepsen.

Some traditions are not worth emulating.

Chapter 61

NFL's Early Success Due to Wrigley Field

The Cubs Even Changed the Course of History for the NFL.

The National Football League owes its existence to the success of the Chicago Bears, and the Chicago Bears in turn owe their success to the Cubs. According to the transitive relationship of mathematics, that means the NFL owes its existence to the Cubs.

The NFL began as the American Professional Football Association in 1920. The Decatur, Illinois, Staleys—founded by George "Papa Bear" Halas and named after the team sponsor (the Staley Starch Company)—was one of the league's charter members. In 1921, Halas moved the team to Chicago and agreed to a one-season, $5,000 deal to keep the team name the same. Playing at the home of the Cubs, the Staleys won the 1921 AFPA championship with a 9–1–1 record, marking the first championship season of any kind at Wrigley Field.

On January 28, 1922, the team was renamed the Bears. According to the Pro Football Hall of Fame, "Halas reasoned that because football players were generally bigger than baseball players, and the city's baseball team was the Cubs, then logically the football team should be the Bears."[26] That same year, the AFPA was renamed the National Football League.

Fans can't help but wonder what the Chicago Bears would have been called had the Cubs not existed. But the Cubs did more than provide inspiration for the Bears' name. They also gave them a home so large (thanks to temporary stands erected for the football season) that Halas' team had a significant advantage. Their crosstown rival, the Chicago Cardinals, played at Normal Field and Comiskey Park, but never assembled a successful team—meaning seating capacity wasn't really a concern. The Bears had the advantage of both a better team and playing in one of the most popular stadiums in the country. In fact, it can be argued that the Cardinals clung to their very existence from their first game, in which they beat the Chicago Tigers 6–0 in 1920 with the loser agreeing to leave town. The Cardinals won, but never put a team on the field that could consistently compete with the Bears.

In 1922, the Bears averaged an NFL-high 7,000 spectators per game, while the Cardinals had only 4,600.[27] Attendance figures for early NFL games are hard to establish because of the lack of media coverage and the fact that teams would appear for a season only to disappear the next. But Joe Horrigan, curator of the Pro Football Hall of Fame, sifted through old newspaper accounts to determine that during the first years of the NFL, while the average attendance per game was 5,000 people, the Bears increased their average attendance in the mid 1920s to 10,000 per game at Wrigley Field.[28]

In 1925, Halas signed star Harold "Red" Grange. Approximately 36,000 fans packed Wrigley Field for his debut game, against the Cardinals, who fought to a 0–0 draw, holding Grange to just 36 yards.

The Bears called Wrigley Field home for the next 45 years, playing their last game at the Cubs' home stadium on December 13, 1970 (a 35–17 drubbing of the Green Bay Packers). The Bears began playing at Soldier Field in 1971.

The Bears won eight NFL championships during their tenure at Wrigley Field, with four being won at Wrigley Field (1933, 1941, 1943, and 1963). That means the only championships won at Wrigley Field have been those by the Bears, not the Cubs, whose last championship was in 1908, eight years before the team began to play at Wrigley Field.

Despite teams coming and going, the NFL succeeded through its tumultuous first several decades because of the constant presence of Halas, who kept his team at Wrigley Field for 50 years because the sellout crowds increased excitement in the fan base and provided his team with solid income while allowing them to avoid building a stadium of their own. Without Wrigley Field, the Bears would not have become the cornerstone franchise that allowed the NFL to flourish. It's just too bad that every championship won at the Friendly Confines since 1916 has been on the gridiron, rather than the diamond.

Chapter 62

Only Entertainer Ejected from MLB Game

Only One Person Has Ever Been Ejected from a Game for Their Rendition of The Seventh-Inning Stretch—And In This, Too, The Bears and the Cubs Share a Connection.

Ozzy Ozborne deserved to be ejected for his muttering version of "Take Me Out to the Ballgame" in 2003. Jeff Gordon ensured that he would never be invited back after flubbing the lyrics in 2005. But neither performer "topped" Chicago Bears defensive lineman Steve "Mongo" McMichael, the only person ever ejected during the seventh-inning stretch.

On August 7, 2001, the Cubs defeated the visiting Colorado Rockies 5–4. But in the bottom of the sixth inning, plate umpire Angel Hernandez called third baseman Ron Coomer out in a play at home plate. When McMichael took the microphone in the middle of the following inning, he shared his opinion about the call, saying, "Don't worry, I'll have some speaks with that home plate umpire after the game." (GeoVerse™210) The crowd of 40,266 raucous fans loved it, but Hernandez did not: he deemed McMichael's words a threat, and ejected him from the game.

While McMichael's theatrics were entertaining (except to the officials), Cubs manager Don Baylor was angered because of the risk he felt it had posed to his team. "I worried about a forfeit," Baylor said in Bill Jauss' *Chicago Tribune* story.[29] "A lot of people do not realize that was a possibility. I told the umpire we do not condone what [McMichael] did."

History of course proves that Baylor was correct. In 1995, the Dodgers were forced to forfeit a game to the St. Louis Cardinals when fans threw promotional giveaway baseballs onto the field. In 1979, the Chicago White Sox were forced to forfeit the second half of a doubleheader to the Detroit Tigers when the infamous "Disco Demolition Night" caused a riot with fans storming the field. And in

1974, the Indians were forced to forfeit a game to the Texas Rangers when fans fueled by dime-beer night got out of control.

Jauss' story revealed that years earlier a general manager had been ejected for cursing at officials, but that exchanged happened in a minor league game. That gives McMichael the rare distinction of being the only press box guest ejected from a major league game for what he said rather than anything he physically did.

Chapter 63

Religious Evangelism Industry
Created by Former Cubbie

Religious Evangelism, Frank Sinatra, and a Hall of Fame
Songwriter Were All Aided by a Cubs Outfielder Who Did More
for Church Attendance Than Any Other Player In Sports History.

Frank Sinatra fans who have sung along to one of the most famous tunes of the twentieth century were actually singing about a former Chicago Cub—though most never knew it.

"Chicago (That Toddling Town)" is one of the tunes most identified with the Windy City (along with "Sweet Home Chicago" by Robert Johnson). Written by Fred Fisher in 1922, the song is a celebration meant to embody the attitude of the town where this aspiring songwriter lived for years when he was starting out. The author of dozens of popular hits during the early 1900s, Fisher was enshrined in the Songwriter Hall of Fame[30] for his lifetime of achievements. But none of his songs will ever be more popular than "Chicago," with its upbeat tempo and fun lyrics. What few baseball fans realize is that the song also immortalized a former Cubs player, referenced in the lyric: "The town that Billy Sunday couldn't shut down."

It's doubtful if any song was as special to Fisher as "Chicago," considering the multiple elements of his life that he poured into the words. Though born in Germany, Fisher lived in Chicago at the turn of the century. One of the first jobs he held in the United States was serving as music leader for an up-and-coming evangelic preacher using a new approach to create a nationwide following the likes of which nobody had ever seen. Eschewing temporary tents and bland sermons for his traveling church services, this preacher built new wooden tabernacles and laced his preaching with vivid stories about his life in baseball. He performed on stage, jumping, yelling, and pretending to throw and catch the ball. The preacher's name was Billy Sunday, a man who had been a talented base runner before he traded in his bat for a pulpit.

Much to Fisher's delight, Sunday had a unique way of presenting music to his congregation, replacing the traditional organ and choir with 12-piece orchestras hired in every town they visited. Sunday was a showman like nobody else, and he was changing the world of church services. He soon became synonymous with straight-talk sermons about the evils of drinking, drugs, and loose morals. He became the most influential traveling preacher in the nation, the first professional evangelist to claim a following of millions from coast to coast. He toured the country nonstop, building tabernacles and churches wherever he went. Sunday would also become a staunch supporter of Prohibition, which made him close friends with some of the most powerful men in the world, including U.S. presidents Theodore Roosevelt, Woodrow Wilson, and Herbert Hoover, and oil tycoon John D. Rockefeller.

Gifted with feet faster than a good rumor, Sunday first caught the attention of Cap Anson, who signed him to play for the Cubs (then called the White Stockings). He played for the Chicago NL team from 1883 to 1887, patrolling the outfield, where Anson put him to take advantage of his blazing speed. Anson claimed Sunday was the fastest man in baseball and could round the bases in 14 seconds (which would also make him the fastest player in the MLB today, according to *Baseball America*[31]). But Anson also pointed out that Sunday's less than stellar hitting (he struck out in his first 13 at-bats with Chicago) and poor outfield judgment needed his blazing speed. In addition to turning ground-outs into base hits with his fast legs, Sunday also had to use his speed to run down catches misplayed in the field.

During one game in particular, in the era before outfield fences, Sunday's speed paid off handsomely in an unexpected way. According to the Sunday biography *Home Run to Heaven* by Robert Allen, on June 10, 1886 (baseball records indicate the game was actually played on July 10), during a game in Detroit, a hitter cracked a long fly ball in Sunday's direction. The future preacher initially misjudged the ball's trajectory. Without a fence to mark an outside boundary to the outfield, Sunday prayed to God to give him some help to catch the ball. Running as hard as he could, Sunday pushed fans aside and dove for the catch, tumbling at the feet of an approaching horse-drawn carriage. The outfielder jumped up with the ball in his hand.

The first person to congratulate Sunday for his fabulous play was former Cleveland mayor Tom Johnson. "Here is $10, Bill," Johnson said. "Buy yourself the best hat in Chicago. That catch won me $1,500. Tomorrow go and buy yourself the best suit of clothes you can find in Chicago."

Little did Sunday know that someday his congregation would cheer and applaud every time he recited this story. Whenever a member of the congregation asked if he'd kept that $10, Sunday would reply, "You bet I did!"[32]

Sunday's past as a popular baseball player helped cement his appeal to his congregations, but it was his determination to turn his back on the vice of the big city while playing in Chicago that truly earned the preacher his first followers.

It was baseball that took this country boy from his hometown of Ames, Iowa, and transported him to a completely different world in Chicago. Where Ames was quiet and God-fearing, Chicago was bustling and filled with every form of temptation. It was baseball that introduced Sunday to the sins of the flesh when he went out on the town with his teammates, many of whom were known carousers. Sunday did drink, but rarely got drunk. He was a trusted teammate who, though only 5'10" and 160 pounds, fought for his fellow players when provoked on or off the field.

But everything changed for Sunday one summer night on State Street in 1886. While roaming from bar to bar, Sunday and his teammates paused to take a seat on the curb because Mike "King" Kelly, the ringleader of the party crowd on the team, was too drunk to walk. According to Robert Allen, teammates John Clarkson, Abner Dalrymple, and George Gore were with Sunday and Kelly that night. While trying to clear their heads, the teammates heard singing. The sound was pouring out of the Pacific Garden Mission (formerly located on State Street between Harrison Avenue and Polk Street, since razed in 2012 to make way for new construction).

According to Allen, Dalrymple said, "Let's listen. I like singing."[33]

While the group listened, Sunday realized he knew the hymn that was floating across the dirty street to their ears. It was "Where Is My Boy Tonight," and Sunday immediately recalled hearing it at the Methodist church in Iowa to which his mother used to take him and his brothers. The lyrics spoke to Sunday in a way that his teammates didn't fully understand:

Where is my wandering boy tonight
The boy of my tenderest care,

The boy that was once my joy and light,
The child of my love and prayer?

"That's a song my mother used to sing," Sunday said, pulling himself to his feet.[34] While several players tried to convince Sunday to sit back down, Dalrymple told his friends to stop and let Sunday do as he wished. Which is precisely what Sunday did. He began attending services at the Pacific Garden Mission that summer, and his days of partying with teammates ended. It wasn't an easy decision; Sunday worried about whether his hard-partying teammates would accept him once he traded carousing for nighttime church services at the mission. He needn't have worried. Kelly himself told Sunday, "Bill, I'm proud of you. Religion's not my long suit, but I'll help you all I can."[35]

Sunday devoted his life to helping the needy after that summer, working for the Young Men's Christian Association (YMCA). His tenure in Chicago ended when the Pittsburgh Alleghenys purchased his contract for $2,000 in 1888. He played for Pittsburgh until he was traded to the Philadelphia Phillies in 1890. At age 27, Sunday was a backup outfielder at the crossroads of a major decision: accept an offer of $400 per month from the Phillies or take a job for $68 per month helping the YMCA. Sunday choose the latter, walking away from baseball for a pay cut. But the move proved to be the right one in the long run, as his popularity as a preacher was on the rise.

By the time Fisher joined Sunday's staff in 1900, the traveling preacher was holding one- and two-week revivals in Iowa, Minnesota, Illinois, Nebraska, and Missouri. At the time, Sunday used tents when he couldn't find a local church to suit his congregation's needs. However, in 1905 one of those tents collapsed in Colorado, and though nobody was hurt (since the collapse occurred at night), Sunday decided to build wooden tabernacles for his flock from that time forward. These buildings included nurseries (since Sunday hated having his sermons drowned out by crying babies). According to *Home Run to Heaven,* each one also housed a post office box so that the zealous preacher could quickly mail the names of new converts to the pastors in their home towns, allowing local church leaders to continue what Sunday had started. The wooden floors of Sunday's tabernacles were covered in sawdust to reduce the noise so as not to compete with his preaching. His evangelical tours were soon dubbed "the Sawdust Trail" in reference to this sound-dampening solution.

Sunday's organization had the foresight and planning of a military invasion. Months before reaching a town for a revival, Sunday's group dispatched organizers to local communities to hold nightly prayer meetings at homes to increase the turnout for the upcoming event. For example, in Scranton, Pennsylvania, during a three-week period prior to a Sunday revival, organizers arranged for 4,137 prayer meetings at private homes with a combined attendance of 68,360 worshippers, ensuring Sunday would be met with overflowing crowds every day he preached.[36] As many as 100 ushers were trained in the offering procedure that Sunday devised so that collections could be taken from as many as 8,000 people in less than three minutes. These offerings were used for the maintenance of the tabernacles, revival management, and the YMCA—except for the offering on the final day of a revival, which was given to Sunday as his payment.[37]

This system proved profitable for everyone, particularly when Sunday's revivals hit the East Coast. According to Allen, one last-day collection at a revival in New York City in 1917 netted $124,600. Though Sunday donated that collection to the YMCA and the Red Cross, it was clear that this evangelist could afford to be giving. Sunday had become the richest preacher in America.

As the United States crept closer to entering World War I, Sunday began to ramp up his sermons against alcohol, exhorting parishioners to give up drinking for the good of God and country. Sunday's sermons began to affect Americans who had never even entered his tabernacles. He delivered his "Booze" sermon (GeoVerse™220) often and with as much aggressiveness as if he was chasing down a fly ball. Speaking of drunken men who return home to threaten a wife or child, he'd swing a chair to the floor until it splintered. He pounded his fist on a table so hard that some in the crowd thought he had broken his hand. He preached for more than an hour at a time. It became common for bars and saloons to close their doors in the weeks after a Sunday revival due to the lack of patrons. Many cities also reported lower crime rates in the wake of his revivals.[38]

Sunday soon began incorporating soldiers into his "Booze" sermon, arranging for dozens of uniformed men to march across the stage behind him carrying American flags as he railed against alcohol, shouting: "The saloon feeds on our boys and destroys the young manhood of our country! Are you going to let these boys be destroyed, or are you going to take your stand for God and country? Can you be counted on to protect your wives and homes, your mothers and the children and the manhood of America?"[39]

By the time the United States entered World War I in 1918, Sunday had done as much as any single American, including President Woodrow Wilson and any governor in the country, to be sure that every American male in his audience had enlisted. He even urged that women should not consider marriage proposals without first seeing the man's enlistment papers.

But Sunday's greatest victory was still to come. After more than 20 years of preaching against alcohol, delivering his "Booze" sermon so frequently that many attendees knew the stories by heart, Sunday helped create what he believed to be the best thing possible for both God and country: prohibition. Teetotalers like Wilson and Rockefeller worked with Sunday behind the scenes while the preacher carried the message to the masses to convince the nation that banning alcohol would be best for everyone. On January 16, 1919, Congress approved the 18th amendment to the Constitution—called the Volstead Act due to its legislative sponsor, Representative Andrew J. Volstead of Minnesota, but known to most as Prohibition. For the first time in American history, alcohol was illegal. Which was just the way Sunday wanted it.

Everyone working in any field affiliated with alcohol (including brewers, bar owners, managers, servers, bar backs, singers, entertainers, truck drivers, etc.) was either out of work or forced to hide their occupation. Average Americans wanting a beer or a glass of wine at the end of the day were suddenly forced to disguise their consumption. But neither government officials nor Sunday had expected the sudden proliferation of illegal bars called "speakeasies" that flourished in the absence of legal access to alcohol. Chicago, the city that spawned Sunday's hatred of drinking, became known for its many speakeasies, with Al Capone and other gangsters controlling the industry. And therein lies the root of Fisher's famous lyric describing Chicago as "the town that Billy Sunday couldn't shut down."

What began on State Street in 1886 at the Pacific Garden Mission led to a religious movement, Prohibition, and a famous song about a town that wouldn't stop swinging. Sunday's biographer estimated that by the time the enormously successful preacher died in 1935 at age 73, he had preached in front of more than 85 million people. His Sawdust Trail organization had reached every state in the union.

Despite those impressive achievements, most people today know Sunday only from his inclusion in the song that helped make Sinatra one of the most famous singers of the twentieth century. But Sunday can take solace in the fact that he isn't the only former Cub remembered more for his portrayal in the arts than his playing career. Our next Cub changed the world of film when the portrayal of his unusual circumstances became one of the most popular and highest-grossing baseball movies of all time. This man's life was far from an ideal movie script. And while he did have the honor of being played by Robert Redford, he had to get shot to make it happen.

Chapter 64

Cubs Shooting Leads to Movie History

The Actions of a Deranged Fan Led to One of the Most Critically Acclaimed Baseball Films of All Time and Made One Cub More Well-Known for Being Shot Than for His Performance in the Infield.

No other team in professional sports history has had more team members shot under mysterious circumstances than the Chicago Cubs. It isn't a record to be proud of, but it's also undeniable.

In 1932, shortstop Billy Jurges was shot by Violet Valli, a lovesick girlfriend who also helped blackmail the former player. In 1951, pitcher Hi Bithorn was shot and killed by a Mexican police officer who was eventually found guilty of murder and sentenced to eight years in prison. In 2012, former Cubs manager Dave Sveum was accidentally shot in the back and ear while quail hunting with Brewers icon Robin Yount. But none of these incidents had the historic impact of the story of Eddie Waitkus, who was shot by an obsessed teenager with a .22 rifle in 1949. Waitkus' life became the basis for one of the most popular baseball movies of all time, *The Natural.*

Released in the second week of May 1984, *The Natural* debuted at No. 1, where it stayed for most of May thanks largely to the big-screen presence of star Robert Redford in the role of Roy Hobbs, a baseball player shot by deranged fan Harriet Bird (played by Barbara Hershey). Based on Bernard Malamud's novel of the same name, *The Natural* was a fictional story largely based on Waitkus' shooting by obsessed fan Ruth Ann Steinhagen on June 14, 1949.

The Natural is the tenth-highest grossing baseball film of all time,[40] having earned $47 million in box office receipts, and most critics rank it as one of the best baseball films ever made. When the editors of ESPN.com ranked the all-time best moments in baseball film history,[41] *The Natural* took three of the top ten scenes—including the No. 1 moment, in which Hobbs' knocks out a home run that hits a light tower. The other two were Hobbs' home run off the clock tower, ranked No. 5, and Hobbs' striking out "the Whammer," ranked No. 10. (The only other film in ESPN's list to earn more than one mention was *Major League*, which had two spots in the list of top 10 moments and, as we've already discussed, had its own connections to the Cubs.)

ESPN.com also listed the Waitkus shooting as one of the top 10 real-life shocking moments in baseball history, placing it seventh on the list.[42] The Waitkus shooting is fascinating for several reasons. First, Waitkus was a war hero, having served in the army in 1944 and 1945 in the Pacific theater and earning four battle stars. Second, Waitkus didn't even know Steinhagen. This real-life attempted murderer was even more deranged than her counterpart in *The Natural*, who had at least met Hobbs before shooting him. Third, the shooting brought Waitkus, a former All-Star, closer to death than any action he saw in World War II and this strange, horrible incident altered Waitkus' personality and career for the worse. Finally, while few athletes are ever attacked by a fan, and fewer still are shot by one, none have ever had a Hollywood icon the likes of Redford play them in a box-office hit about their story like *The Natural*.

After returning home from World War II, Waitkus proved himself a welcome addition to the 1946 Cubs, hitting .304 with 55 RBI and committing only four errors at first base. He finished 13th in Most Valuable Player voting in his first full season (he played only 12 games for the Cubs in 1941 before being drafted), and was "acknowledged as the best fielding first baseman in the league."[43] After going through a sophomore slump, Waitkus rebounded and was voted an All-Star in 1948 and 1949 (although he received the second nod largely for sentimental reasons after he was shot).

Waitkus was one of the few bright spots on an otherwise moribund Cubs team that finished under .500 for five straight seasons. That brought him some notoriety, which would normally be great for any up-and-coming starter. But Waitkus' newfound fame garnered him the unfortunate attention of Steinhagen, a troubled young woman. After the shooting, Steinhagen confessed that as a child, she had killed the family's pet canary and wanted to hurt her family members, saying, "At 10 or 12 years of age, I had a feeling I was going crazy, and a little later on I had a horrible desire to kill my mother."[44] Steinhagen later said that once she saw Waitkus, she became obsessed with him to the point that she saved every photo of him; created a shrine to him in her home; and pretended that he was walking, talking, and even eating dinner with her.[45]

On December 14, 1948, the Cubs traded Waitkus to Philadelphia in a four-player swap. Steinhagen was mentally and emotionally crushed. She sent letters to the Cubs and local newspapers beseeching them to bring Waitkus back. Her parents, knowing Steinhagen was unbalanced, took her to two psychiatrists, but nothing seemed to work. With the object of her fixation in Philadelphia, Steinhagen began talking about how she was going "to get Eddie."[46]

Knowing the Phillies were scheduled to play in Chicago in mid-June, Steinhagen bought a rifle at a pawn shop to avoid having to get a gun permit and made a reservation at the Edgewater Beach Hotel (GeoVerse™ 230), where the Phillies stayed when they were in town.[47] On Monday, June 13, she checked into the Edgewater and was given the keys to room 1297-A, where she unpacked a three-and-half inch paring knife and a .22 caliber rifle. Her plan was to kill Waitkus with the knife and then kill herself with the rifle.

Steinhagen did not attempt to contact Waitkus during her first night at the hotel, having drinks in her room with a friend, Helen Farazis, instead. Farazis later told authorities that Steinhagen had talked about her plans "to get Eddie." But Farazis hadn't taken the comments seriously.

Sadly, the next day the world would learn just how serious the 19-year-old typist was. Prior to checking in to the hotel, Steinhagen had carefully prepared a note to lure Waitkus to her room. She paid a bellboy $5 to deliver her note, which read:

> It is extremely important that I see you as soon as possible. We're not acquainted, but I have something of importance to speak to you about. I think it would be to your advantage to let me explain this to you as I am leaving the hotel the day after tomorrow. I realize this is out of the ordinary, but as I say, it is extremely important.[48]

Shortly after 11:00 p.m., Waitkus called Steinhagen's room. She gave him her room number and asked him to come over immediately. Steinhagen let the ballplayer in. Moments later, she calmly said, "I have a surprise for you," then pulled out her rifle and pointed it at Waitkus, ordering him to move toward the window. "For two years you've been bothering me and now you're going to die," she said, pulling the trigger.[49] The bullet ripped through the right side of Waitkus' chest, collapsing his lung before lodging near his spine.

"Baby, what did you do that for?" Waitkus asked, according to Steinhagen, who knelt by his side. Looking into his shooter's eyes, Waitkus realized the horrible truth: "You like this, don't you?"[50]

Steinhagen rose to her feet, called the front desk, and emotionlessly stated, "There's a man shot in my room."[51] When police questioned Steinhagen, her lack of sympathy was evident:

> I'm not really sorry. I'm sorry Eddie has to suffer so. I'm sorry it had to be him. But I had to shoot somebody. Only in that way could I relieve the nervous tension I've been under the last two years. The shooting has relieved that tension.

Steinhagen also told police that Waitkus reminded her "of so many people, especially my father" and that "whatever I am in the mood for, I eventually do. . . . I just wanted to do away with him. I just wanted something exciting in my life." When asked if she shot him for a thrill, Steinhagen replied, "Maybe that was it. I didn't want to go back to typing."[52]

Two weeks later, a grand jury found Steinhagen legally insane and committed her to a local psychiatric ward, where she received electric shock treatment. She was released in April 1952, less than three years after the murder attempt.

Waitkus recovered from his wounds and was voted to the All-Star Game in 1949 despite only playing in 54 games that season. Sympathy was on his side, not just because of the shooting but because he didn't press charges against the mentally ill Steinhagen. The year that his attacker was released from her mental institution was also the last year Waitkus played a full season. His playing time and production had steadily declined after the shooting, and 1955 saw the end of his career.

As he grew older, Waitkus tried to put the notoriety of the shooting behind him. When reporters asked him about it, he joked that "Air conditioning is okay, but it should never be done with lead in the cool of the evening." He also said that if a woman ever gave him a note asking to meet again, he would give her a note back telling her to meet him at a local department store where he'd have "her frisked before going in."[53]

But according to biographer John Theodore, although Waitkus attempted to put a light-hearted spin on this ugly event, he was never able to get past what had happened to him. He developed a drinking problem, had a nervous breakdown, and suffered a failed marriage before he died in 1972 at age 53.

Steinhagen returned to the same Chicago neighborhood where she had grown up and lived a quiet life until her death in 2012 at age 83, her sordid history unknown to any of her neighbors until reports of her death caused her background to be revealed.

Section VII

Baseball

Chapter 65

All-Star Game Was Windy City Invention

Baseball's All-Star Game Was Created By One Future Cubs Owner Despite The Initial Opposition Of The Owner At That Time.

The idea of a midseason game featuring the best players in both leagues has been around since 1933, the year an employee of a future owner of the team proposed the idea to baseball officials. The owner in question wasn't William Wrigley Jr., who died in 1932, or his son, Philip, who sold the team to the *Chicago Tribune* in 1981.

Arch Ward was a sports reporter for the *Chicago Tribune* from 1925 to 1930, at which time he took over as sports editor until his death in 1955. In 1933, the newspaper's publisher, Colonel Bertie McCormick, summoned Ward into his office for a meeting with the city's mayor, Edward J. Kelly. Kelly's leadership would keep the city solvent and moving forward during the most difficult financial times in America's history, the Great Depression and World War II. Elected to four terms, Kelly served as mayor from 1933 to 1947 and was the first to engage the African American community in city politics (which helped the Chicago Machine achieve the Democratic dominance it has held for decades). But Kelly's greatest contribution went beyond Chicago, benefitting the entire nation—for it was his prodding that led to the creation of the All-Star Game, which baseball fans now enjoy every summer.

Almost immediately after winning the mayoral election on April 13, 1933, Kelly went to the publisher of the *Chicago Tribune* looking for help in mitigating the effects of the Depression that had gripped the nation since 1929. To rekindle business and innovation, Kelly wanted to convince local business leaders to celebrate the city's centennial year with a gala exhibition that would become known as Chicago's World's Fair.

To build civic involvement, Kelly wanted to plan a major sporting event to occur simultaneously, but he wasn't sure what exactly it should be.[1] But he did know the right man for the job: Ward. The newspaperman immediately suggested resurrecting an idea that had met with stern resistance from baseball officials back when it was first proposed by F. C. Lane, editor of *Baseball Magazine*, in 1915.[2]

"Thinking ahead as always, Ward knew just what he wanted to do," wrote biographer Tom Littlewood in his book *Arch: A Promoter, Not a Poet*: revive "the idea of having a baseball game between the best players of the American League and the best players of the National League."[3]

Where Lane had failed 18 years earlier, Ward would succeed. He had two major things on his side that Lane had lacked: the backing of the powerful and influential *Chicago Tribune* and a knack for knowing just who to woo. Shrewd and circumspect, Ward did not approach MLB commissioner Kenesaw Mountain Landis, whose office was only four blocks from the *Chicago Tribune*. Instead, he went to American League president Will Harridge, whose office was also only blocks away, leaving it to him to convince Landis and the other AL owners. Harridge "agreed enthusiastically that the All-Star Game would be good for baseball,"[4] and consented to push the idea in the AL, allowing Ward to focus on the National League.

Pressured by the support his AL counterpart was giving the idea, NL president John Heydler also agreed to push the plan—which wasn't easy. Several NL teams, including those in St. Louis, Boston, New York, and, unfortunately, Chicago, opposed the idea.

Ward worked his magic on the ownership of each of those teams, creating a "blizzard of telegrams and telephone calls"[5] that salted away the opposition in three of the cities. As for the Chicago Cubs, Ward approached team president William Veeck, rather than going directly to Wrigley. While the substance of their meetings remains a mystery, Ward obviously made it clear to Veeck that the Cubs' current owner, Wrigley, would be unwise to oppose any ideas supported by the team's future owner, the *Chicago Tribune*. "Veeck reminded [Wrigley] of the potential harm in antagonizing the *Tribune*," MLB's first official historian, Jerome Holtzman, wrote. "Wrigley had second thoughts. Reluctantly, Wrigley gave his approval."[6]

Although Ward was able to convince all the baseball owners to agree to his idea, there were still grave concerns, particularly for McCormick, who was paying for the entire extravaganza. What if, for example, it rained? What if the tickets didn't sell? It was one thing to get baseball owners to share their players for a huge event, but McCormick was paying for it. Though the *Tribune* would benefit from organizing the fan voting, it was still a financial risk. Still, plans went forward. Ward's son, Thomas Ward, told Holtzman for a 1990 *Tribune* column, "When Colonel McCormick said, 'What happens if nobody shows up?' Dad said, 'You can take the losses out of my paycheck.' And the Colonel said, 'If you're that confident, we'll underwrite it.'"[7]

On July 6, 1933, 49,200 fans stuffed Comiskey Park and witnessed history in the third inning when Babe Ruth belted the first home run in an All-Star Game, giving the AL a 4–2 win in what was dubbed "the Game of the Century."

MLB's All-Star Game, created by the *Chicago Tribune* at the behest of Mayor Kelly, has been played every year since except for 1945. In honor of the man who made it happen, the award given to the Most Valuable Player in the game was originally called the Arch Ward Memorial Award (though it has since changed names several times).

Wrote *Chicago Tribune* columnist Rick Morrissey on July 13, 2003[8:]

These days, if a sports editor ever tried to be a promotional partner with a professional sports league, he and his unethical butt would be thrown out on the street. Most of us try to keep an emotional distance from the people we cover. That way, when we sit down to write, we don't feel beholden to them in any way. We are free to write what we want, with no strings attached to our fingers.

Is it better this way? I think it is, but I also know that whatever innocence we might have had is long gone. The relationship between athletes and the media isn't always adversarial, but sometimes it resembles a rugby scrum.

Ward would go on to pioneer other similar events before his death in 1955, including the College All-Star Game (played between the reigning NFL champion team and a team of college all-stars) and the Golden Gloves boxing tournament, which became so popular that Pope Pius XII once invited the participants as guests to the Vatican.[9]

"[Ward] was one of the most influential sports editors of the century," wrote Chicago historian Laura Enright in her 2003 book *Chicago's Most Wanted*.[10]

Chapter 66

Interleague Play Began As Chicago Idea

A Cub Came Up with the Idea of Interleague
Play 75 Years Before It Became Official.

Baseball fans can only wonder where the MLB would be today if a Cubs executive had become commissioner instead of a former car salesman. Bud Selig was voted MLB's commissioner in 1998 after a career as owner of the Milwaukee Brewers, president of Selig Executive Lease Company, and owner of several used-car dealerships in Wisconsin. Although he is credited with one of the most popular changes in baseball, the innovation was first suggested by Chicago Cubs president William Veeck decades earlier.

Reported Richard Justice for MLB.com on May 18, 2012:

> Since it began in 1997, Interleague games have drawn an average of 33,285 [fans]. That number is 12 percent higher than baseball's average in other contests. Last season [2011], Interleague Play drew an average of 33,606. That was an 18.2 percent jump over what regular-season games had drawn to that point. Even when warmer weather, weekend dates and school being out are factored in, there's no arguing the popularity of Interleague Play.[11]

There is also no arguing whose idea it was, according to Holtzman. "In a National League meeting in 1922, [Veeck] proposed a schedule of interleague games at the midpoint of the championship season," Holtzman wrote in a column for the *Chicago Tribune* on June 5, 1997, days before MLB's interleague action finally began.[12] "It was dismissed out of hand and never came to a vote."

So what changed between 1922, when Veeck first suggested the idea, and 1997, when MLB finally warmed up to it? That's easy, professional baseball reached its lowest point. There was no World Series in 1994 due to a player strike that lasted from August 1994 until the two sides signed a new agreement in

March of 1995. This was a first—even World War II hadn't been able to cancel a World Series. Neither did the 1989 Loma Prieta earthquake, which registered an 8.3 on the Richter scale moments before the start of Game 3 of the World Series between the Oakland A's and the San Francisco Giants. Fighting between players and owners managed to do what neither Mother Nature nor the Nazis could.

When the two sides finally agreed to terms and play resumed in 1995, Selig knew baseball had to do something to boost dreadful (yet predictable) attendance figures. How could they bring back the fans who felt wronged by the custodians of the national pastime? One of the first announcements after play resumed was the creation of an interleague schedule, a decision that fans, according to Justice's story, clearly welcomed.

It shouldn't be a surprise that it was a Chicagoan who suggested this idea, considering that the Cubs and the White Sox had their own interleague series, called the City Series, beginning back in 1903. When Veeck brought up his idea during a 1922 meeting of baseball officials, the suggestion had already been market tested for nearly 20 years in Chicago. But the idea was simply ahead of its time.

In 1903, James Hart, owner of the Cubs (then called the Colts), and Charles Comiskey, owner of the White Sox, agreed to have their teams play at the end of the regular season whenever either team was not in the World Series. They called the contests the City Series back then, but today it goes by several nicknames, including the Crosstown Classic and the Red Line Series. The games were technically exhibitions, not postseason games (nor did they count in official MLB record books).

Other cities and teams followed Chicago's lead. In 1903, Philadelphia's Athletics and Phillies played a similar series, as did St. Louis's Cardinals and Browns, and cross-state rivals Cleveland and Cincinnati. New York baseball fans were denied the chance to see such a series, however, as the NL's Giants and Dodgers refused to play their AL counterpart, the Americans (later renamed as the New York Yankees).

The Colts and the White Stockings played their first game on October 1, 1903, but only the local bookies were impressed. According to many reports, betting was heavy, but it was clear to newspaper reporters that the players had no interest in exhibition games after a grinding 140-game season. Increasing the players' apathy was the fact that the two greedy owners staged the first City Series as a best-of-15 series.

"Chicago's Colts met their local rivals the White Stockings yesterday for the first time in baseball history, on the West Side Grounds, and there was absolutely nothing to it," was how the *Chicago Tribune* described the Colts' 11–0 victory.[13] Realizing he needed to motivate his players, Comiskey offered his team a $2,500 bonus if they won the series. The White Stockings rebounded accordingly, tying the series at seven games apiece. But a deciding game scheduled for October 16 was never played because NL player contracts expired on October 15, and the players wouldn't play if they weren't being paid. Of course, the players *could* have negotiated payment for one more game, but the Colts players voted the idea down, citing shortstop Joe Tinker's wedding as a good enough excuse as any to call the season to an end. Comiskey viewed the tie as a victory and gleefully paid his players the $2,500 bonus.

The South Siders continued to get the better of their North Side rivals in coming years, winning 19 of the 26 City Series, including each one from 1931 to 1942, the final year of the exhibition.

In 1949, the Cubs and White Sox began their exhibition competition anew, this time as a single game played during the season with the proceeds benefitting the Chicago Park District's baseball leagues. These games, which were very popular with fans, lasted until 1972. The Cubs fared better in this single-game format, winning 13 of the 23 contests. In 1986, the Windy City Classic revived the intercity battle, with the Cubs and White Sox playing a single game during the season until 1995.

Official interleague play began for all MLB teams in 1997, with the Cubs and White Sox playing a three-game series at both ballparks each season. But with a series dating back to 1903, the Cubs and the White Sox were playing interleague games before many teams even came into existence.

"Like a glacier, big-league baseball moves slowly and so it has taken a while— 75 years—but William L. Veeck's idea of a round robin of interleague games will begin," Holtzman wrote in his 1997 *Chicago Tribune* column.[14]

"SELIG HAD IT RIGHT ON INTERLEAGUE PLAY" read the headline of Justice's 2012 column. But for justice to truly be served, fans need to remember that it was Veeck, the former Cubs president, who had it right first. Not Selig.

Chapter 67

Throw It Back! The Copying of a Cubs Original

A Tradition Begun at Wrigley Field Has Been Called the "Worst" and "Stupidest" Trend in Sports, While Others See It as A Source of True Pride. Whichever Side You Take, There's No Denying It's Now a National Tradition That Has Expanded Well Beyond Wrigley Field.

During the 2011 World Series, St. Louis slugger Albert Pujols put his name in the record books in the ninth inning of Game 3 by hitting his third home run of the game. Only Reggie Jackson and Babe Ruth have hit three home runs in a World Series game (Ruth actually did it twice). Despite seeing history happen before their eyes, the fans weren't cheering much until the person in the stands who caught the ball threw it back onto the field. Then the crowd roared. You see, the game was at Rangers Ballpark in Texas and the fan who threw the ball back was a Rangers diehard, not a Cardinals one.

Wrote ESPN.com columnist Jim Caple:

The baseball gods gave Jordan Hartsell a piece of history during Game 3 of the World Series. And due to the worst tradition in baseball, she threw it back in their faces. . . . Far too many fans are throwing home run balls back onto the field, copying a stupid tradition started by Cubs fans. Why anyone would happily copy a tradition begun by baseball's ultimate losers is beyond me."[15]

Throwing back a home run hit by the opposition began at the Friendly Confines in 1969 and has since become a national tradition—even if journalists despise the trend.

"THROW IT BACK! A STUPID TRADITION" read the headline to Mike Vacarro's *NY Post* column on September 5, 2010,[16] in which he lamented, "It was very charming when the old Bleacher Bums did it at Wrigley Field back in the day; now everyone does it." There's no doubt that the trend has caught on in every ballpark across the country, nor is there any doubt where it began and, according to some, where it should remain.

"I mean, the Cubs haven't much of anything else to cherish, so why take even that away from them? You shouldn't," debated Terence Moore in a 2012 column for MLB.com arguing that the Cubs tradition should stay just that—a *Cubs* tradition. "It was only a Wrigley Field tradition for years—and even for decades—and then it wasn't. It was everywhere."[17]

The tradition began in 1969 with the Bleacher Bums, a group of diehard fans who wore yellow construction helmets and ruled the outfield bleachers. During the summer of '69, Chicago sports radio personality Mike Murphy was one of the Bums who cheered Ron Santo and the Cubs into a pennant race that eventually broke fans' hearts. But along the way, the Bums began a national tradition. Murphy cited Ron Grousl, who he dubbed "the president of the Left Field Bleacher Bums," as the originator of the practice.

"It was totally unplanned," Murphy recounted in Doug Helpingstine's book *The Cubs and White Sox: A Baseball Rivalry, 1900 to Present*:

> I was standing next to Ron when it first occurred. Hank Aaron hit a home run into the left field bleachers, which Ron caught on the fly. He looked at the ball and said, "We don't want this stinking ball . . . it's an enemy homer!" With that he wound and flipped it on the fly behind second base. There was stunned silence for a moment—no one had ever seen anything like this before. Then the crowd went nuts. Cheering, laughing, jeering of the great Hank Aaron. Yes, the fans had just illustrated love for their favorite team. Fanaticism was personified in the act and in the discarded ball. From then on, enemy home runs hit into the Wrigley Field bleachers were expected to be thrown back.[18]

Most, if not all, MLB teams have rules against throwing objects onto the field. So there's a real chance that anyone who throws back a home run may be ejected from the ballpark. But is there any better way to prove your true allegiance to your team than being ejected for rejecting an opponent's home run? Not if you're a Cubs fan. Apparently, a nation of copycat baseball fans agrees.

Chapter 68

A Victim of Two 'Called Shot' Home Runs

Only One Pitcher In Baseball History Has The Illustrious Distinction of Being Part of Not One but Two "Called Shot" Home Runs.

Some people are remembered for what they did to others, while some are remembered for what others did to them. Unfortunately for Guy Bush, he became the latter. Raised in Aberdeen, Mississippi, Bush was one of the best-dressed players on the Cubs squad and always drove an expensive car. With a toad-like hop to his delivery and a Southern drawl, Bush stood out from both other pitchers and the rest of his teammates. He was also the only Cub ever acquired in exchange for a jug of corn whiskey and $1,200.[19] During 12 seasons with the Cubs, Bush, nicknamed "the Mississippi Mudcat," had a career record of 152–101 and recorded at least 15 wins for seven consecutive seasons, helping the Cubs win the pennant in 1929 and 1932.

The secret to Bush's success was an ointment applied to his arm by team trainer Andy Lotshaw.[20] Bush dutifully reported to Lotshaw for his special treatment before each game he pitched. Reporters and fans asked Bush about the secret liniment, but the right-hander never gave up the secret. Why? Because he didn't know it himself. Lotshaw refused to tell the superstitious pitcher what the dark liquid was. The tactic worked: Bush recorded 18, 15, 16, and 19 wins, respectively, from 1929- to 1932. Frustrated at coming oh-so-close to 20 wins four years in a row, the Mississippi Mudcat asked fans to send him four-leaf clovers to improve his luck. The next season, he went 20–12.

Lotshaw continued to rub the mysterious dark liniment on Bush's arm until the pitcher was traded to the Pirates after the 1934 season. It was only then, when Bush needed to tell the Pittsburgh trainer what the liniment was, that Lotshaw was forced to admit the truth: the magic substance was nothing more than warm Coca-Cola.

While that "special ointment" made for a funny story, what wasn't amusing to Bush was the fact that he was at the heart of not just one supposed "Called Shot" home run, but two, both by the same hitter—none other than baseball's biggest star of all time, Babe Ruth.

Ruth's "Called Shot" home run in Game 3 of the 1932 World Series was, as we've already proven, not really a "called shot" but rather a series of coincidences that Ruth, who loved the attention, never bothered to publicly correct as he aged. But the verbal assaults and insults the Cubs threw at the entire New York Yankees squad, and Ruth in particular, have never been questioned. One of the most vocal Cubs was Bush, whose Southern voice made it easy to distinguish his taunts from the other players'. It was Bush who Ruth supposedly replied to after the second strike, reminding the Mississippi Mudcat that Charlie Root still needed to get a third strike past him—just before belting his unforgettable home run into the stands.

Bush was fortunate to be in the dugout rather than on the mound that day. But karma has a funny way of reminding us of our past misdeeds. The superstitious Bush should have remembered that when he faced Ruth years later for what would become Ruth's second "Called Shot," still honored by Pittsburgh fans decades later.

Ruth's career came to an end in 1935. He played for the Boston Braves during his final season. On May 25, the Braves played at Pittsburgh's Forbes Field with Red Lucas starting for the Pirates. Lucas lasted only one out into the first inning, giving up a two-run homer to Ruth in the opening frame. Pirates manager Pie Traynor immediately called for a relief pitcher—Bush. In the third inning, Ruth stepped to the plate and faced the pitcher for the first time since the 1932 World Series, when the Mississippi Mudcat and others had called the dark-skinned hitter such foul names that he and his teammates earned a rebuke from Commissioner Landis himself. The Bambino belted a home run, his penultimate career homer.

Karma wasn't through with Bush, however. Traynor left the right-hander in the game until the seventh inning, when Ruth came to bat once more. "[Ruth] pointed to a group of old guys clapping for him and said he'd put it over the roof," Pittsburgh fan Paul Warhola, who was at the game, told the *Pittsburgh Post-Gazette*.[21]

And that is precisely what Ruth did; the final home run of the Bambino's career, his 714th, was the first home run ever to clear the 86-foot high roof in right field at Forbes Field, as well as his second of the day off the Mississippi Mudcat and his third that day overall.

Bush is the only pitcher in history to be a part of not just one "Called Shot" home run, but two, both by Ruth. Adding insult to injury, Bush is now remembered not for his service as a workhorse pitcher for the Cubs for years, but as the pitcher who surrendered Ruth's final two home runs.

The lesson appears to be simple: don't taunt a tiger or you just might get swatted—not once, but twice.

Chapter 69

Cubs Brothers Set Baseball History

*Two Brothers Who Were Also Cubs Share a Special
Place in the Baseball Record Books.*

The 2013 season saw brothers B. J. and Justin Upton take the field together in the starting lineup for the Atlanta Braves. But as special as their feat was, they were just the latest in a long line of brothers who were also teammates; in fact, Major League Baseball lists nearly 100 sets of such siblings.[22] But Cubs pitchers Paul and Rick "Big Daddy" Reuschel were the only two to pitch a shutout together.

On August 21, 1975, Cubs starting pitcher Rick Reuschel gave the Cubs a 5–0 lead against the visiting Los Angeles Dodgers, scattering five hits until he was pulled with one out in the seventh inning. His relief pitcher was his older brother, Paul, who gave up just one hit the rest of the game as the Cubs defeated the Dodgers 7–0. Only 8,377 fans witnessed the historic feat, in part because the game was on a Thursday afternoon. And of course the 1975 Cubs simply weren't very good, finishing tied with the Montreal Expos for last place in the NL East (75–87). Despite how few people saw it actually happen, that was the only time in baseball history that two brothers combined to pitch a shutout.

"I didn't even realize it until I saw it in the paper the next day," said Paul, in a 1985 story with the *Chicago Tribune* story.[23] "I figured with all the brother combinations that had pitched, that it had to have been done somewhere before."

Actually, Dizzy and Paul Dean were the only brothers to achieve something close to (and some would say better than) the Reuschels—they won two games apiece to lead the St. Louis Cardinals to the 1934 World Series.

According to MLB.com, the only other brothers to play on the same team for the Cubs organization were Larry and Mike Corcoran (1884, Chicago White Stockings), Jiggs and Tom Parrott (1893, Chicago Colts), and Danny and Hal Breeden (1971).

Born in Quincy, Illinois, the Reuschel brothers shared the special experience of playing for their favorite childhood team. Paul's playing career lasted only six years, ending in 1979, while Rick's lasted for 19 years (1972–91), during which time he was an All-Star three times, once for the Cubs and once each with Pittsburgh and San Francisco.

Paul was quite clear about where his loyalties stood, as both a brother and a Cubs fan. "When Rick [pitched] against the Cubs, I root against the Cubs until he's out of the game. Then I root for the Cubs," Paul said. "I always will be a Cubs fan. After 35 years, it's hard to switch."[24]

Chapter 70

Baseball Trade History That Will Never Be Topped

Many Unusual Trades Have Happened in Baseball, But One Cubs Trade Was So Unusual That It Is Unlikely to Ever Be Repeated.

The Chicago Cubs are no stranger to unusual trades. But there's only one trade in the team's history so unusual that it will probably never be repeated. To underscore the uniqueness of this trade, it helps to examine some of the other highly unusual trades in Cubs history that were rare, but not unprecedented.

In 1987, Cubs pitcher Dickie Noles was traded to the Detroit Tigers for a player to be named later; he appeared in only four games for the Tigers before being named as the player to be traded the next month—completing a trade for himself. But Noles was actually the third of four players to be exchanged for himself in baseball history. The others were Harry Chiti (1962, Mets/Indians), Brad Gulden (1982, Yankees/Expos), and most recently John McDonald (2005, Tigers/Blue Jays).

On May 4, 1960, Cubs owner Philip Wrigley swapped manager Charlie Grimm, whose team opened the season 6–11, for WGN announcer Lou Boudreau, who had been in the booth for two seasons after managing for 15 combined years for the Indians, the Red Sox, and the Athletics. The swap did nothing for the Cubs, however, who ended in seventh place in the NL (60–94), prompting Wrigley to begin his "College of Coaches" the following season.

Wrigley's unusual swap of Boudreau for Grimm was just the first of several managers hired from the broadcast booth, though at least Boudreau had previous managing experience. There was no such history on the resumes of Larry Dierker (1997, Houston), Bob Brenly (2000, Arizona), and Buck Martinez (2000, Toronto), who were all hired to take over a team that they had been covering as a broadcaster in the years prior to becoming skipper. No, none of the teams'

323

former managers took over the broadcasting duties for their team, making the the Grimm/Boudreau trade the only one in history in which a manager and a broadcaster changed duties.

On May 30, 1923, the Cubs and the Cardinals completed a trade that was unique because it involved a doubleheader, something that MLB teams hate to schedule. The Cubs traded Max Flack for the Cardinals' Cliff Heathcote after the first game of a doubleheader between the teams. Then Flack reported to the St. Louis locker room and Heathcote went to Chicago's. In the first game, both players had been hitless for their teams. Flack started in right field for the Cubs and went 0-for-4, while Heathcote went 0-for-3 and started in center field. In the second game, Flack went 1-for-4 for St. Louis, again starting in right field; Heathcote went 2-for-4 and also started in right field. This incident marked the only time in MLB history that two players were traded for each other and then played for two teams on the same day.

Since the 1920s, doubleheaders have become an increasingly rare part of the game, and their future seems doubtful. Teams are reluctant to schedule doubleheaders because they feel that playing two games on one day reduces their revenue. Nearly all doubleheaders today are the result of rained-out games forced into the schedule as necessary. There were 34 doubleheaders in 2011, and only 20 in 2012. The 2013 season had only one doubleheader scheduled before the start of the season.

Only two other players in MLB history experienced what Flack and Heathcote went through physically and emotionally that day in 1922. On August 4, 1982, Joel Youngblood helped the New York Mets beat the Cubs 7–4 in a day game at Wrigley Field with a single in the third inning. Then, in the middle of the game, he was told he had been traded to the Montreal Expos, who were playing in Philadelphia that night. Youngblood left the Friendly Confines, hopped on a plane, and made it to Philadelphia for the evening game, in which he hit a single in the top of the seventh inning off Phillies pitcher Steve Carlton. That feat made Youngblood the only player in MLB history to have a hit with two different teams on the same day (since Flack and Heathcote were both hitless in the first game of their doubleheader). A dearth in doubleheaders combined with players usually taking the full 72 hours to report to their new team after a trade make Flack, Heathcote, and Youngblood the only players in league history who will likely ever play for two teams on one day.

While team executives are not known for their caring ways with players' emotions, Jose Cardenal shared the emotional reason why no other player will likely achieve the unusual feat. On August 2, 1979, the reserve outfielder, a former Cub known mostly for his huge afro, was traded from the Phillies to the New York Mets during a doubleheader. A backup on the bench, Cardenal did not play in the first game for the Phillies and, between games, reported to the Mets locker room. After several Mets players joked that he was in the wrong locker room, Cardenal suited up for the second game of the doubleheader, but asked Mets manager Joe Torre to keep him out of the game because he couldn't handle facing his former teammates only hours after being traded.

"I couldn't do it," Cardenal told *Sports Illustrated* afterward.[25] "I was in shock."

Chapter 71

First World Series Ejection in History

*One Hall of Fame Cubbie Is Credited with Both the
Greatest Season Ever and the Creation of One of the Most
Infamous (and Beloved) Traditions in Baseball.*

Long before anyone called them the "Lovable Losers," the Chicago Cubs were
one of the most successful and aggressive teams in all of baseball, known for
employing an "any means necessary" approach. The curses and threats employed
by the Cubs were once so offensive that early shepherds of the sport such as Judge
Kennesaw Mountain Landis feared the crude behavior would be detrimental to
the future of the game. Players shouted vulgar taunts loudly enough for fans to
hear every stereotypical, racial, or religious taunt they could imagine.

This was turn-of-the-century baseball, when the Cubs dominated the game.
Openly racist player/manager Cap Anson led the organization to championship
seasons during the 1880s and 1890s, when the team was known as the White
Stockings, the Colts, and the Orphans. Frank Chance, a card player, drinker,
part-time boxer, and overall intimidating presence (at 6' and 188 pounds), joined
the team in 1898 playing first base. His acumen on the field would endear him to
sports fans everywhere as part of the famous Tinkers-Evers-Chance double-play
combination.

But it was as manager of the Cubs that Chance, aka "the Peerless Leader,"
etched his name in the annals of baseball history for both good and bad. In
1905, Chance replaced the clean-living Anson as manager, and his impact was
immediate. A "man's man" to the bone, Chance did not trust anyone who didn't
drink or play cards. In fact, he urged his players to bet on horses and play poker
because he felt it increased their mental acuity and competitiveness. He set a 25¢
betting limits on card games, and fined anyone caught breaking his rule $25.

Once, when he couldn't stop himself and played beyond the limit, he even fined himself.

"When we'd get rained out," former Cubs infielder Jimmy Archer recalled in the book *Wrigleyville* by Peter Golenbock, "we'd be sitting around the clubhouse. Then Chance would come in. 'What have I got here, a Sunday school club?' he'd say. We'd all go to a saloon. You couldn't buy a drink. Chance would buy them all."[26]

When teammate Heinie Zimmerman—who was later banned from baseball for life due to his nefarious activities—tried to form a group of players to conspire against Chance, "the Peerless Leader" quickly took matters into his own hands, literally. The manager/player confronted Zimmerman, offering him a deal: they would have a fistfight, and if Zimmerman won, Chance would quit as manager. Foolishly, Zimmerman took the bet, forgetting (or perhaps unaware) that Chance was an experienced boxer. Chance destroyed Zimmerman, and the clubhouse squabble disappeared instantly.

Former Cubs manager Lou Piniella is probably the closest modern equivalent to Chance in many ways. Like Chance, Piniella was a former player turned manager before he skippered the Cubs from 2007 to 2010. Along the way, Piniella proved to be a combustible character who would just as soon fight umpires on calls (and be gloriously ejected) as he would players on his own team if he felt they weren't trying hard enough. When he managed the Cincinnati Reds, Piniella infamously went after his own pitcher, Rob Dibble, in 1992.

While he may not know it, Piniella owes Chance a nod for creating the very thing for which Piniella is known: ejections. Chance's fiery temper earned him an infamous mark in history so well known that it won him his own Facebook page, created 86 years after his death[27]: he was the first manager to be thrown out of a World Series game. (BaseballAlmanac.com[28] credits two other managers with being ejected before Chance: Detroit's Hughie Jennings in 1907 and Bill Donovan, also from Detroit, in 1909. However, multiple other sources, including the National Baseball Hall of Fame, credit Chance's 1910 ejection as the first.[29])

If asked, we're sure that Piniella could empathize with Chance ejected for arguing with future Hall of Fame umpire Tom Connolly about a called home run in the third inning of the 1910 World Series. After all, a few years earlier, in 1906, Chance and the Cubs became the first team ever to record 116 regular-season victories (a record that still has not been bettered), only to lose 4–1 to the Connie Mack–led Philadelphia A's in the championship.

Like Piniella, Chance was demanding and tough, treating his players as men, not boys, but allowing them their fun away from the field. Both Cubs managers demanded perfection on the field in exchange for turning a blind eye to minor vices off it. The 1906 Cubs team gave Chance the closest thing to perfection that any team has ever given their manager in exchange for his trust: the most wins ever (116) in the regular season. That season was a product of a Cubs dynasty that won four pennants in five years (1906–10) thanks in large part to the guidance of Chance, "the Peerless Leader."

The team's 116–36 record is also the best win-loss record of any team ever. Only one team has equaled Chance's Cubs: the Seattle Mariners, who went 116–46 in 2001, tying the Cubs on wins, but failing to top the 1906 Cubs' win ratio (.763 to .716).

Who was the Chance-like manager of the 2001 Seattle Mariners?

Lou Piniella.

Chapter 72

Baseball's First Spring Training Firing

Only Three Managers Have Been Fired During Spring Training—One For Over-Managing, One for Lying, and a Cubbie Who Was Fired for Telling the Truth.

On March 17, 1999, Toronto Blue Jays manager Tim Johnson was fired for lying about having served in Vietnam as a Marine (he had not), and was replaced by Jim Fregosi. Johnson's firing was surprising to baseball fans, many of whom had never heard of a manager getting a pink slip during spring training. But as the Associated Press story that went out over the wires reminded readers the world over, this was not the first time a baseball manager had been fired so early in the season.

"Firing a manager in spring training is rare, but not unprecedented," the AP story read that day. "Phil Cavarretta was fired by the Chicago Cubs in March 1954."[30]

The massive difference between Johnson's firing and Cavarretta's was that the Cubs' manager was actually let go for telling the truth., where his Toronto counterpart was not. (In 1978, San Diego manager Alvin Dark was fired in spring training for his reluctance to keep members of upper management updated while simultaneously alienating his coaching staff and creating an adversarial atmosphere in the clubhouse with players.)

Cavarretta was one of the most popular Cubs players in franchise history due to the fact that he was drafted by the Cubs straight out of Lane Tech High School, less than two miles from Wrigley Field. A local boy playing for the hometown team needs to do little more than avoid screwing up to keep fans on his side, and the first baseman/outfielder did more than that. In his first game with the Cubs, Cavarretta, then just 18 years old, belted a home run. Manager Charlie Grimm soon bestowed upon him the nickname "Phillibuck," which stuck for the rest of his career.

During his 20-year career with the Cubs, Cavarretta was named an All-Star three times and was the NL MVP in 1945, leading the Cubs to their most recent World Series appearance. During the 1951 season, the Cubs fired manager Frankie Frisch and made Cavarretta the team's player/manager. Unfortunately, the hometown hero's success as a player didn't carry over into managing, in large part because his team just didn't have the talent. The Cubs went 27–47 in Cavarretta's half of the 1951 season, then 77–77 in 1952 and 65–89 in 1953.

March 1954 found Cavarretta in despair, knowing that his team lacked the offensive power, defensive prowess, and overall drive to succeed. Bob Lewis, the Cubs' traveling secretary, urged Cavarretta to speak frankly with team owner Philip Wrigley. Cavarretta recalled the conversation in the book *Wrigleyville*:

> Why don't you have a meeting with Mr. Wrigley tomorrow. He'll listen to you, Phil. Tell him what's on your mind. Go over the whole ball club. Tell him who you think will help the club and the guys who won't.[31]

It would prove to be very bad advice.

The following day, Wrigley and Cavarretta took seats in the right-field bleachers and went over the starting lineup. After highlighting a few players who seemed to have solid futures in baseball, Cavarretta told Wrigley that too many of the players who general manager Wid Matthews had acquired, particularly aging star outfielder Ralph Kiner, were not going to help the club.

Said Cavarretta:

> Some of the things I said, especially about my outfield and pitching staff and my catching, I guess I shouldn't have said. I wasn't very kind, but I was being honest. . . . It was a mistake on my part. See, Wid Matthews, our general manager, was in Florida at the time, and in a way, I shouldn't have done this. Wid Matthews didn't like what I had to say, and I don't blame him. I should have waited until Mr. Matthews came back so the three of us could have sat in a room and gone over the club. I admit I pulled the trigger a little too quick on what I had to say, but again, I was telling the truth. I wanted Mr. Wrigley to understand that.[32]

Days later, Cavarretta was called to the team hotel to meet with Matthews, who had returned from Florida. Recalled Cavarretta:

> He got to the point real quick. These were the words, "We feel that it's necessary to make a change in managers." I was quiet for a while, and I said, "Change

of managers in spring training?" He said, "We're going to make a change in managers. We're going to bring in Stan Hack to take over the ballclub."

Matthews and Wrigley wanted Cavarretta to take over the Cubs' AAA team in Los Angeles, but the lifelong Cubbie refused.

"When he picked everyone but us to finish in the first division, he was licked before he started," Wrigley told the Associated Press concerning Cavarretta's firing. "He had sort of given up on the boys, so to speak, feeling that they were not pennant material."

Sadly, history proved Cavarretta right. The 1954 Cubs finished seventh in the NL East with a record of 64–90, and the team's once league-leading attendance dropped to fifth out of eight teams.

The White Sox signed Cavarretta to play on the South Side, hoping to benefit from the Chicago native's fan base. However, after 20 years of playing baseball, the 37-year-old was at the time of his career to begin coaching, rather than continue playing. He played in only 71 games for the White Sox in 1954 and appeared for only a few weeks of the 1955 season before the organization released him.

Cavarretta never managed in the major leagues again.

Recalling Matthews' curt dismissal at the team hotel back in 1954, Cavarretta said, "I was almost in tears. That really was one of the saddest moments in my life. To this day I still can't get over it."[33]

Chapter 73

Ugliest Incident in Cubs Brawl History

*The Game with the Most Suspensions in Baseball History
Was Arguably Also the Ugliest Moment in Cubs History.*

For better or worse, brawls are part of the game of baseball. For example, right or wrong, fans loved seeing 46-year-old Nolan Ryan put 26-year-old Robin Ventura into a headlock and rain blows down on his head after the younger player rushed the mound in 1993. (Ryan stayed in the game after the incident and no-hit Ventura's White Sox to add insult to cranial injury. We mention this last part because, well, we're Cubs fans.) The 2003 fight between the Yankees and the Red Sox that led to 32-year-old Boston pitcher Pedro Martinez throwing 72-year-old Yankee coach (and former Cubs manager) Don Zimmer to the ground was also unforgettable to most fans.

We could list a dozen more memorable baseball fights, but one in particular tops the list: the three-sided fight between the Los Angeles Dodgers, the Chicago Cubs, and fans at Wrigley Field on May 16, 2000, that ended in a record-setting 19 Dodgers being suspended from play. The incident is known to most fans as "the Rumble in Wrigley."

The suspensions were especially stunning given that all 19 players were from the same team. The prior record for suspensions in a game (16), which had happened less than a month earlier on May 22, 2000, involved the Detroit Tigers and the Chicago White Sox. The total of games suspended for all 19 Dodgers players was 84 total games, also a record for an MLB game (82 games combined in the Tigers-White sox battle).

The Cubs-Dodgers fight was eerily reminiscent of the "Malice in the Palace," on November 19, 2004, an NBA brawl between the visiting Indiana Pacers and the Detroit Pistons at the Palace in Auburn Hills that spilled over into the stands with players fighting fans. Nine players were suspended for a total of 143 games; the incident was the nadir of the NBA's fan-player relations.

It was during the ninth inning of the Dodgers' 6–5 victory when a fan sitting in the seats behind the visiting pitchers' bullpen (some of the most expensive seats at Wrigley Field) decided he wanted a souvenir: Dodgers catcher Chad Kreuter's cap. The fan snatched Kreuter's cap, apparently hitting him in the head in the process. The Dodgers' bullpen, both coaches and players, then charged into the stands to retrieve the stolen property.

Anyone who has attended a game at Wrigley Field knows how close the seats are to the bullpen (only a waist-high brick wall separates them). Security was present, as always, but nobody had planned for such an assault, and it took nine minutes to restore order. When the dust cleared, 16 Dodgers players and three Dodgers coaches were suspended, the Cubs dropped charges against the fan who instigated the entire affair, a criminal judge threw out charges against two other fans, and the Dodgers paid another fan $300,000 for injuries sustained in the fight.

While no charges of public intoxication were filed as a result of either the "Rumble in Wrigley" or the "Malice in the Palace," alcohol was strongly suspected to have played a role in both incidents. Los Angeles coaches and players said the fans were dousing them with beer just prior to the fight. The Cubs changed their alcohol sales policies as a result, moving last call for alcohol sales in the stands to the seventh inning.

Author's note: I remember the Rumble in Wrigley very well because it marked the end of my brief radio career in Los Angeles. In 2000, I was the sports editor for a small Chicago newspaper. I had befriended a Los Angeles radio producer in Chicago during a press conference weeks before the incident. He asked me to be a weekly guest on his L.A. show as a "Chicago sports insider." Was I an insider? No. But I've always enjoyed doing radio, so I agreed. The first two weeks went well, with our on-air conversations lasting about ten minutes. The third week of our arrangement happened just after the Rumble in Wrigley. In our next on-air interview, he asked whether his hometown Los Angeles Dodgers or the drunk fans at Wrigley Field were to blame. "The Dodgers, of course," I replied. "Drunk fans are at every game. I'll never make excuses for drunk fans. They ruin a good time for everyone. But the Dodgers' coaches and players are paid millions of dollars to be professional baseball players, not try to be professional fighters." Not surprisingly, it was the last time I was asked to appear on the show.

Chapter 74

The Most Dominant Pitching Performance in MLB History

The Most Dominant Pitching Performance in Baseball History Was Delivered by a Cubs Pitcher Who Wasn't Old Enough to Buy Himself a Celebratory Beer After the Game.

The most dominating pitching performance in baseball wasn't delivered by Nolan Ryan, who had seven no-hitters, or Sandy Koufax, who had four. Nor did it come from legendary pitchers Roger Clemens, Cy Young, Tom Seaver, Randy Johnson, Bob Feller, Christy Mathewson, or Bob Gibson. The best pitching performance in baseball history came from a 20-year-old Chicago Cubs pitcher taking the mound in just his fifth major league game.

Kerry Wood became known as Kid K on May 6, 1998, when he announced his presence to the world with the most dominating pitching performance in the history of baseball. According to the Bill James' pitching statistic known as "Game Score," Wood had the No. 1 most-impressive showing for a pitcher ever that day, striking out 20 Houston Astros batters in a 6–0 win and giving up one hit, one balk, one hit batter, and no walks. Within 24 hours of the final out, the National Baseball Hall of Fame called to ask for parts of his uniform to enshrine at Cooperstown. Wood had been in the big leagues for only 24 days when he became a part of baseball history.

Wrote ESPN.com columnist David Schoenfield:

I'll never forget walking into the office that May afternoon in 1998 and having excited co-workers ask, "Did you see what just happened?" His pitches were moving like whiffle balls thrown in the middle of the Columbia River Gorge, except they were moving at 95 miles per hour. The Astros had no chance.

They managed one infield single and Wood hit a batter, so it wasn't a perfect game or even a no-hitter. But by the Bill James Game Score method, it was the best game ever pitched. Game Score rewards pitchers for strikeouts, and subtracts points for runs, hits and walks. There have been just nine starts of nine innings in which a pitcher scored 100 or better. Ryan (twice), Johnson, Curt Schilling, Warren Spahn and Brandon Morrow scored 100; Ryan (with a 16-strikeout, two-walk no-hitter) and Sandy Koufax (his 14-strikeout perfect game) scored 101. Kerry Wood's game? 105.[34]

The formula for figuring out a pitcher's Game Score is as follows: begin with 50 points, then add one point for each out recorded (three points per inning), add two points for each inning completed after the fourth inning, and add one point for each strikeout. Then subtract two points for each hit allowed, four points for each earned run allowed, two points for each unearned run allowed, and one point for each walk. The highest possible result is 114.

After San Francisco pitcher Matt Cain recorded a perfect game on June 13, 2012, ESPN researched the numbers to find the best pitching performance in baseball history using the Game Score statistic as their guide. Wood's 105 was the best, followed by a three-way tie at 101 between Cain's 2012 perfect game, Ryan's 1991 perfect game, and Koufax's 1965 perfect game.

Wood's one-hitter was benefitted by his awe-inspiring 20 strikeouts, lifting his performance above any of the perfect games in history (at least using the Game Score formula). *USA Today* writer Peter Barzilai took it a step further, pointing out that Wood's performance was not just statistically better than anyone else's, but that he also faced a much better team than Cain, Ryan, or Koufax did in their performances. Barzilai reminded readers:

> Wood faced an Astros team that finished 102–60 and led the NL in runs. Cain faced an Astros team that [was at the time] 26–36, eighth in the NL in runs and whose lineup had six hitters 25 or younger. Ryan faced a Blue Jays team that finished 91–71 and was 11th in the AL in runs. Koufax faced a Cubs team that finished 72–90 and was seventh out of 10 teams in NL in runs.[35]

Wood was named Rookie of the Year in 1998, but the celebration was short-lived. The stress of his pitching forced him to miss the entire 1999 season following elbow surgery. Baseball fans everywhere could only wonder what Kid K could have been. While Wood recovered and had a 14-year career, he was never fully the same. Cubs fans were forced to question if something was wrong with the team's use of strong-armed pitchers when, just a few years later, pitcher Mark Prior joined Wood in the starting rotation only to have his career cut short because of arm problems as well. Like Wood, Prior dominated the league during his rookie season in 2003 and was selected an All-Star. In April 2007, Prior had shoulder surgery; although doctors claimed at the time that it wasn't a career-ending move, they were wrong. Prior never pitched in the major leagues again.

Cubs fans will always recall the magical 2003 season, when Wood was voted to the first of his two All-Star Games (the other came in 2008), where he appeared alongside Prior making his lone All-Star appearance.

Added Schoenfield in his ESPN.com column:

[Wood] does have one important lasting legacy, beyond that 20-strikeout game: In part because of what happened to Wood (and teammate Mark Prior and others), teams are more careful with how they handle young starters. You won't see 20-year-old kids throwing 130 pitches in a game, no matter their ability. One reason we're seeing so many good young pitchers now and declining levels of offense is that pitchers are healthier and not flaming out in the minors or early on in their major league careers. Sure, maybe teams are *too* cautious with this approach, but I'd rather see that than what happened with Wood. He undoubtedly won't view himself as an unfortunate trailblazer, but rather as a pitcher who grinded his way through 14 major league seasons, giving his best.

And during one game in 1998, Wood's best proved to be better than anyone else's ever.

Chapter 75

First No-Hitter of Its Kind in History

*The Only No-Hitter of Its Kind Came from One of
the Most Unique Pitchers in Cubs History.*

Mediocrity was never a part of Carlos Zambrano's game. His highs and lows were always superlative in either their grandeur or their despicability. But what he did on the night of September 14, 2008, was a first in baseball history unlikely to be equaled any time soon.

It's unfortunate for Zambrano's legacy that most baseball fans remember him for his fights with other players more than his pitching ability. While fighting has always been a part of baseball, Zambrano tended to throw down against his own teammates rather than opponents. First, there was his dugout fight with catcher Michael Barrett in 2007. Then in 2010, he and first baseman Derrek Lee went nose-to-nose in the dugout before teammates separated the two.

After the second incident, Cubs manager Lou Piniella sent Zambrano home. The Venezuela native was absent from the team for weeks attending anger management therapy. It was hardly what the Cubs had expected when they handed him a five-year, $91-million contract in 2007, giving him one of the top five player salaries in the game at the time.

But nothing about Zambrano was normal or average. He was the modern day reincarnation of Fergie Jenkins, only better. A home run–hitting, fastball-throwing pitcher who could win a major league game both as a pitcher and a hitter, Zambrano stood 6'4", weighed 275 pounds, and was built more like a football player than a baseball man. (By comparison, Chicago Bears linebacker Brian Urlacher was 6'4" and 260 pounds and Bears defensive end Julius Peppers was 6'6" and 280 pounds.)

Zambrano beat Jenkins' record of 13 home runs by a Cubs pitcher, hitting 23 during his 11 seasons with the Cubs. He won the Silver Slugger Award (given annually to the best hitter at his position) three times, in 2006, 2008, and 2009. When he won the award in 2008, Zambrano became the first player in MLB history to win the Silver Slugger and throw a no-hitter in the same season.

It was that no-hitter on September 14, 2008, that put Zambrano's name in the record books. That was because his blanketing of the Houston Astros happened in Milwaukee's Miller Park, the first time in baseball history that a no-hitter was thrown at a neutral site. Hurricane Ike forced MLB officials to relocate two games from Houston to Milwaukee that year. Playing the games at Wrigley Field would have given Chicago an obvious advantage, but playing in Milwaukee proved to be little different in the long run. It was the 13th no-hitter in Cubs history and the first since Milt Pappas' in 1972, which was one walk shy of a perfect game. It was also the first no-hitter at Miller Park—even though no Brewers players were on the field.

Zambrano was coming off a rotator cuff injury when he led the Cubs to a 5–0 win in front of 23,441 fans at Miller Park. While the game was officially a neutral site, it was certainly not a bipartisan crowd. Cubs fans so overwhelmed the stadium that according to the Associated Press, "a fan wearing a Brewers jersey was booed when he appeared on the video board in center field."[36]

Given the rarity of neutral site games, Zambrano's no-hitter will likely remain the only one of its kind for years to come. According to records on the Cubs Website, the Cubs played 29 neutral-site games between 1885 and 2013.

The good times didn't last long, however, as Zambrano soon went back to his petulant ways, bumping officials and getting in a screaming match with Lee later in the season. The end of Zambrano's Cubs career came about in a way very similar to Sammy Sosa's quiet exit. On August 12, 2011, Zambrano surrendered back-to-back home runs in the fifth inning, giving the Braves an 8–1 lead. Angry and seeking retaliation, Zambrano threw at Chipper Jones, but missed the Braves icon. Zambrano was still ejected. He cleaned out his locker and claimed he was going to retire. Nobody took him seriously, however, in part because of his history of histrionics, but mostly because he was still due $18 million from the $91-million contract he had signed in 2007. Predictably, a contrite Zambrano apologized to his teammates days later, but Cubs management wasn't listening and suspended him for the rest of the season. On January 4, 2012, the Cubs traded Zambrano to the Miami Marlins for pitcher Chris Volstad, who went 3–12 in his one season with the Cubs before being waived.

Zambrano went 7–10 and hit one home run during his only season in Miami. As part of the trade, Chicago agreed to pay roughly $15.5 million of Zambrano's $18-million salary. Miami made no attempt to sign Zambrano to a new contract, making the Marlins the second team unwilling to put up with his antics. No other team showed interest in signing Zambrano until the Philadelphia Phillies signed him to a minor league deal six weeks into the 2013 season, but the organization released him two months later.

Author's note: I feel obligated to state for the record that I worked with Zambrano for months on his 2007 autobiography *Como Llego A Ser Grande Carlos Zambrano* (the English title was *The Big Z: The Carlos Zambrano Story*), and enjoyed his company despite what others have had to say about him. Working with Alderman Daniel Solis and the City of Chicago, we were able to have October 10, 2007, declared as Carlos Zambrano Day in the neighborhood of Pilsen. You have to understand Chicago geography to appreciate the weight of such an undertaking. Pilsen, a Hispanic community, is located in White Sox territory on the South Side of Chicago, miles from the Friendly Confines. But with Solis' approval, we were able to get the city to shut down 18th Street in Pilsen so local television shows could broadcast what proved to be the largest Spanish-language book signing in Chicago's history. With the area closed to traffic, nearly 1,000 fans filled the streets. Zambrano joked often, his eyes squinted tight, his mouth open wide in a loud, toothy laugh, his head bobbing back and forth. Even if you didn't get the joke (I usually didn't, since he spoke too quickly for my Spanish), you could not help but laugh along with him because he seemed to be having such fun. When he wasn't cracking jokes, his other two topics of serious interest were politics and home-cooked Venezuelan dishes. While there's no denying he was a problem for the Cubs, but I enjoyed working with Big Z.

Chapter 76

Highest Scoring Game in MLB History

The Two Highest-Scoring Games in Major League History Happened within the Walls of the Friendly Confines.

Perseverance and patience are attributes that both Cubs players and fans have had to learn over the years. Rarely have these traits been as necessary as they were during the two highest-scoring games in MLB history.

Many fans probably think the highest-scoring game in baseball history took place on May 17, 1979, when the Cubs rallied against the Phillies with three runs in the eighth inning (off five singles) to tie the game 22–22 before Philadelphia's Mike Schmidt hit a solo home run in the top of the 10th inning to give the Phillies a 23–22 victory before 14,952 fans at Wrigley Field. *New York Times'* baseball blogger Tyler Kepner referred to it as "the Holy Grail of high-scoring games."[37]

But with all due respect, Kepner was wrong. It was only the second-highest scoring game in baseball history. The real Holy Grail of baseball scoring occurred more than a half-century earlier, oddly enough also between the Cubs and the Phillies.

On August 25, 1922, the Phillies were at the Friendly Confines (then called Cubs Park) when one of the most unusual offensive displays in baseball history began. Chicago jumped to a 25–6 lead after the fourth inning, leading the 7,000 fans in the stands to believe that the hometown team was in the midst of a walk-away win. But as Cubs fans have learned in the decades since, nothing is ever as clear as it seems when it comes to a Cubs victory. After scoring eight runs in the eighth and six runs in the ninth, the Phillies closed the score to 26–23. The bases were loaded when replacement center fielder Bevo LeBourveau, who had already gone 3-for-4 in the game, came to the plate. A home run would give the Phillies the lead, while a base hit could tie the game. Thankfully for the Cubs and their fans, relief pitcher Tiny Osborne managed to strike out LeBourveau to preserve the victory.

According to baseball historian John Snyder, several records were set or tied that day beyond total scoring. The 51 total hits in the game (the Phillies had 26) is still a record for a nine-inning game. Chicago center fielder Cliff Heathcote tied a league record by reaching base all seven times he came to plate, going 5-for-5 with two walks, and teammate Marty Callaghan tied another league record with three at-bats in one inning.[38]

Those two games were just two more lessons to a group of fans who already know that nothing is ever guaranteed when it comes to Cubs baseball. Chicago nearly blew its massive lead in 1922, allowing Philadelphia to come within a base hit of embarrassing the club. But in 1979, the Cubs reminded the Phillies—and fans everywhere—that anything can happen if you try hard enough, coming back from deficits of 17–6 and 21–9 to force extra innings with a small-ball rally in the eighth inning that nearly won the game.

The traits the Cubs displayed in those two historic games—a never-give-up attitude combined with a stick-to-it approach—were just pixilated details in the grand portrait of the Chicago Cubs and their fans.

Chapter 77

Longest Championship Drought in Major League History

The World's Longest Championship Drought In Professional Sports At The Highest Level Of Competition.

We now must finally address the one thing that the Cubs are most known for: losing. The Chicago Cubs have the world's longest championship drought in any professional franchise's history among teams playing in leagues at the highest level in their respective sport. There are a few other teams around the globe who know the year after year frustration that Cubs fans, players, and executives feel—but even in this "elite" group, the Cubbies have them beat.

As of 2013, the Cubs have gone 105 years since last winning the World Series, in 1908. Most professional sports leagues weren't even in existence yet when the Cubs lost to the Detroit Tigers that year. The Cubs had already had two dynasty runs (1880–90 and 1906–10) before the creation of the National Hockey League (1917), the National Football League (1920), the National Basketball Association (1946), and Major League Soccer (1996).

In the NHL, the Toronto Maple Leafs have the longest championship drought, having last won the Stanley Cup after the 1966–67 season. The longest championship drought in the NBA belongs to the Sacramento Kings, who joined the league in its third season (as the Rochester Royals) and won the championship in 1951—but haven't won the title since. In the NFL, the Arizona Cardinals are the only charter member of the league never to win the Super Bowl. Major League Soccer launched in 1996, and each of the charter teams in the league has since played in the championship, though only three have never won (New York, New England, and Dallas).

Sports outside of the United States complicate our comparison because of the practice of relegation, which forces the lowest two or three teams (depending on the sport) to a lower level and promotes the best two or three teams in that lower level to the higher level. In major sports outside of America that do not employ relegation, the Australian Football League's Western Bulldogs, founded in 1877, have the longest championship drought in the league, winning the title last in 1954. The Japan Baseball League, founded in 1936 and reorganized in 1950 as Nippon Professional Baseball, is the highest level of baseball other than MLB play. The Hiroshima Toyo Carp have the longest championship drought in the NPB, last winning the Japan Series in 1984.

Wading into the murky comparisons of sports that do not have relegation takes us to cricket, one of the world's oldest organized sports (evidence of the game dates back to the 1500s in England). Cricket has remained mostly an amateur sport, which is one reason that comparing it to major league baseball is difficult. Clubs have largely been made up of amateurs competing for bragging rights, rather than professionals in organized leagues. There are also different variants of the game, with one-day and multiple-day matches. Yet even in this realm, the Cubs have a longer streak of futility. In 1967, The Professional Cricketers' Association was founded to oversee pro cricket in England and Wales, while American Pro Cricket was created in 2004 and the Indian Premier League began play in 2008. In Australian cricket, generations of athletes have competed for the Sheffield Shield, the country's oldest competition, which began in 1892. Only six teams compete for the trophy. After Tasmania won for the first time in 2006–07, each team had claimed the championship at least once. Similar to the Sheffield Shield, the County Championship is England's most revered cricket championship, with 18 teams competing for the title since 1890. There are three clubs that have never won: Gloucestershire, Northamptonshire, and Somerset. However, each of these teams has now been relegated to Division Two, ending their inclusion in our comparison with elite teams at the highest level of play.

That brings us to soccer (or football, or *futbol*, depending on where you were born), a sport with several teams whose fans can empathize with Cubs backers. Yet here again we find that the Cubs have a claim to history like no other team in the world. While MLB is the unquestioned dominant league in the world in its sport, soccer has six national leagues that experts regard as being at the top of their sport: Spain's La Liga, England's English Premier League (EPL), Germany's Bundesliga, Italy's Serie A, France's Ligue 1, and Brazil's Brasileirao.

However, several of these leagues are relatively new compared to MLB and its nearly 150-year history. The EPL began play in 1992, Brasileirao in 1971, and Bundesliga in 1963, eliminating any teams in those leagues from any comparison to a championship drought begun in 1908. Serie A was founded in 1929, and eight of the founding teams have never won the championship, but each of them has been relegated to Serie B for most of the intervening decades and were not playing in Serie A as of 2013. That brings us to two top-flight soccer teams. Spain's La Liga was founded in 1928, and charter member R.C.D. Espanyol has never won the championship. Likewise, France's Stade Rennais was part of Ligue 1 in its inaugural year of 1932 and is the league's only team still playing at the highest level without winning the title (the team has been relegated several times over the past decades, however, so we include them here reluctantly). While fans of Espanyol and Stade Rennais may know something like the pain of Cubs fans, the Cubs still claim the victory: their century-plus without a championship tops that of Espanyol's, which began in 1928, and Stade Rennais, which started in 1932.

The Cubs are the only team playing at the highest level in their sport that has not held their championship trophy over the course of several generations. So why would fans continue to cheer for them? No other professional sports team can make such a claim, and yet the organization is still as popular as ever. Cubs attendance totals have fallen below the top half of the NL's rankings only once since 1983. And even then, when the Cubs went 65–97 in 2000, the team still finished with the ninth-highest attendance numbers out of 16 NL teams.

An old-fashioned ballpark that reminds fans of yesterday is surely part of the answer. Another element is the leisurely attitude of the Friendly Confines, which encourages adults to play hooky from work and relax at a game. Still, there must be more to it than that.

One reason fans are so dedicated to seeing the Cubs succeed is the desire to see history unfolding before our eyes. Whether the event is positive (Barack Obama's 2008 victory speech in Chicago's Grant Park) or negative (the morning of the 9/11 attacks), everyone has a visceral desire to say "I was there" or "I saw it happen." Each moment of witnessed history allows average Americans to think that anything is possible. In 2004, the Boston Red Sox overcame a 3–0 deficit against the hated rival New York Yankees to win the AL Championship Series 4–3 (becoming the first MLB team to overcome such a deficit in the postseason), and in so doing they provided generations of sports fans with the knowledge that anything is possible. The Cubs winning the World Series would be even bigger than that. Cubs fans return to the Friendly Confines every year just like the swallows to Capistrano because they want to have a ticket stub from the season when the Cubs finally win it all. They want to say that they saw it happen in person, that they were part of it. And if that game doesn't end up as part of history, it's okay. They had a good time anyway sharing the day with friends and family.

And that is the next reason why millions of Cubs fans continue to support the team: family tradition. Few things in life can be shared between generations. Children rarely enjoy the same things their parents and grandparents did. But all those differences are forgotten in the realm of sports. Worries can be dismissed for a brief spell when generations talk about their favorite team. And that is why, even though the child of a Cubs fan may not know the score of the previous day's game, when the Cubs finally win the big one, that son or daughter will smile, knowing they are seeing something their parent always hoped to see.

Through it all, the Cubs provide hope. More than a century of failing to reach the big game is not the same thing as losing. The Cubs haven't gotten there in a long time, but they will. And that is the lesson that the Cubs have taught the world. After all, is it not the journey, rather than the destination, that is the point of life?

Like most sports writers, I was a frustrated athlete growing up who was always second string. Whether the sport in question is baseball, football, soccer, softball, tennis, darts, or even adult kickball, I own no championship trophies for any of the dozens of teams for which I have played. But whenever the score was against us and my team began to drag, I would call my teammates together and say the same thing: "Look at that score. Look at how bad we are losing right now. Just imagine how great our story will be when we tell everyone how we overcame this deficit to win!"

This same philosophy is why the Cubs have changed the world more than other team. They provide hope to millions of sports fans around the world who know that one day, the Chicago Cubs will win the World Series—and when they do, we'll finally get to say "I told you so."

Acknowledgments

Creating the world's first book to be powered by GeoVerse™ has taken a legion of supporters who helped in a wide variety of ways. It has taken longer than expected, but it would never have happened without the aide and assistance of many people from many walks of life.

To my mother, Polly, my father, Don, and my brother, Mark, I want to say thank you for bearing with me during this process.

One of my biggest debts of gratitude goes to everyone at Shedd Aquarium who taught me how to teach through engagement and entertainment.

Without the Chicago Public Library I don't know if it would have been possible to create this book. Thank you for your great collections.

Thank you to the staff at the Chicago Historical Society for your research help.

To the staff at the National Underground Railroad Freedom Center thank you for your patience and research help.

Several authors proved to be of help even though we never met because their books proved to be great sources of information including Peter Golenbock, Glenn Stout, Richard Johnson, John Snyder and George Vass.

Thank you to Jerome Holtzman, the one Cubs author who I did know personally and am proud to have had as a colleague. I will never forget eating together at The Bagel.

To Adam Schneider with GPS Visualizer for helping with GPS coding and my slow learning curve.

The West Side Rooters Social Club proved to be of great help, thank you for a great site.

Thank you to Blythe Hurley, a great editor, and Patricia Frey, a wonderful designer.

To Tim Mollette-Parks, thank you for being such a great friend and the best musician I know.

To Allan Zarach, thank you for your great voice and patience.

To Ziggy, I know you will never read this but having you at my feet every day was a constant calming presence. Thank you for the dog walks.

But mostly I want to thank Drew Balac for supporting me at all times and in all ways. None of this would have happened without you. Thank you. I love you.

Sources

Section I: Politics

1. Ronald Regan, *An American Life* (New York: Simon and Schuster, 1990), 80.
2. Laton McCartney, *The Teapot Dome Scandal* (New York: Alfred A. Knopf, 2008), 159.
3. Ibid., 311.
4. Neil Steinberg, "Ugly Presidential Campaigns Hit Their 100-Year Mark," *Wilmette Life,* December 6, 2012, http://wilmette.suntimes.com/news/elections/16155258-505/ ugly-presidential-campaigns-reach-their-100-year-mark.html.
5. Herbert S. Duffy, *William Howard Taft: A Biography* (New York: Minton, Balch & Co., 1930), 219.
6. Richard D. White Jr., *Roosevelt the Reformer* (Tuscaloosa, AL: University of Alabama Press, 2003), 91.
7. Duffy, *Taft,* 221.
8. Duffy, *Taft,* 275.
9. Duffy, *Taft,* 275–76.
10. "President William Taft Baseball Game Attendance Log," *Baseball Almanac,* http://www.baseball-almanac.com/prz_cwt.shtml, accessed June 4, 2013.
11. Presidential Baseball Famous Firsts," *Baseball Almanac,* http://www.baseball-almanac.com/firsts/ prz_1st.shtml, accessed June 4, 2013.
12. Eldon L. Ham *"Broadcasting Baseball: A History of the National Pastime on Radio and Television* (Jefferson, NC: McFarland, 2011), 87.
13. "Ethan Allen, Cadaco-Ellis, and All-Star Baseball," *Baseball Games,* April 2011, http://baseballgames.dreamhosters.com/CadacoASB.htm.
14. Mike Sielski, "Baseball's Original Nerd Magnet," *The Wall Street Journal,* July 18, 2011, http://online.wsj.com/article/SB10001424052702303661904576452363862242304.html.
15. Erik Arneson, "Ethan Allen's All-Star Baseball Game," http://boardgames.about.com/od/ gamehistories/p/ethan_allen.htm, accessed June 4, 2013.
16. "President George Bush Baseball Related Quotations," *Baseball Almanac,* http://www.baseball-almanac.com/prz_qgb.shtml, accessed June 4, 2013.
17. Josh Robbins, "Flyovers: Valuable aids or flights of fancy?" *Orlando Sentinel,* February 10, 2008, http://articles.orlandosentinel.com/2008-02-10/sports/flyovers10_1_flyovers-air-force-force-base/2.
18. John Snyder, *Cubs Journal* (Cincinnati: Emmis Books, 2005), 276.
19. Ibid.
20. Peter Golenbock, *Wrigleyville: A Magical History Tour of the Chicago Cubs* (New York: St. Martin's Press, 1996), 237–38.
21. Ibid, 238–39.
22. Ibid, 238.
23. Ibid, 234–39.
24. Jerome Holtzman, "Oct. 1, 1932 The Yankees' Babe Ruth Gestures Toward Wrigley," *Chicago Tribune,* October 1, 1987, http://articles.chicagotribune.com/1987-11-01/ sports/8703230677_1_babe-ruth-cub-bench-world-series-history.
25. Ronald Reagan, *An American Life* (New York: Simon and Schuster, 1990), 116, 124.
26. Golenbock, *Wrigleyville,* 186.

27. Golenbock, *Wrigleyville*, 190.
28. Jimmy Greenfield, *100 Things Every Cubs Fan Should Know & Do Before They Die* (Chicago: Triumph Books, 2011), 275.
29. Ibid.
30. Ibid.
31. John C. Skipper, *Wicked Curve: The Life and Troubled Times of Grover Cleveland Alexander* (Jefferson, NC: McFarland, 2006), 14.
32. "Stepping Up to the Plate," *Chicago Baseball Museum*, http://www.chicagobaseballmuseum.org/files/ Stepping%20Up%20to%20the%20Plate%20-%20Rockford%20Peahces.pdf, accessed June 4, 2013.
33. Carrie Muskat, "Wrigley lights up the night for 20 years," MLB.com, http://chicago.cubs.mlb.com/ news/article.jsp?ymd=20080806&content_id=3267314&fext=.jsp&c_id=chc, accessed June 4, 2013.
34. Snyder, *Journal*, 325.
35. *Gerald Bazer and Steven Culbertson*, "President Called Baseball a Wartime Morale Booster," *National Archives*, 2002, http://www.archives.gov/publications/prologue/2002/ spring/greenlight.html, accessed June 7, 2013.
36. Snyder, *Journal*, 325.
37. Muskat, "Wrigley."
38. Snyder, *Journal*, 326.
39. Bob Verdi, "Sobering News For Cubs Followers," *Chicago Tribune*, October 13, 1987, http://articles.chicagotribune.com/1987-10-13/sports/8703170583_1_herzog-cub-followers-wrigley-field.
40. Paul Sullivan, "Cubs may have to reset their clocks," *Chicago Tribune*, March 3, 2012, http://articles.chicagotribune.com/2012-03-03/sports/ct-spt-0304-cubs-chicago--20120304 _1_cubs-convention-soriano-and-derrek-lee-manager-dale-sveum.

Section II: Society

1. John Toland, *The Dillinger Days* (New York: First Da Capo Press, 1995), 23.
2. Ibid.
3. Ibid.
4. G. Russell Girardin and William J. Helmer, *Dillinger: The Untold Story* (Bloomington and Indianapolis: Indiana University Press, 1994), 19.
5. Ibid., 190.
6. Ibid., 272.
7. Ibid., 184–85.
8. Dary Matera, *John Dillinger: The Life and Death of America's First Celebrity Criminal* (New York: Da Capo Press, 2005), 305.
9. Ibid., 162.
10. Girardin and Helmer, *Dillinger*, 277-278.
11. Ibid., 221.
12. Ibid., 226.
13. Girardin and Helmer, *Dillinger*, 226.
14. Ellen Poulson, *Don't Call Us Molls* (Little Neck, NY: Clinton Cook Publishing Corp., 2002), 341.
15. Elliott Gorn, *Dillinger's Wild Ride* (New York: Oxford University Press, 2011), 178.
16. Fergie Jenkins with Lew Freedman, *Fergie* (Chicago: Triumph Books, 2009), 19.
17. "Two Theories As To Fire's Origin," *Chicago Daily Tribune*, August 6, 1894.
18. Robert Wiggins, *The Federal League Of Base Ball Clubs: The History Of An Outlaw League 1914-1915* (Jefferson, NC: McFarland, 2011), 272.
19. John Snyder, *Cubs Journal* (Cincinnati: Emmis Books, 2005), 147.
20. David Anderson, *More Than Merkle: A History of the Best and Most Exciting Baseball Season in Human History* (Lincoln: Bison Books, 2003), xi.
21. "Fred Merkle Obituary," *Baseball Almanac*, http://www.baseball-almanac.com/deaths/fred_merkle_ obituary.shtml, accessed June 7, 2013.

22. Keith Olbermann, "The Goof That Changed the Game," SI.com, September 23, 2008, http://sportsillustrated.cnn.com/2008/magazine/09/23/merkle/.

23. Bruce Levine, "Santo's ashes to be scattered at Wrigley," ESPN.com, December 10, 2010, http://espn.go.com/blog/chicago/cubs/post/_/id/2893/santos-ashes-to-be-spread-throughout-wrigley.

24. Jimmy Greenfield, *100 Things Cubs Fans Should Know & Do Before They Die* (Chicago: Triumph Books, 2012), 259.

25. Glenn Stout and Richard Johnson, *The Cubs: The Complete History of Chicago Cubs Baseball* (New York: Houghton Mifflin Company, 2007), 192.

26. Malcolm Gladwell, *The Tipping Point: How Little Things Can Make A Big Difference* (New York: Back Bay Books, 2007).

27. Dave Seminara, "Still Stung by Failure, Cubs Fans Convene to Refresh Faith," *The New York Times*, January 17, 2010, http://www.nytimes.com/2010/01/18/sports/baseball/ 18cubs.html?_r=0.

28. Paul Sullivan, "Priest who blessed dugout says Cubs chairman threw him 'under the bus,'" *Chicago Tribune*, January 20, 2009, http://articles.chicagotribune.com/2009-01-20/ sports/0901190610_1_billy-goat-curse-greek-orthodox-priest-cubs-convention.

29. Shankar Vedantam, "Persistence of Myths Could Alter Public Policy Approach," *The Washington Post*, Tuesday, September 4, 2007, http://www.washingtonpost.com/wp-dyn/content/article/2007/09/03/AR2007090300933.html.

30. Cheryl Lavin, "Home Based: Ex-ball girl Marla Collins Is A Fan Of Motherhood Now," *Chicago Tribune*, October 4, 1989, http://articles.chicagotribune.com/1989-10-04/ features/8901190333_1_ball-girl-cubs-marla-collins.

31. Mike Royko, "Bottom Line On The Collins Case," *Chicago Tribune*, July 23, 1986, http://articles.chicagotribune.com/1986-07-23/news/8602220995_1_cub-marla-collins-ball-girl.

32. Peter Golenbock, *Wrigleyville: A Magical History Tour of the Chicago Cubs* (New York: St. Martin's Press, 1996), 422.

33. Jerome Holtzman, "Tinkering With Cub Double-Play Legend," *Chicago Tribune*, May 14, 1992, http://articles.chicagotribune.com/1992-05-14/sports/9202120912_1_gonfalon- bubble-evers-bear-cubs.

Section III: Race

1. Robin Doak, *Struggling to Become American* (New York: Chelsea House Publishers, 2006), 57.

2. "Players by Place of Birth (Number of players)," Baseball-Reference.com, http://www.baseball-reference.com/bio/, accessed June 11, 2013.

3. "Player's Slayer Sentenced," Associated Press, October 3, 1952.

4. David L. Fleitz, *Cap Anson: The Grand Old Man of Baseball* (Jefferson, NC: McFarland, 2005), 111–12.

5. Ibid., 112.

6. Ibid.

7. David W. Zang, *Fleet Walker's Divided Heart: The Life of Baseball's First Black Major Leaguer* (Lincoln, NE: University of Nebraska Press, 1995), 42–43.

8. Ibid., 42.

9. Ibid.

10. Ibid., 43.

11. Clyde Hughes, "Prestige of 1st black major leaguer likely no longer belongs to Toledo," *The Blade*, February 7, 2005, http://www.toledoblade.com/frontpage/2005/02/07/Prestige-of-1st-black-major-leaguer-likely-no-longer-belongs-to-Toledo.html#vRliVzSF48Avt80t.99.

12. James E. Elfers, *The Tour to End All Tours: The Story of Major League Baseball's 1913–14 World Tour* (Winnipeg: Bison Books, 2003), 6.

13. Peter Golenbock, *Wrigleyville: A Magical History Tour of the Chicago Cubs* (New York: St. Martin's Press, 1996), 26–27.

14. Richard Peterson, *Only the Ball Was White: A History of Legendary Black Players and All-Black Professional Teams* (New York: Oxford University Press, 1992), 25.

15. Alfred M. Martin and Alfred T. Martin, *The Negro Leagues in New Jersey: A History* (Jefferson, NC: McFarland, 2008), 142.

16. Fleitz, *Anson*, 153.

17. Zang, *Fleet*, 55.

18. Golenbock, *Wrigleyville*, 27.

19. Joel Zoss and John Bowman, *Diamonds in the Rough: The Untold History of Baseball* (Winnipeg: Bison Books, 2004), 173.

20. Fleitz, *Anson*, 153.

21. Zoss and Bowman, *Diamonds*, 173.

22. Fleitz, *Anson*, 154.

23. Sol White, *Sol White's History of Colored Baseball with Other Documents on the Early Black Game, 1886–1936* (Winnipeg: Bison Books, 1996), 76–77.

24. Golenbock, *Wrigleyville*, 346.

25. Jonathan Eig, *Get Capone* (New York: Simon & Schuster, 2010), 51.

26. John Thorn, *Baseball in the Garden of Eden* (New York: Simon & Schuster, 2011), xiii.

27. Deidre Marie Capone, *Uncle Al Capone* (New York: Recap Publishing, 2011), 45.

28. Golenbock, *Wrigleyville*, 220.

29. Nate Bruce Hendley, *American Gangsters, Then and Now: An Encyclopedia* (Santa Barbara, CA: ABC-CLIO, 2009), 34.

30. Ibid.

31. Capone, *Capone*, 43–44.

32. Capone, *Capone*, 44.

33. Ibid.

34. Ibid.

35. Gus Russo, *The Outfit* (New York: Bloomsbury, 2003), 80.

36. Capone, *Capone*, 44.

37. Ibid.

38. Ibid.

39. Ibid.

40. Ibid.

41. Ibid., 45.

42. Ibid., 46.

43. Frank James, "Martin Luther King Jr. in Chicago," *Chicago Tribune*, August 5, 1966, http://www.chicagotribune.com/news/politics/chi-chicagodays-martinlutherking-story,0,4515753.story.

44. Richard Dozer, "Cubs Sign Negro Coach," *Chicago Daily Tribune*, May 30, 1962.

45. Glenn Stout and Richard Johnson, *The Cubs: The Complete History of Chicago Cubs Baseball* (New York: Houghton Mifflin, 2007), 241.

46. Steve Wulf, "The Guiding Light," *Sports Illustrated*, September 19, 1994, http://sportsillustrated.cnn.com/vault/article/magazine/MAG1005706/index.htm.

47. George Castle, *The Million-to-One Team: Why the Chicago Cubs Haven't Won a Pennant Since 1945* (South Bend, IN: Diamond Communications, 2000), 120.

48. Ibid.

49. Buck O'Neil and David Conrads, *I Was Right on Time* (New York: Simon & Schuster, 1997), 14–15.

50. Phil Rogers, *Ernie Banks: Mr. Cub and the Summer of '69* (Chicago: Triumph Books, 2011), 13.

51. Keith Olbermann, "Passing the Buck," NBCNews.com, February 28, 2006, http://www.nbcnews.com/id/11478921/#060301a.

52. Wulf, "Light."

53. Golenbock, *Wrigleyville*, 347.

54. Lisa Winston, "Baker was a blazer of many trails," MLB.com, February 11, 2008, http://www.milb.com/news/article.jsp?ymd=20080207&content_id=345146&vkey=news_milb&fext=.jsp.

Section IV: Vice

1. Sean Deveney, *The Original Curse* (New York: McGraw Hill, 2009), 107.
2. Glenn Stout and Richard Johnson, *The Cubs: The Complete History of Chicago Cubs Baseball* (New York: Houghton Mifflin, 2007), 104.
3. Deveney, *Curse*, 107.
4. Ibid., 5.
5. Ibid., 106.
6. Stout and Johnson, *Cubs*, 99.
7. Ibid., 103.
8. Bill Veeck and Ed Linn, *Veeck as in Wreck* (Chicago: University of Chicago Press, 1962), 36.
9. Stout and Johnson, *Cubs*, 106.
10. John Snyder, *Cubs Journal* (Cincinnati: Emmis Books, 2005), 206.
11. Stout and Johnson, *Cubs*, 106.
12. Virginia Gardner, "Jurges' Girl Friend Blames Shooting on 'Too Much Gin,'" *Chicago Daily Tribune*, July 8, 1932.
13. Edward Burns, "Girl Who Shot Cubs' Player Goes Free," *Chicago Daily Tribune*, July 15, 1932.
14. Ibid.
15. Ibid.
16. "Police Hold Chief of Jurges Blackmail Plot," *Chicago Daily Tribune,* August 14, 1932.
17. Peter Golenbock, *Wrigleyville: A Magical History Tour of the Chicago Cubs* (New York: St. Martin's Press, 1996), 252–53.
18. Snyder, *Journal*, 276.
19. Golenbock, *Wrigleyville*, 231.
20. Roberts Ehrgott, *Mr. Wrigley's Ball Club: Chicago and the Cubs During the Jazz Age* (Lincoln, NE: University of Nebraska Press, 2013), 121.
21. Bill Chastain, *Hack's 191* (Guilford, CT: Lyons Press, 2012), 4.
22. John O'Brien, "The St. Valentine's Day Massacre," *Chicago Tribune*, February 14, 1929, http://www.chicagotribune.com/news/politics/chi-chicagodays-valentinesmassacre-story,0,1233196.story.
23. David Pietrusza, *Judge and Jury: The Life and Times of Judge Kenesaw Mountain Landis.* (South Bend, Indiana: Diamond Communications, 1998) 401.
24. Clifton Blue Parker, *Fouled Away: The Baseball Tragedy of Hack Wilson* (Jefferson, NC: McFarland, 2000), 117.
25. "Famous Cases and Criminals," FBI.gov, http://www.fbi.gov/about-us/history/ famous-cases/al-capone, accessed June 18, 2013.
26. Veeck, *Veeck*, 35–36.
27. "Gambling Scandals in Sports," SI.com, http://sportsillustrated.cnn.com/multimedia/photo_gallery/0707/gambling.scandals/content.1.html, accessed June 18, 2013.
28. Peter Golenbock, *The Spirit of St. Louis: A History of the St. Louis Cardinals and Browns* (New York: Avon Books, 2000), 106.
29. David Pietrusza, *Judge and Jury: The Life and Times of Judge Kenesaw Mountain Landis* (South Bend, IN: Diamond Communications, 1998), 316.
30. Golenbock, *The Spirit of St. Louis*, 316.
31. Golenbock, "The Spirit of St. Louis," op. cit., p Ibid., 99.
32. "Hornsby Was Sold Because Of His Debts," *Sarasota Herald-Tribune*, January 19, 1927, http://news.google.com/newspapers?nid=1755&dat=19270119&id=aBseAAAAIBAJ&sjid=EGQEAAAAIBAJ&pg=1349,6123740.
33. Ibid.
34. Golenbock, "The Spirit of St. Louis," op. cit.,p 270-271.
35. William McNeil, *Gabby Hartnett: The Life and Times of the Cubs' Greatest Catcher* (Jefferson, NC: McFarland, 2004), 147.
36. Pietrusza, *Judge*, 318.
37. Golenbock, *Wrigleyville*, 229–30.

38. Pietrusza, *Judge*, 318.
39. Robert C. Alexander, *Rogers Hornsby: A Biography* (New York: Holt Paperbacks, 1996), 280.
40. Ibid., 279.
41. "Wife Says Hornsby Used Her Inheritance," *The Register-Guard*, May 30, 1953, http://news.google.com/newspapers?nid=1310&dat=19530530&id=emxWAAAAIBAJ&sjid=ueIDAAAAIBAJ&pg=3788,4397973.
42. "$25,000 Left to Hornsby In Will of Suicide Victim," *Pittsburgh Post-Gazette*, September 9, 1953, http://news.google.com/newspapers?nid=1144&dat=19530909&id=JuYeAAAAIBAJ&sjid=rU0EAAAAIBAJ&pg=7380,2053561.
43. Alexander, *Hornsby*, 280.
44. Pete Cava and Bob Logan, *Amazing Tales from the Chicago Cubs Dugout* (New York: Skyhorse Publishing, 2012), 104.
45. Jimmy Greenfield, *100 Things Cubs Fans Should Know & Do Before They Die* (Chicago: Triumph Books, 2012), 96.
46. Leo Durocher and Ed Linn, *Nice Guys Finish Last* (Chicago: University of Chicago Press, 1975), 11.
47. Greenfield, *100*, 125.
48. Roger Khan, *The Era 1947-1957: When the Yankees, Giants and Dodgers Ruled the World* (Winnipeg: Bison Books, 2002), 36.
49. Durocher and Linn, *Nice,* 238.
50. Ibid., 243.
51. George Raft as told to Dean Jennings, "Break With Durocher Was Painful," *St. Petersburg Independent*, January 26, 1958.
52. "Laraine Day Divorce Upheld In California," UP, May 9, 1947.
53. Lyle Spatz, *The Team That Forever Changed Baseball and America: The 1947 Brooklyn Dodgers* (Lincoln, NE: University of Nebraska Press, 2012), 53.
54. Robert Shaplen, "The Nine Lives of Leo Durocher," *Sports Illustrated*, June 6, 1955.
55. Ibid.
56. Khan, *Era*, 30.
57. Durocher and Linn, *Nice*, 244.
58. Ibid., 245.
59. "Albert Benjamin 'Happy' Chandler," MLB.com, http://mlb.mlb.com/mlb/history/mlb_history_people.jsp?story=com_bio_2, accessed June 18, 2013.
60. "Mary's Hour," *Walteromalley.com*, http://www.walteromalley.com/ biog_ss_maryshour.php, accessed June 18, 2013.
61. Peter Hernon and Terry Ganey, *Under the Influence: The Unauthorized Story of the Anheuser-Busch Dynasty* (New York: Avon Books, 1992), 246.
62. Golenbock, *Spirit*, 512–13.
63. Hernon and Ganey, *Under*, 246–47.
64. Ibid.
65. Golenbock, *Spirit*, 113.
66. Golenbock, *Wrigleyville*, 101.
67. Anthony Castrovince, "Baseball world teams up to strike out epilepsy," MLB.com, May 8, 2012.
68. Bruce Newman, "Just Happy to Be Here," *Sports Illustrated*, April 17, 1989.
69. Barbara L. Dershin, "What To Do, Not Do, In Seizure Cases," *Chicago Tribune*, August 18, 1988.
70. Golenbock, *Wrigleyville*, 186.
71. Golenbock, *Spirit*, 104.
72. Golenbock, *Spirit*, 114.
73. "Scorecard," *Sports Illustrated*, March 16, 1998.
74. Wayne Drehs, "The place to go where no one knows your name," *ESPN.com*, May 20, 2003, http://static.espn.go.com/mlb/s/2003/0515/1554407.html.
75. Fred Mitchell, "RV home on the range," *Chicago Tribune*, May 19, 2003, http://articles.chicagotribune.com/2003-05-19/sports/0305190167_1_winnebago-autograph-triple-a- iowa-cubs.

76. Drehs, *place.*
77. Amy K. Nelson, "'Shooter' Beck lived as hard as he played," ESPN.com, October 12, 2007, http://sports.espn.go.com/mlb/news/story?id=3060456.
78. Ibid.
79. Ibid.
80. Darren Rovell, "Lee Elia: Former Cubs Manager Cashes In On Tirade," CNBC.com, April 28, 2008, http://www.cnbc.com/id/24356505/Lee_Elia_Former_Cubs_Manager_Cashes_ In_On_Tirade.
81. Wayne Drehs, "Fans won't let Elia forget meltdown," ESPN.com, April 29, 2008, http://sports.espn.go.com/mlb/news/story?id=3372891.
82. Drehs, *Fans.*

Section V: Innovation
1. Stuart Shea, *Wrigley Field: The Unauthorized Biography* (Herndon, VA: Potomac Books, 2004), 19.
2. "Timeline," whitecastle.com, http://www.whitecastle.com/company/timeline, accessed June 27, 2013.
3. Ray Kroc, *Grinding It Out: The Making of McDonald's* (New York: St. Martin's Press, 1992), 181.
4. Shea, *Wrigley,* 19.
5. Robert Wiggins, *The Federal League of Base Ball Clubs: The History of an Outlaw League 1914-1915* (Jefferson, NC: McFarland, 2011), 346.
6. Ibid., 163.
7. Press Reference Library, *Being the portraits and biographies of the progressive men of the West: Vol. II* (New York: The New York Public Library, 2011), 419.
8. Roberts Ehrgott, *Mr. Wrigley's Ball Club: Chicago and the Cubs During the Jazz Age* (Lincoln, NE: University of Nebraska Press, 2013), 44.
9. Eldon L. Ham, *Broadcasting Baseball: A History of the National Pastime on Radio and Television* (Jefferson, NC: McFarland, 2011), 17.
10. Glenn Stout and Richard Johnson, *The Cubs: The Complete History of Chicago Cubs Baseball* (New York: Houghton Mifflin, 2007), 13.
11. Bill James, *The New Bill James Historical Abstract* (New York: Free Press, 2003), 65.
12. David L. Fleitz, *Cap Anson: The Grand Old Man of Baseball* (Jefferson, NC: McFarland, 2005), 72.
13. James, *Abstract,* 65.
14. Stout and Johnson, *Cubs,* 13.
15. S. Derby Gisclair, "History of New Orleans Baseball," neworleansbaseball.com, http://www.neworleansbaseball.com/history.html, accessed June 27, 2013.
16. Charles Fountain, *Under the March Sun: The Story of Spring Training* (New York: Oxford University Press, 2009), 11.
17. Fleitz, *Anson,* 134.
18. Fountain, *Under,* 12.
19. David Broughton, "Clubs give winter homes a branding boost," *SportsBusiness Journal,* February 27, 2012, http://www.sportsbusinessdaily.com/Journal/Issues/2012/02/27/Research-and-Ratings/Spring-training.aspx.
20. Peter Golenbock, *Wrigleyville: A Magical History Tour of the Chicago Cubs* (New York: St. Martin's Press, 1996), 20.
21. Stout and Johnson, *Cubs,* 9.
22. Robert Elias, *The Empire Strikes Out: How Baseball Sold U.S. Foreign Policy and Promoted the American Way Abroad* (New York: The New Press, 2010), 20.
23. "The 'Secret History' Of Baseball's Earliest Days," npr.org, March 16, 2011, http://www.npr.org/2011/03/16/134570236/the-secret-history-of-baseballs-earliest-days.
24. Daniel Helpingstine, *The Cubs and the White Sox: A Baseball Rivalry, 1900 to the Present* (Jefferson, NC: McFarland, 2010), 40.
25. Shea, *Wrigley,* 269–70.
26. John Snyder, *Cubs Journal* (Cincinnati: Emmis Books, 2005), 465.
27. William M. Bulkeley, "Chicago's Camera Network Is Everywhere," *The Wall Street Journal,* November 17, 2009, http://online.wsj.com/article/SB10001424052748704538404574539910412824756.html.

28. Danny Wild, "Umpire tosses music intern in Daytona," *milb.com*, August 2, 2012, http://www.milb.com/news/article.jsp?ymd=20120801&content_id=35977786&vkey=news_milb&fext=.jsp.

29. Stout and Johnson, *Cubs*, 236.

30. Paul Sullivan, "Theo stresses the 'Cubs way' as camp opens," *Chicago Tribune*, February 18, 2012, http://articles.chicagotribune.com/2012-02-18/sports/chi-cubs-file-in-to-camp-on-opening-day-20120218_1_chicago-cubs-cubs-way-cubs-way.

31. "Sports – Baseball, 1982-Present," boxofficemojo.com, http://boxofficemojo.com/genres/chart/?id=baseball.htm, accessed June 27, 2013.

32. John Frascella, *Theology* (New York: Cambridge House Press, 2009), 46.

33. David Haugh, "Haugh: Epstein always calculating," *Chicago Tribune,* February 26, 2013, http://articles.chicagotribune.com/2013-02-26/sports/ct-spt-0227-haugh-cubs-chicago-- 20130227_1_theo-epstein-cubs-fans-rooftop-owners.

34. Harlan Lebo, *Casablanca: Behind the Scenes* (New York: Simon & Schuster, 1992), 9–10.

35. Greg Couch, "Theo asking Cubs fans to believe," *FoxSports.com*, October 3, 2012, http://msn.foxsports.com/mlb/story/chicago-cubs-theo-epstein-worst-team-in-franchise-history-100212.

36. Frascella, *Theology*, 59.

37. Terry Francona, *Francona: The Red Sox Years* (New York: Houghton Mifflin, 2013), 272.

38. Frascella, *Theology*, 62.

39. Dr. Christopher D. Green, "America's first sport psychologist," *Monitor on Psychology*, April 2012, Vol. 43, No. 4.

40. Ibid.

41. Ibid.

42. Ibid.

43. Pat Putnam, "Evil In The Eye Of An Older Beholder," *Sports Illustrated,* January 23, 1978, http://sportsillustrated.cnn.com/vault/article/magazine/MAG1093249/1/index.htm.

44. "Ben Finkle Makes Living As 'Eye-Opener'—But Not As Any Startling Beauty," *Sarasota Herald-Tribune*, January 14, 1942, http://news.google.com/newspapers?nid=1755&dat= 19420114&id=kJYcAAAAIBAJ&sjid=e2QEAAAAIBAJ&pg=5547,913871.

45. Bill Veeck and Ed Linn, *Veeck as in Wreck* (Chicago: University of Chicago Press, 1962), 46.

46. Ibid.

47. Jerome Holtzman, "Psychologists' Roles In Baseball Aren't Shrinking," *Chicago Tribune*, December 18, 1990, http://articles.chicagotribune.com/1990-1218/sports/9004150127_1_cub-footnote-in-baseball-lore-alan-lans.

48. Putnam, "Evil."

49. Jerome Holtzman, "College Of Coaches Got Failing Grade From AD Whitlow," *Chicago Tribune*, February 20, 1994, http://articles.chicagotribune.com/1994-02-20/sports/9402200477_1_training-remember-philip-wrigley.

50. Jimmy Greenfield, *100 Things Cubs Fans Should Know & Do Before They Die* (Chicago: Triumph Books, 2012), 51.

51. Golenbock, *Wrigleyville*, 380.

52. Holtzman, "College."

53. Golenbock, *Wrigleyville*, 371.

54. Snyder, *Cubs*, 420.

55. Shea, *Wrigley*, 223.

56. Stout and Johnson, *Cubs*, 242.

57. "Gym, Health & Fitness Clubs in the US: Market Research Report," ibisworld.com, May 2013, http://www.ibisworld.com/industry/default.aspx?indid=1655.

58. David Quentin Voight, *American Baseball: From Gentleman's Game to the Commissioner System* (University Park, PA: Pennsylvania State University Press, 1983), 17.

59. Mike Roer, *Orator O'Rourke: The Life of a Baseball Radical* (Jefferson, NC: McFarlane, 2006), 99.

Section VI: Entertainment

1. Glenn Stout and Richard Johnson, *The Cubs: The Complete History of Chicago Cubs Baseball* (New York: Houghton Mifflin, 2007), 13.
2. Jerome Holtzman and George Vass, *The Chicago Cubs Encyclopedia* (Philadelphia: Temple University Press, 1997), 171.
3. Stout and Johnson, *Cubs*, 21.
4. Marty Appel, "Slide, Kelly, Slide," appelpr.com, http://www.appelpr.com/ARTICLES/ A-slidekelly.htm, accessed July 2, 2013.
5. Martin Gardner, *The Annotated Casey at the Bat* (Mineola, NY: Dover Publications, 1995), 188.
6. Charles Billington, *Wrigley Field's Last World Series* (Chicago: Lake Claremont Press, 2005), 173.
7. Peter Golenbock, *Wrigleyville: A Magical History Tour of the Chicago Cubs* (New York: St. Martin's Press, 1996), 296.
8. Golenbock, *Wrigleyville*, 296.
9. Golenbock, *Wrigleyville*, 297.
10. Gary Reinmuth, "Ex-Cub Player, Coach Harry 'Peanuts' Lowery Dies," *Chicago Tribune*, July 4, 1986, http://articles.chicagotribune.com/1986-07-04/sports/8602180119_1_cubs-third-base-coaches-leo-durocher.
11. Leo Durocher and Ed Linn, *Nice Guys Finish Last* (Chicago: University of Chicago Press, 1975), 327.
12. Durocher and Linn, *Nice*, 325.
13. Phil Silvers and Robert Saffron, *The Laugh Is on Me* (Upper Saddle River, NJ: Prentice-Hall, 1973), 204.
14. Rob Neyer, *Rob Neyer's Big Book of Baseball Lineups* (New York: Touchstone, 2003), 179.
15. Mitch Williams and Darrell Berger, *Straight Talk from Wild Thing* (Chicago: Triumph Books, 2010), vi.
16. Chris Nashawaty, "A League Of Its Own," *Sports Illustrated*, July 4, 2011, http://sportsillustrated.cnn.com/vault/article/magazine/MAG1187813/index.htm.
17. "Sports - Baseball, 1982-Present," boxofficemojo.com, http://boxofficemojo.com/genres/chart/ ?id=baseball.htm, accessed July 2, 2013.
18. "AFI's 100 Years . . . 100 Movie Quotes," afi.com, http://www.afi.com/100years/ quotes.aspx, accessed July 2, 2013.
19. "TV Ratings: 1958–1959," classictvhits.com, http://www.classictvhits.com/tvratings/1958.htm, accessed July 2, 2013.
20. David Fury, "Chuck Connors," riflemanconnors.com, 1992, http://www.riflemanconnors.com/ chuck_connors_in_memory_of.htm.
21. "Chuck Connors Cowboy Hall of Fame," riflemanconnors.com, http://www.riflemanconnors.com/ chuck_connors-cowboy_hall_of_fame.htm, accessed July 2, 2013.
22. Fergie Jenkins with Lew Freedman, *Fergie* (Chicago: Triumph Books, 2009), 90.
23. Gil Bogen, *Tinker, Evers and Chance: A Triple Biography* (Jefferson, NC: McFarland, 2003), 86.
24. Robert Cantwell, "The Music of Baseball," *Sports Illustrated*, October 3, 1960, http://sportsillustrated.cnn.com/vault/article/magazine/MAG1071836/1/index.htm.
25. Moira McCormick, "Cubs Go to Bat for Charity," *Billboard*, October 13, 1984.
26. "Nicknames," profootballhof.com, http://www.profootballhof.com/history/nicknames.aspx, accessed July 2, 2013.
27. James Quirk and Rodney D. Fort, *Pay Dirt: The Business of Professional Team Sports*, second ed. (Princeton, NJ: Princeton University Press, 1997), 335.
28. Quirk and Fort, *Pay Dirt*, 334.
29. Bill Jauss, "Cubs to McMichael: You're out!" *Chicago Tribune*, August 9, 2001, http://articles.chicagotribune.com/2001-08-09/sports/0108090252_1_umpire-forfeited-cubs.
30. "Fred Fisher," songwritershalloffame.org, http://songwritershalloffame.org/index.php/exhibits/bio/ C259, accessed July 2, 2013.
31. J. J. Cooper, "Billy Hamilton Hits a Stand-Up Inside-The-Park Home Run," *Baseball America*, July 16, 2012, http://www.baseballamerica.com/blog/prospects/2012/07/ billy-hamilton-hits-a-stand-up-inside-the-park-home-run/.

32. Robert Allen, *Billy Sunday: Home Run to Heaven* (Fenton, MI: Mott Media, 1985), 48.
33. Ibid., 43.
34. Ibid.
35. Ibid., 47.
36. Ibid., 63.
37. Ibid., 82–83.
38. Ibid., 87.
39. Ibid., 93–94.
40. "Sports - Baseball, 1982-Present," boxofficemojo.com, http://boxofficemojo.com/genres/chart/?id=baseball.htm, accessed July 2, 2013.
41. "Readers: Best baseball movie moments," espn.go.com, http://espn.go.com/page2/s/list/readers/baseballmovie/moments.html, accessed July 2, 2013.
42. "Shocking moments in baseball history," espn.go.com, http://espn.go.com/page2/s/list/baseball/shocking/moments.html, accessed July 2, 2013.
43. Jerome Holtzman and George Vass, *The Chicago Cubs Encyclopedia* (Philadelphia: Temple University Press, 1997), 67.
44. "Girl in Waitkus Shooting Pens Her Life Story," *Chicago Daily Tribune,* June 24, 1949.
45. Ibid.
46. "Waitkus Life in Balance After Shooting by Girl Admirer," *Chicago Daily Tribune,* June 16, 1949.
47. Ibid.
48. Ibid.
49. Ibid.
50. Ibid.
51. "Waitkus Shot; Quiz Girl," *Chicago Daily Tribune,* June 15, 1949.
52. "Waitkus Life in Balance After Shooting by Girl Admirer," *Chicago Daily Tribune,* June 16, 1949.
53. John Theodore, *Baseball's Natural: The Story of Eddie Waitkus* (Carbondale, IL: Southern Illinois University Press, 2002), 67–68.

Section VII: Baseball

1. Jerome Holtzman, *The Jerome Holtzman Baseball Reader* (Chicago: Triumph Books, 2003), 120.
2. Ibid., 121.
3. Thomas Littlewood, *Arch: A Promoter, Not a Poet* (Iowa City: Iowa State Press, 1990), 67.
4. Ibid., 70.
5. Holtzman, *Reader,* 122.
6. Ibid.
7. Ibid., 121.
8. Rick Morrissey, "Arch would approve," *Chicago Tribune,* July 13, 2003, http://articles.chicagotribune.com/2003-07-13/sports/0307130450_1_arch-ward-century-of-progress-exposition-college-all-star.
9. Ibid.
10. Laura Enright, *Chicago's Most Wanted: The Top 10 Book of Murderous Mobsters, Midway Monsters and Windy City Oddities* (Dulles, VA: Potomac Books, 2005), 190.
11. Richard Justice, "Selig had it right on Interleague Play," MLB.com, May 18, 2012, http://mlb.mlb.com/news/article.jsp?ymd=20120516&content_id= 31423316&vkey= news_mlb&c_id=mlb.
12. Holtzman, *Reader,* 194.
13. "Colts Smother White Stockings," *Chicago Daily Tribune,* October 2, 1903.
14. Holtzman, *Reader,* 192.
15. Jim Caple, "Don't throw that home run ball back!" ESPN.com, October 26, 2011, http://espn.go.com/espn/page2/story/_/id/7151065/throw-home-run- ball-back-certainly-copy-cubs-fans.
16. Mike Vaccaro, "'Throw it back!' a stupid tradition," *New York Post,* September 5, 2010, http://www.nypost.com/p/sports/more_sports/throw_it_back_stupid_ tradition_ jCOFmNyChhzDYwHUWq5jmJ.

17. Terence Moore, "Baseball rituals have lost their uniqueness," MLB.com, June 27, 2012, http://mlb.mlb.com/news/article.jsp?ymd=20120627&content_id= 34015014&vkey= news_mlb&c_id=mlb.

18. Daniel Helpingstine, *The Cubs and the White Sox: A Baseball Rivalry, 1900 to the Present* (Jefferson, NC: McFarland, 2010), 37.

19. Jerome Holtzman and George Vass, *The Chicago Cubs Encyclopedia* (Philadelphia: Temple University Press, 1997), 236.

20. John Snyder, *Cubs Journal* (Cincinnati: Emmis Books, 2005), 236.

21. Rick Shrum, "Parting shots: Two local men recall being witness to Babe Ruth's final three home runs," *Pittsburgh Post-Gazette*, May 10, 2006, http://www.post-gazette.com/stories/sports/pirates/parting-shots-two-local-men-recall-being-witness-to-babe-ruths-final-three-home-runs-433325/.

22. "Brothers as teammates in MLB history," MLB.com, January 24, 2013, http://mlb.mlb.com/ news/ article.jsp?ymd=20130124&content_id=41133556&vkey=news_mlb&c_id=mlb.

23. Linda Young, "Pau Returns To His Roots And A Life In The Country," *Chicago Tribune,* July 16, 1985, http://articles.chicagotribune.com/1985-07-16/sports/8502160213_1_farm-prices-major-leagues-playground-accident/2.

24. Ibid.

25. "Youngblood always was a team player," *sportsillustrated.cnn.com*, August 4, 1982, http://sportsillustrated.cnn.com/motorsports/2001/indy500/news/2001/05/25/double_dippin/.

26. Peter Golenbock, *Wrigleyville: A Magical History Tour of the Chicago Cubs* (New York: St. Martin's Press, 1996), 106.

27. "Frank Chance Of The Chicago Cubs 1st Player Ejected In A World Series Game," facebook.com, https://www.facebook.com/pages/Frank-Chance-Of-The-Chicago-Cubs-1st-Player-Ejected-In-A-World-Series-Game/309832391800?sk=info, accessed July 3, 2013.

28. "World Series Ejections," baseball-almanac.com, http://www.baseball-almanac.com/ws/wsmgrej.shtml, accessed July 3, 2013.

29. "Chance, Frank," baseballhalloffame.org, http://baseballhall.org/hof/chance-frank, accessed July 3, 2013.

30. "Blue Jays fire manager," Associated Press, May 17, 1999.

31. Golenbock, *Wrigleyville,* 322.

32. Ibid., 323.

33. Ibid.

34. David Schoenfield, "Kerry Wood and the greatest game pitched," ESPN.com, May 18, 2012, http://espn.go.com/blog/sweetspot/post/_/id/24585/kerry-wood-and-the- greatest-game-pitched.

35. Peter Barzilai, "Where does Matt Cain's perfect game rank?" *USA Today,* June 14, 2012, http://content.usatoday.com/communities/dailypitch/post/2012/06/matt-cain-perfect-game-sandy-koufax-kerry-wood/1#.UXrmMytoSPd.

36. Chris Jenkins, "Neutral site, Cubbie crowd: Big-Z no-hits Astros," *USA Today,* September 15, 2008, http://usatoday30.usatoday.com/sports/baseball/2008-09-15-2915802103_x.htm.

37. Tyler Kepner, "The Wildest Game in Modern History," *The New York Times,* May 16, 2009, http://bats.blogs.nytimes.com/2009/05/16/the-wildest-game-in-modern-history/.

38. Snyder, *Journal,* 220.

Index

About the Author

Scott Rowan is a publishing executive and former newspaper sports reporter whose love of sports came mostly from being second string while playing football, baseball, golf and tennis growing up. After balancing his life between working on more than 1,000 published sports books and volunteering at Shedd Aquarium, where he taught the public about marine animals and conservation, he invented GeoVerse™ as a way to take fun topics like sports and turn them into engaging ways to teach fans about the world we inhabit. He has lived for 10 years close enough to Wrigley Field to learn (and hopefully never forget) that cheers and boos sound nearly the same from just a short distance away. This is his second book.